Helping Parents Practice

Ideas for Making it Easier

Volume I

Edmund Sprunger

Yes Publishing
St. Louis • Ann Arbor

Caveats:

- *Characters in this book are composites drawn from the author's life experience and work as a teacher and clinician. The use of first names only indicates that details of parents and students have been changed to protect confidentiality.*
- *This book is meant to educate and should not be used as an alternative for professional care. The author and Yes Publishing shall have neither liability nor responsibility to any person or entity with respect to any loss or damage caused, or alleged to have been caused, directly or indirectly, by the information contained in this book.*

Published in the United States by
Yes Publishing • St. Louis, Missouri
yespublishing.com

Editing by Erin V. Obermueller, PhD
Book Design by Edmund Sprunger
with assistance from Ken Botnick and Zeuler Lima

Set in Minion with Univers headings

Printed in the United States of America

Permissions and copyright acknowledgments will be found in Notes and Sources, beginning on page 263.

Unattributed quotations are by Edmund Sprunger

Library of Congress Control Number: 2005902431

Library of Congress Cataloging-in-Publication Data
Sprunger, Edmund.
Helping parents practice: ideas for making it easier, volume I/Edmund Sprunger.
–First ed.
Includes bibliographical references
ISBN 0-9767854-3-9

To my father, Max Truman Sprunger,
the Mennonite version of Mr. Miyagi,
who made me rotate the tires on the car
when it wasn't necessary;
so I would know how to change a tire
when it was.

acknowledgements

I owe a debt of gratitude to the following people for the assistance they gave me, the opportunities they provided, and for pointing my thinking in directions that made this book possible: Loren Abramson, Geri Arnold, Debbie Baker, Marvin Bartel, Joanne Bath, Marvin Blickenstaff, Ken Botnick, John Bowers, Pam Brasch, Linda Case, Mary Ellen Clifford, Ronda Cole, Reinaldo Couto, Winifred Crock, Jacqueline DeFrancesco, Sally Dunning, John Edwards, Irene Fast, Bart Feller, Chuck Fisher, Bernard Gerdelman, Siri Gottlieb, John Gutoskey, Carol Kaplan-Lyss, Martin Katz, John Kendall, Marilyn Kesler, Edward Kreitman, Ray Landers, Cathy Lee, Alice Joy Lewis, Allen Lieb, Donna Lim, Lynn Malley, Anna Martin, Joanne Martin, Dee Martz, Kay Collier McLaughlin, Mordecai Miller, Jesse Nichols, Erin V. Obermueller, Mary Palmer, Lauren Papalia, Dwarky Rao, Sandy Reuning, Gail Seay, Susan Sermoneta (and the rest of the Creative Non-Fiction class at Columbia University in the fall of 2001), Martha Shackford, Lon Sherer (his quote on page 5 gives you just a glimpse of how fortunate I was to have this amazing man as my college violin professor...), Hugh Shirato, Diane Shoemaker, Dale Simmerman, William Starr, Ramona Stirling, Shin'ichi Suzuki (who carried the brightest torch), Barbara Wampner, Thomas Wermuth, Mary Ann Yaeger (and The School of Architecture at Washington University in St. Louis for use of Seminar Room 118, when I desperately needed to lay out this entire book), Esther Yoder Strahan, Sanna Yoder, Andrea Zuercher…and, of course, Zeuler.

And all the parents who have shared their joys and frustrations with me over the years.

contents

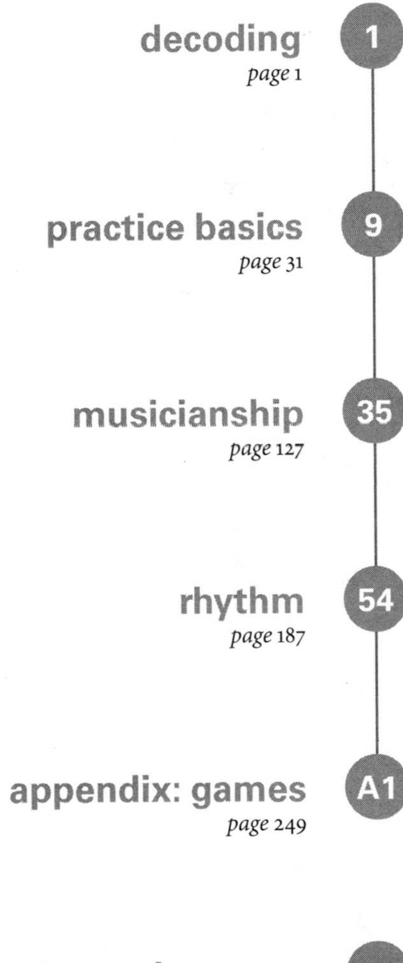

Every child "talks" in code;
every parent's job is to
break the code.

Peter Ruderman, MSW

decoding

1

8

decoding

E. L. Doctorow once said that "writing a novel is like driving a car at night. You can see only as far as your headlights, but you can make the whole trip that way." You don't have to see where you're going, you don't have to see your destination or everything you will pass along the way. You just have to see two or three feet ahead of you. This is right up there with the best advice about writing, or life, I have ever heard.

Anne Lamott
Bird by Bird

[Practice] is intensely personal, and as variable and individual as it is necessary. It is a blending of music, instrument, soul and body into artistic entity....Practicing well involves discipline and self-knowledge along with healthy measures of self-respect and even self-forgiveness.

Lon Sherer, A Mus D
Practicing:
A Liturgy of Self-Learning

1

You Don't Have to Do it All

At the parent sessions I have done at workshops, institutes, and seminars, I usually ask parents to write their questions and concerns on note cards. In this fairly anonymous format, I tell them that I'm particularly interested in the concerns they are afraid to bring up with their regular teachers, other parents, or perhaps even their spouses. As I've read these questions aloud over the years, I've watched hundreds of parent faces smile nervously in recognition when I read questions such as "Why is it that whjen I ask my child to repeat something, he just sighs like I've just asked him to do something totally impossible?" I've also seen those same faces begin to relax when they discover that they are not alone in their struggles.

I have listened to the concerns of parents in other ways as well–comments between classes, cafeteria line questions, and discussions while driving me to and from airports. And this is what I've discovered: parents worry.

So I want to get two things out of the way, right away.

First of all, your child doesn't need for you to be a perfect parent. I like the way the British pediatrician D.W. Winnicott put it: every child needs an "ordinary devoted" parent. And a parent's anxiety about being a *perfect* parent isn't a substitute for this ordinary devotion that every child needs. To Winnicott's ideas, I add the following: even when practicing an instrument with your child, perfection is still not required. However, as with parenting in general, your consistent presence is important.

If you're like most of the parents I have worked with over the past twenty years–and I'm sure you are–you want to know how to practice with your child in ways that maximize your usefulness and minimize your interference. This book is here to help you do that. In ordinary ways.

Here's the second thing to get out of the way: you don't have to read this entire book for it to be helpful or for it to make sense. It's not like a series of math courses in which you can't take algebra because you missed the class on addition. You're a parent. I know you're busy.

Of course, if you *want* to read this book cover to cover, you may. You could also use it as a reference book, reading just the sections that address your immediate needs. Or use it as a daily dose, reading one or two sections a day before starting practice. Or use it as a textbook, reading just the portions your teacher assigns.

You may find yourself reading a chapter one day, a small section three weeks later, and the rest of the book in six months. Many sections have cross-references, which allow you to hop around the book as your needs and interests dictate. Or you can just ignore the cross-references altogether. My hope is that you find a way to make the book useful for *you.*

I've organized this book into "neighborhoods." Each chapter has several separate sections, or "blocks," within those neighborhoods. Now you know why the table of contents looks like a subway map.

As you make your way through the book, you'll discover that many of the same concepts and themes keep reappearing. That's by design. Just as it's handy to have a neighborhood store where you can grab a quick loaf of bread, it's important to have the staples of practice where you need them. That's why they're all over the book. For example, all of the chapters reflect a common set of concerns and values that are difficult to exhaust, such as how to make practices both pleasant and productive. Each chapter is also unique. Every neighborhood has a place to grab a jug of milk; but not every neighborhood has a place to buy a sheet of birch plywood.

The idea that "repetition is the heart of learning" is one of the most important ideas I picked up during the year I studied with Shin'ichi Suzuki, founder of the Suzuki Method™. He constantly cycled through the basics of playing the violin–something his teaching was famous for–and in the process I came to understand the importance and richness of these basics. I believe that the staples in this book, which come from a variety of disciplines, not just music, are at the heart of practicing any instrument with your child. Actually, they are more than staples. I think of them as soul food.

2

You Are Unique–And So Are Your Challenges

Written in calligraphy and simply framed, the words "Monotony is the enemy of music," hung in Shin'ichi Suzuki's studio, and he referred to them often when our playing got, well, *boring*. Sometimes he read the words out loud himself. Sometimes he had us read them out loud. And sometimes he just pointed.

Suzuki was also quite fond of something else the Spanish cellist Pablo Casals once said:

> Each second we live is a new and unique moment of the universe, a moment that never was before and will never be again. And what do we teach our children? We teach them that two and two make four, and that Paris is the capital of France. When will we also teach them what they are? We should say to each of them: Do you know what you are? You are a marvel. You are unique. In all of the world there is no other child exactly like you. In the millions of years that have passed there has never been another child like you. And look at your body–what a wonder it is! Your legs, your arms, your cunning fingers, the way you move! You may become a Shakespeare, a Michelangelo, a Beethoven. You have the capacity for anything. Yes, you are a marvel.

I think it's helpful for every parent to understand something similar: *there is no other parent in the world quite like you.* Of all of the parents around you, none is able to care about your child the way you do. As a parent, you are unique. And you and the child you happen to be practicing with at any moment make a unique combination. In all the years that have passed, there has never been another parent just like you. There has never been a relationship just like your relationship with the child you practice with. (If you have more than one child, of course, you have more than one unique relationship.)

There is not one single way to be a parent, just as there isn't a single way to be a student–or a teacher, for that matter. Because of my respect for the uniqueness of each parent and his or her situation in life, it is impossible for me (or anyone else, in my opinion) to write a manual that tells you exactly what to do in each and every practice situation you face. Without a manual to consult, you're left with learning how to assess the situation as you go.

I like to think of daily practicing–and much of parenting in general–as a journey in which you come upon one yellow light after another. While red and green lights are pretty clear-cut–red means stop, green means go–a yellow light means that the driver has to check out the traffic conditions and make a decision in a split second. You've got more time when you're practicing, but still, you're facing a yellow light if you tell your child to play "Lightly Row" and "French Folk Song" comes out instead. Your reaction is likely to vary from that of another parent. Another parent might decide that it's important for the child to develop an awareness of directions, and stop the child immediately. You, on the other hand, knowing that your child is usually pretty good at following directions but currently has a distracting paper cut, may be grateful that anything at all came out of the instrument. So you simply point out that the last note was particularly lovely. Both of these reactions are appropriate. As the driver, you're the one who must decide.

A professional (such as myself) who lives outside of your unique traffic patterns can offer you a kind of "driver's ed."–information and knowledge that will enrich your understanding and skills. But I can't predict the specifics you'll encounter. That's why the idea that practice happens during a yellow light is one of the central themes of this book. There's a yellow light on the cover, and I like to think of the gray circles that surround the section numbers as yellow lights. I encourage you to take whatever enrichment you get from this book to that string of yellow lights you and your child approach during your daily practices.

Even though each parent/child relationship is unique, it's still important to teach children basic facts that *aren't* unique. They do need to know that 1 + 1 = 2 and that Paris is the capital of France. As important as these facts are, however, it is equally important that we find opportunities to teach them in ways that preserve the uniqueness of each child. One of those ways is by recognizing the uniqueness of each parent. I don't expect that this book will make all parents practice exactly alike. My aim is to help you develop basic skills, such as listening to your child's feelings, listening to your *own* feelings, and doing what you can to enjoy the journey of learning. The way you and your parent colleagues put those skills into practice will be different, perhaps just subtly. That's o.k. You're unique.

3

The Dirt that Lettuce Grows in Isn't Bad

After three days in the parent discussion group I was leading, the silent father finally spoke:

"I've been listening to all of the questions people are asking about practicing, and they really don't have anything to do with music–it seems like they're all about how you're getting along."

Bingo. In order to be effective, parents don't generally practice with their children over the phone, through e-mail, via fax, or even by shouting instructions from another room. Practicing happens in a very close–often intense–relationship. When the emotional environment of this relationship gets either too hot or too cold, practicing gets more difficult, just as it would if the physical environment went to one extreme or the other.

One way this upbeat book is here to help you is by acknowledging the darker, coarser side of the practicing relationship. This book understands that even though few things are more annoying than biting into a piece of dirty lettuce, lettuce actually grows in dirt. The dirt doesn't make the lettuce bad. Similarly, relationships often grow in conflict. The presence of conflict doesn't necessarily indicate that the relationship is bad.

Any close relationship is likely to have its share of conflict. People don't tell a librarian that they found a book out of place the same way they tell their spouse about, say, finding the remote in the refrigerator. Again. It's not the absence of conflict that determines the health of a relationship, but the way in which the conflict is acknowledged, managed, and–everyone hopes–eventually worked through.

I think of the conflicting, gritty moments of practice as a signal, not a report card. I hope that this book can help you determine whether a specific signal you're getting in your practice indicates that real work is happening–and you should keep at it–or that it's time to make some changes. Grittier moments don't mean that you, the parent, are being bad and need to be scolded. What you probably need are lots of ideas for how to make your practices more positive, so that your child doesn't end up overwhelmed with conflict, because just as dumping a truckload of dirt on a sprout prevents it from growing, too much conflict can suffocate a child. Still, when parents and children work through these rougher moments together, children can and do absorb the emotional nutrients that they contain.

At the outset of lessons, however, neither parent nor child counted on the struggles that can often come between them during practices. First lessons often start after parents and children have seen other children performing–or perhaps even playing fun games in a group class. The parent-child duo takes up an instrument with beautiful images of working together happily to produce delightful sounds. There's usually a honeymoon period, but before long, parents begin to realize that the work of practicing resembles gardening with your bare hands more than arranging fresh flowers in a vase. (And don't be fooled: even the parents who appear to have practices as graceful as ikebana also run into a thorn now and then.)

An important truth from gardeners can help parents who practice with their children: you can't tug on a plant to make it grow. You have to trust the process. But there's nothing wrong with fertilizing, watering, and generally caring for a plant. That's what gardeners do. Parents need to do it as well. In the process of tending beautiful flowers and nutritious vegetables, gardeners also encounter weeds. And pests. They also get some dirt under their fingernails. In their own way, so will parents.

I know about this grit in the practice relationship because of the kinds of questions parents have asked me over the years. The most common parental concerns have to do with conflicts during practice. A cloud of disappointment and confusion commonly goes along with these questions. Parents expected that there would be some work involved in practicing, but they didn't expect to come into contact with so much abrasiveness.

Sure, there's more to their practices than conflict, and parents want to know more than just how to avoid it. They want to know if they are practicing in a way that helps their children develop musical skills, along with ownership, responsibility, and rising to expectations. Still, the questions about resistance and struggle–conflict–are the most prominent.

At the core of all these questions is one fundamental question: "Am I a good parent?" It's no wonder that this core question is there. Parents have been entrusted not only with caring for their children physically, but also with nurturing their children's emotional and moral development. The stakes are high. Of *course* parents worry about whether or not they're doing the right thing.

One source of the worry is the fact that parents rarely get feedback. Parents lack what most important occupations have: a supervisor, someone who monitors what they're doing and might even offer a "Yes-that's-it" or "How-about-giving-this-a-whirl?"

A parent's own background may not provide much assistance either. Many parents who practice with their children didn't grow up that way themselves. They either didn't study music at all or they practiced alone. Those who did grow up practicing with their parents know that it was helpful, but they may want to spare their children some of the difficulties they had, so they don't want to do it the same way. Or they are somewhat baffled when they find out that their children aren't the way they themselves were as children. They feel stuck.

Your friends and parent-colleagues may sometimes have helpful ideas, but they don't have *your* child. Besides, they're not *you*. The more I think about how little feedback parents get, the more I realize that asking other parents "What piece is your child on?" is not always the adult version of the sandbox boast "My Dad's Bigger Than Yours." Instead, it's often merely a means of seeking reassurance. On the inside the parent is calculating: "Let's see…if your child and my child started lessons at about the same time and now we're more or less on the same piece…I must be doing an o.k. job as a parent." But gauging parent effectiveness this way is about as accurate as measuring the humidity with a plastic fork.

There's one more little snag: spouses don't always agree about what to do.

Teachers want to help out, but parents usually have to wait a week between lessons–which can leave you worried about the prospect of facing five more practices like the one you just had. Then, unfortunately, when you parents finally do get to a lesson, we teachers are often limited in our ability to comment on the practice relationship. Partly we are limited because the many other things we have to accomplish during a lesson usually win the battle for our attention.

We teachers are also limited because the quality of the child's playing and the rate of its growth are often our usual criteria for determining whether or not the parent is doing an adequate job. If progress on the instrument seems to be going along well, we often don't stop and ask how the practicing is going. The quality of a student's playing, however, is not always an accurate representation of the quality of the parent-child relationship during practice. It is possible for a child to play really well and have wonderful, nurturing, supportive parents. It is also possible for a child to have less than stellar musical skills and *still* have wonderful nurturing, and supportive parents. Just because a child is playing well at lessons doesn't mean a parent isn't struggling and worrying at home.

What to do? Just remember that you're not a bad parent if your child doesn't do everything perfectly. You might even want to remind yourself that good doctors, even *great* doctors, have patients who die. I'll admit that it's a grim comparison, but my point is that not everything is under your control, no matter how loving or caring you are. While you do have the enormous responsibility of giving your child the best you can give during your daily practice sessions–and I realize that your best will fluctuate from day to day–you alone are not responsible for the way your child plays. You do, however, have total responsibility for how you, yourself, behave during practice. It's a colossal responsibility, and this book is here to help you.

Through daily practice–spending time in the garden–you'll begin to see it more and more closely. This awareness of your garden will help you know what it needs to help it grow.

4

Listen to the Actions First

A scraped knee followed by a Band-Aid and a little TLC from a parent–and a child is soon back at it. In some ways, children are rugged. But at a very basic level, they're extremely vulnerable. Without someone to take care of them, they die. The younger they are, the truer this is, but even a ten-year-old would have a difficult time surviving without help from an adult. In a place deep inside themselves, a place that doesn't express itself in words, children sense their vulnerability and their vital dependence on their parents. The violin teacher and grandparent Joanne Bath often talks to groups of parents about this aspect of the parent-child relationship. "Children want to look good in the eyes of their parents," she says at nearly every one of her talks. For me, that comment says it all. If a child senses that he looks good in his parent's eyes–is loved–then he knows that he will be taken care of. If he doesn't look good in the eyes of his parent, then a crucial but voiceless part of him feels significantly at risk.

Actions speak louder than words, and it's usually through actions–not words–that children express their core vulnerability. You'd never guess it though, because the language of actions is often difficult to understand during practice. Many parents report that their children scream, cry, defy them, and argue irrationally, even about the simplest of directions. Usually, the directions are the same ones the child heard so easily when his teacher gave them at the lesson.

Picture this scenario: wanting to be helpful, Luther's mom–and she actually does have a name, it's Angela–seeing that Luther is trying to figure out where to start, calmly says "It's B on the A string, honey." Whereupon Luther explodes. Angela, feeling hurt and rejected after one too many practices like this–she was, after all, just trying to be helpful–finally reaches her limit and explodes back: "If you're not willing to follow directions, I give up!" The practice comes to a screeching halt, with Luther upset and irritated–and also scared. Angela is confused and feeling guilty.

This had not been what she had in mind when Luther expressed enthusiasm about the violin and she and her husband decided to give their son "the gift of music."

Luther's behavior is not attractive. How could a snarling child possibly be seeking love? Yet the vulnerability is embedded in these actions. It doesn't have to make obvious sense, and in fact it often doesn't. We generally have difficulty reading these actions because in the process of becoming adults who could function in a civilized world, we appropriately learned to think rationally and to put most of our feelings into words instead of actions. For example, we pay the cashier the total instead of waiting for her to grab it out of our hand. In the process of becoming civilized, however, we may have forgotten much of the language of actions.

So let me do some interpreting. Irritating behaviors such as creating a fuss, arguing, and poking may be a child's way of telling his mother that he hopes she will pay attention to him. (In hopes of getting publicity, the obnoxious behavior of rock stars often mimics this strategy to the nth degree.) Though he doesn't have words to express his vulnerability–which would, of course, be much easier for both the parent and the child–the child's actions are saying that he wants to stay connected to his mother. Even if the connection is unpleasant, the child's hope is that by keeping her attention, she will remember to take care of him. It's not a very sophisticated strategy, but without even thinking it through, a child's gut discovers that it works. Though the parental attention that this behavior generates is not particularly sweet for children, it does keep them fed.

Wanting to look good in the eyes of the person he counts on for survival may cause a child to explode, the way Luther did. It can also sometimes explain what first appears to be an opposite reaction.

In an effort to protect their status in their parent's eyes, some children tune out when their parents give them instructions. It doesn't matter that the instructions usually mean exactly what the parents say, nothing more. For example, wanting to look good in the eyes of her parent, the emotional insides of a child don't hear "Play it again and check to see if the bow hairs stay in one spot on the string." What they hear instead might be something completely different–"If you don't keep the bow hairs in one spot on the string, I'm going to stop loving you." Instead of responding to this fear with an explosion the way Luther did, a child may simply disregard her mother's instructions, in the hope that it will be as if her mother never noticed the bow hairs and there were no instruction in the first place. In essence, it's only a slightly more advanced form of peek-a-boo. If the child were able to speak with words instead of actions, the child's insides would say something like "Maybe if I don't do it, my mom will just forget."

Nice try. Mom usually remembers. Children who act this way are often expressing a very normal fear–that they have done or will do something that is so bad that their parents will stop loving them.

"You're kidding, aren't you?" I can hear many parents ask.

No, I'm not. Not at all. It really happens. I've observed it happening countless times, and I've heard about it over and over in the stories that parents–good parents–tell me. These feelings would be much easier if children could attach words to them, but they usually can't do that very well. So the feelings come out in actions. They are technically known as "unconscious" feelings. As the noted psychologist Irene Fast once told me, "Nobody would care about unconscious feelings if they stayed unconscious." But they do speak. They speak through actions. And we adults need to pay attention to them.

Of course, in addition to needing to feel cared for, there are other things going on in the life of a developing child. The actions of a child may be speaking about something other than feeling at risk. For example, children have a deep wish for things to be instant and easy and are frustrated when they aren't. A child's strategies for getting out of the difficulty and struggle of work may include fussing in hopes that the parent will back down, ignoring in hopes that she will forget, and other similar types of unpleasant behavior.

And the person a child is usually unconsciously frustrated with is the parent, not the teacher. It's not because the teacher is a better person, it's because the teacher doesn't have the history that the parent has with the child. After all, when a child was a baby, it was the parent, not the teacher, who was the original magician who made necessities like food and transportation appear. So there's often a part of a child's emotional insides that senses the parent to be magical. It's the part of your child that feels–but doesn't have words to express–that you're just hiding your magic wand

and that you actually *could* make it possible for her to learn the instrument effortlessly if you would just go to your room right now and get that wand out of the drawer you hide it in. You can offer your child a dose of reality and a shot of love if you say something such as "Wouldn't it be *great* if I had a magic wand and could make this instantly easy for you? I don't have a wand and I'm not magic...but if I did have a wand, I'd use it to make this easy for you. But since there's no wand and no magic, you'll just have to practice it..."

A fear of completely losing your love may not explain every behavior of your child's any more than a nearly empty gas tank explains why a car's brakes aren't working. Like the gas gauge, however, it's important to pay attention to how "full" of your love your child feels during practice. And it's crucial that you read your *child's* gauge, not your own. You probably have enormous amounts of love in the pumps in *your* station, but a child whose own tank is running low is going to need a fill-up. That fill-up will have to come from you, the person in the parent role, the only one who can supply him with this necessary fuel–and it will not necessarily come from what you say, but from the strategies you use during practice. Be forewarned that it may take a while to fill up the tank. This book can help.

(Note: though the adult who practices with the child may be the grandparent, guardian, etc., throughout this book, when I use the word "parent," "mother," and "father," I mean the person who is functioning in the parental role.)

...**Then**–and only then–**Respond to the Actions**

Parents are usually relieved to know that the emotional struggles of a developing child are often behind the struggles in the daily practice arena–that it's not their incompetence as parents that makes practices difficult. But the relief is not enough–nor should it be. When I talk to groups of parents about these issues, there's usually a hand that shoots up:

"O.K., I get it, but what do I *do*? I still have to tell my kid if it's a wrong note, don't I? At some point they have to learn how to handle constructive criticism, right? I mean, I can't just lie and say it was wonderful when it wasn't–or should I?"

I know these concerns are pervasive because, as if on cue, the heads of the other parents start nodding together in agreement. From my vantage point, it's a bit like watching the Rockettes kick.

The first step in addressing these concerns is simply understanding the general vulnerability of children, as outlined in the previous section. Assuming vulnerability will generally save the two of you lots of difficulties during practice. It's like setting the iron at a very low setting for what you think is a piece of nylon. If you start out on a high setting, you may find yourself with a sticky stubborn, difficult mess, as I discovered one Halloween–I must have been about eight–when I made a coolie wig out of old nylons and tried to iron the pigtail.

Once you actually start to do the ironing, you need to check to see whether your initial setting is working. You might want to try gradually turning up the heat as you go along, testing it in an inconspicuous place that doesn't really matter. Or you might try a pressing cloth. If a higher temperature doesn't work, you can't blame the nylon for being nylon anymore than you can blame a child for feeling vulnerable.

So the most important thing in dealing with a child's vulnerability is simply to notice whether or not your words and actions contribute to a useful result. This seems like an obvious step. But like a hamster running on a wheel, we adults are commonly so occupied with doing what we're doing, we forget to check to see if it's getting us anywhere. This quirk seems to be especially true during practice.

Children do need to learn how to handle constructive criticism, but without support from adults, we can't expect them to be able to do it any more than we can expect them to take the casserole out of the oven with their bare hands. We adults need to be vigilant when it comes to noticing the ways in which our words help them develop the confidence–the oven mitts–they need in order to handle that criticism. Feeling safe in the parent's love and care is one of the basic raw materials of that confidence.

Criticism is also easier to handle if it's built on previous success. We need to notice if our words are moving the practice forward, whether forward means developing the musical craft or the child's confidence. There's nothing wrong with giving children information that seems neutral to you. But if children feel at risk–whether it's rational or not–even the mildest of "suggestions" can often cause a meltdown.

When these meltdowns occur–and they come in a variety of unpleasant forms–adults then do the best they know to do. If they haven't been given other alternatives, they typically attempt to improve the situation with rational words. They start slinging facts:

"If you'll just do it this once, you'll know what I mean."

–or maybe–

"I'm not making this up, see? It really is a B-flat–it says so right here in the book!"

Given that actions speak louder than words, these parent words are not nearly at the same volume as the child's actions. When stating facts doesn't work–and it rarely does when a child is feeling vulnerable–parents can start to feel powerless as well, which frequently leads them to wonder if they're a good parent and if playing an instrument is worth all the fuss. The nylon melts *and* the iron gets clogged up. In the worst case scenarios, parents who feel disregarded and hurt retaliate against their children by being overly harsh, which, of course, makes the child feel even more vulnerable, and escalates the problems.

Clearly, parents need lots of options that will help them lead the parent-child practice relationship into more productive and pleasant territory. Productive *and* pleasant. The productive part is a bit like scuba diving–merely connecting to your oxygen supply isn't the point of scuba diving, but you won't get much else done if you don't. Ideas for making practice pleasant and productive can come from many sources: teachers, lectures, other parents, articles, and books.

Most of the options and ideas in this book are ordinary. At some point, you or another parent would probably figure them out. In fact, many of the ideas come from typical parents who eventually did just that. If you find yourself wondering "Why didn't I think of that?" it's probably because you were busy practicing. In the heat of practicing–not to mention all of the millions of other things parents have to do–generating solutions can be difficult. Like the emergency room physicians whose preparation helps them avoid being freaked out by gruesome and grave situations, preparation during calmer moments can help increase the likelihood that instead of working from an impulse that may or may not be what you need, you'll be working from a plan that has some care and concern behind it. If you should slice your finger when attempting to repair a lawnmower and the doctor in the emergency room screeched "Oh no! You've cut your finger! Blood!" you would likely feel a lot differently than if the doctor said "We'll just get you a couple of stitches in that finger and send you on your way." Similarly, getting *yourself* prepared can really help your child be calmer during the difficulties of practices.

The suggestions in this book are also ordinary in terms of supplies. Even though you might find some of the suggestions challenging at first, they'll get easier as you practice them. You won't, however, find yourself spending your precious time wielding a glue-gun to make practice games out of paper plates and shellacked pinecones. I won't be asking you to engage in what my friend John calls "craft abuse."

You'll find a fair amount of detail in this book, detail that will help you generate ideas for responding to your child's actions. Slinging facts isn't always the best way to help a child practice, but knowing those facts can help you feel confident in responding to that imaginary sign that you should always see hanging over the child, the sign that reads "What can I do next that will help the most?" It doesn't really do anybody much good if you have lots of ideas for delivering facts but don't have specific facts in the first place.

Since snazzy generalities and cute sayings don't usually get the job done, this book is chockfull of specific examples–not so that you can do the exact same thing with your child when you practice, but so that you have clear ideas for specific ways in which you might respond to your unique situation.

Speaking of examples, many of them feature younger children. To use them with older children you'll probably need to de-Barney the language, but their essence should still prove useful. I used examples with younger children because the personality is launched in childhood. Understanding where a child has been can help you understand what's happening currently. Back to the image of ironing nylon, it helps to know what you're dealing with when you're working to smooth out the wrinkles.

In my experience, the areas of musicianship and rhythm generally give parents the most confusion about facts. It's no surprise, then, that some of the biggest difficulties during practice come when attempting to work on these issues. That's why sections on musicianship and rhythm figure predominantly in this book. While difficulties in the parent-child practice relationship can hinder the development of musical skills, it can also go the other way around: misunderstandings about musical concepts, particularly rhythm and musical expression, can sometimes put undue stress on an otherwise happy relationship. While working on rhythm and musicianship may not be the easiest for you and your child, knowing some facts–along with specific strategies for passing them on to your child–can greatly ease the burden. Otherwise, when we adults say things to a child such as "Could you, like, um, do it again and sort of slow down in that one part so it sounds a little bit better–like I know you can do!" the child can feel a little bit like an appendicitis victim whose smiling surgeon hacks away, saying "I know the appendix is in here somewhere..."

Knowing the specific details of where you are and where you're going helps to make practice as pleasant as possible. Even if the detail you know is that the ingredient missing from the child's playing is one that can wait until later. It helps you relax.

When it comes to specific information about the way your child's particular instrument works, you'll have to consult with your regular teacher. Although I'm a violinist, learning how to play the violin, specifically, is outside the scope of this book.

While developing your clear knowledge of facts is important, you'll also notice that this book contains many ideas for transmitting those facts to your child in *indirect* ways. For example, rather than telling your child that it's a C-sharp, not a C-natural, one suggestion is that you share with your child everything you noticed that went well–an incredibly important skill for the official lesson teacher and the parent, or "home teacher"–and then that you merely practice singing the piece away from the instrument before having the child return to playing it on the instrument. For this strategy to work, you'll have to know what was working well, and you'll also have to know that it's a C-sharp.

Many adults wonder how indirect strategies such as this one could possibly help. But they do. They're like the tiny aspirin tablets that we might put in our mouth to address the sprained ankle at the other end of our body. You can't get much more indirect than that, but we don't think of it as indirect because people do this kind of thing all the time. It's usually much more effective than simply yelling at the foot. Or even talking to it sweetly. When direct ways don't work, responding to your child's practice frustrations in indirect ways means that you're responding in the same language as the child's actions, so you stand a better chance of being "heard" and understood.

If you don't always know exactly how to respond to your child's actions during practice–even after reading this entire book, *join the club*! After twenty years of teaching, I'm still frequently stumped during lessons. It's not that I don't have ideas for what to do next, it's that I'm not always exactly sure which one will work. I go down blind alleys, taking the parent and student with me, before I find a place to turn around.

As with teaching, implementing the ideas in this book is likely to be a journey for you. And the journey of a thousand miles begins with a broken fan belt and a flat tire.

But that's o.k. One of the most important pieces of information adults can pass on to children is the idea that learning involves growing and changing; and that it doesn't necessarily happen in a straight line. When we are in the middle of it, we don't always have control over it. Our intentions to do things in new ways get thwarted by our old habits. We want to stop the old thing and go with the new, but we haven't really stopped, and we're not yet to the new place. We have to think about it. For example, a child realizes that the note contains three beats, not two, but still misses the rhythm now and then. Likewise for the parent who understands that it doesn't work to blurt out "Oops!" every time the child's playing trips, but still catches herself doing it on occasion. There's a good reason that old habits die hard: it's risky to test the depth of the water with both feet. Until we're sure of the new thing, it doesn't feel safe to give up the old.

You'll make mistakes. You'll make blunders. Plenty of them. None of them should be life threatening. I don't know a single teacher whose studio has a main entrance and an emergency entrance. I'm never on call, and I don't carry a beeper. You won't make any huge blunders that can't wait for the next lesson. I am saddened when parents find a piece of the information in this book haunting, thinking that it tells them about every way in which they have "ruined" their children. We humans wish that we could always do the right thing so that life would always turn out perfectly. But, that is just a wish.

Oh, and another thing. Some of the suggestions in this book will seem to contradict one another. That's life. I trust you to figure it all out in the moment during your day-to-day practices with your child.

The key to responding to the actions of a child is to notice the results of our well-intentioned responses and to increase and develop a rich vocabulary of options for responding. In other words, think of it this way: it's not what you do first, it's what you do next.

Making it Easier

Always keep in mind that the goal of practice is to make things easier. When the goal of practice is to "fix things," then a child's performance tends to be limited to a hope that all the things you fixed stay fixed–not a set-up likely to give a child's musical soul the freedom it needs to emerge. Practicing to "correct" things tends to have the effect of making children feel like they themselves are in need of correction for their very being, and they are more likely to be resistant during practice.

Sitting there listening to all the things that children are doing wrong, and responding with corrections, will have children–at best–putting up shields. Ignoring you, for example, can often be shielding behavior. At worst, focusing practices on the errors will have children drawing swords–poking you with the bow, hitting, and screaming, to name just a few scenarios that quickly come to mind. If the goal of practice has been to "try hard" at things–getting the rhythm, for example, then the student ends up being anxious about something that can only really work when the body understands it as easily as it understands how to breathe. Finally, if practices and lessons are all about righting the wrong things the teacher and parent bring up, the child ends up working merely to satisfy the concerns of the adults, and the goal of having the child own the playing becomes more difficult to achieve.

But if you focus practice on making things easier, the child can gradually begin to assume full ownership. Such a child who goes on stage to perform no longer needs last-minute reminders–"Remember, Bernadine, *vibrato*"–from a parent or teacher. The things that have been practiced are easy enough that the child reliably and genuinely owns them.

You don't practice something only because the teacher said so. You practice it because some aspect of it is not easy and automatic yet–perhaps it's the draping of the fingers on the bow, or landing smack-dab on the piano key when the left hand crosses over the right. When the focus of practice has been to make things easier, performances are more secure because a student isn't playing in the nervous hope that things will turn out o.k. Instead, the student is playing through the things that have become easy and manageable.

Practicing to make things easier means you spend less and less of your precious practice time attempting to get the child to repeat something because you, the adult, said so. Instead, you gradually bring things into a child's awareness, and then assist your child with repeating what's not yet consistent and reliable–meaning easy. When you practice to make things easier, rhythms can eventually even out. And, when you have practiced to make something easy, a performance is not about struggling to get through a piece, but being able to have the physical aspects of it happen easily enough so that the musical soul of the performer can soar.

There can still be struggle when you're practicing to make things easier. Like Dolly Parton's line "It costs a lot to make a person look this cheap," it takes a great deal of effort for a child's playing to look, to feel, and to sound effortless.

When your goal is moving the playing towards easier and not towards "right," the struggle happens in an appropriate place. You're cooking in the oven instead of the dryer. One of the biggest struggles is dealing with the frustration that children usually have when they bump into the reality that things are seldom immediately easy, and that merely *wishing* to make them easier–no matter how earnestly it's done–just doesn't work. It takes practice. Children are not the only ones who face this frustration: parents and teachers do too! For the child, much of the toil comes in the form of repeating things. For the adults, the struggle is often with figuring out ways to help the child work through the disappointment that accompanies the discovery that the world isn't magic. The adults also have to work out strategies–learned in advance or invented on the spot–to help a child tolerate repeating things until they're easier. The adult who practices with the child needs daily practice, so that over time, he or she gradually learns how to accomplish these enormous tasks.

Practicing is a rich and complex undertaking. Parents sometimes worry that if they don't tell their children that something is bad, the children won't take the work seriously. While this approach can be successful in many ways, it's a much too difficult path to take, and ultimately involves many detours anyway.

This book contains specific strategies for working in ways that are easier–and more effective in the long run–than fixing and correcting bad things. Sometimes the strategies are about practice procedures. At other times they're about giving you ideas that you can use as you deal with that common internal burden, the struggle of answering the question "Am I doing the right thing? and "Am I a good parent?"

The goal of this book is to take you and your child to the land of Easier. It's a nice place to live, but there are still chores to do there.

This Book and Your Child–shhhhh!

Remembering that your child wants to look good in your eyes will help you do your part to create pleasant practices for the two of you. However, you're courting disaster if you take this basic principle, flip it around, and base your moves during practice on your own personal need to look good in the eyes of your child. Though a parent's wish to look good in the eyes of the child may seem equally as valid as the need for the child to look good in the eyes of the parent, it's not. It's like the deadly poisonous mushroom that's nearly identical to the safe one. The distinction matters.

The difference originates with the condition into which babies are born: not knowing they're alive. They gradually come into an awareness that they exist, and much of the time growing up, they are discovering who they are. If they have a sense that their parents genuinely love them, then they have the safe environment they need to discover their own souls. Parents can complicate this discovering, however, if they have a strong need to use their children to satisfy their own emotional needs. One way a parent might use a child in this manner is by forcing her to be a star music student and demanding that she always sit first chair, thus "proving" the parent's own worth. (This situation is very different, by the way, from an insistence on daily practice, which can be very healthy.) The problem in this example comes from the fact that the child risks losing the parent's love because of "disappointing" the parent. The parent may think that sitting first chair will boost the child's self-esteem, but if the parent isn't satisfied unless the child is sitting there, then the child isn't getting the kind of genuine love that only a parent can give. Any "honor" will lack this essential ingredient. Children don't have the capacity to understand that the parent needs to look elsewhere for emotional support.

Another inappropriate way a parent might use a child is by asking the child to approve, or "certify," the parent's job as a parent–as in asking a child if it's o.k. to make him do something that he really shouldn't have a choice about. For example, "Would it be o.k. if you put your clothes on before we go to the grocery store?" [See also section 25, "Make Demands that are Clear, Gentle, and Firm."]

When parents use their children to satisfy their emotional needs, disaster sets in. The disaster comes from the fact that in order to guarantee that their parents will continue to stick around and care for their *physical* needs, children will work to keep the parents' emotional needs satisfied. It's the opposite of what happens during pregnancy, when if nutrients are in short supply, the baby gets the nutrients before the mother. After birth, however, when parents aren't taking care of their own emotional needs, children forfeit their own. Lacking the emotional safety that comes with knowing that parents will take care of themselves, children become too busy monitoring their parent's emotional needs to discover their own selves. The result for the child can be lifelong emotional pain, and much has been written about this phenomenon. The good news is that children can tolerate a bit of this, and that parents who are aware of the issue usually end up being good enough parents for their children. (Remember: you don't have to get it all perfect. You'll mess up some. As I mentioned in section 1 of this book, you just have to be good enough, and most parents are.)

It's crucial, therefore, that someone or something other than the child satisfies a parent's need for approval and self-worth. Approving or disapproving of your job as a parent is certainly not a healthy kind of control for a child to have. Keep in mind that when I say this, it's coming from a person who believes very strongly that children *do* need to have certain kinds of control. But giving your child the option of approving or disapproving of your job as a parent is like giving him the choice between an olive or a twist of lemon with his martini. The problem isn't with the olive and the lemon. This is not to say that it isn't important that you notice what works and doesn't work with your child. You should. You might even ask the child what helps him or her the most. Just remember that there is a huge difference between soliciting information from a child about how your actions make him feel, and looking to the child for approval of what you're doing.

When you are tempted to share the contents of this book with your child, you imagine a voice in your head–a voice that looks and sounds a lot like Sylvester Stallone–saying "Shut up about it." Share this book with other adults, but not with your child.

Here's why: when teachers and parents tell students about the kinds of ideas that are in this book, they are usually–deep down–saying it so that they will feel like they are better parents and teachers, and hoping the child will agree. They want to look good in the eyes of the children. In other cases, adults may present ideas from this book so that the children will automatically do the things the adults need them to do, and then the adult work of setting limits will magically disappear. Sometimes, the adults hope for both. Expecting children to act in these ways, however, is inappropriate. As the adults in the equation, we need to understand that we have the authority to make decisions on behalf of children. We also have the responsibility of paying attention to the results of those decisions and adjusting them if necessary.

Asking a child to take care of your adult emotional needs–for example, tell you that your insistence that she play the scale three times is a really cool and groovy idea so that you don't feel like a meanie when you insist that she practice something she doesn't want to–is very different from your insisting that she play it three times, whether she is thrilled about it or not. After the three times, you may decide that at tomorrow's practice, once or twice may suffice. Or you may decide to give your child a choice about how many times she repeats it. Outside of practicing, it's fine to require a child to do routine behaviors that make living together manageable–such as leaving muddy boots at the back door, and saying "thank you," to mention just two typical examples. The danger is when you expect a child to adore everything you require. Until they're mature adults themselves, it's usually a miracle when children genuinely appreciate reasonable parent requirements that they dislike.

While I do recommend that you refrain from talking about this book with your child, you don't have to keep it hidden in a brown paper bag. If your child takes the initiative and wants to know what the book is about, it would be appropriate to say something such as "I'm reading this book so I can get ideas about how to make our practices more pleasant." Or "I'm hoping to learn ways that I can do all that I can to make the ouchies that happen during practice heal faster." (Obviously, a 12-year-old is going to need slightly different language...)

Please notice that the wording of these responses does not indicate that you, yourself, are 100% responsible for the practice relationship. You're not. While parents need to take the biggest share of responsibility for the way practice goes–maybe up to 99% for an extremely young beginner–it is a mistake to convey to the child that you, the parent, are solely responsible for the way practices turn out. So, when it comes to telling your child about why you are reading this book, avoid saying that you are reading it so that you alone can change the practice sessions.

At this point, even though it may very likely be unclear to you just what your child's responsibility should be during practice, you will save yourself and your child a great deal of grief if you refrain from delivering the message that other people–including you–are 100% responsible for the relationship they have with him or her. Relationships, whether a commercial relationship, such as that between the pilot of an airplane and a passenger, or an intimate one, such as that between spouses, are always a shared responsibility. Much of the advice in this book is designed so that the parent and the child are both engaged in the relationship, though it may never be 50-50. Few relationships ever really are. Although 50-50 is a good set of numbers to aim for, in reality, the numbers are constantly shifting.

Marks on Paper

I fell in love with words the day my college writing professor described a college classmate of hers as being the kind of person who just needed to have "a little raw meat thrown into her cage in the morning." This comment was definitely a case of it-takes-one-to-know-one. Mrs. Hartzler, as this PhD-holding professor preferred we address her, was quite a tiger herself.

During one of the classes before our first assignment was due, Mrs. Hartzler began by snarling "Many of you have asked me how to get started. Well, my mother was an English teacher and when her students asked her how to get started she said 'Make black marks on white paper.'"

While she could be ferocious about slashing clichés and flabby reasoning from our papers, it is also true that a well-turned phrase could make her purr. In fact, in all fairness, I would have to say that she purred a great deal. When it came to marking our papers, she was generous with her red pen. We used to say that our papers came back bloody. But what she had actually written in the margins was an enormous number of curt and direct comments about what worked–and why–as well as what didn't work–and why.

So, how do you get started practicing? Just do something. Anything. Spend some time at it. You can refine as you go. If this book does its job, you'll begin to see what is working in your practices–and why–and you'll also glean ideas for smoothing things out as you go.

"Make black marks on white paper" got us started, and Mrs. Hartzler's instruction moved us beyond it. I hope that this book can do the same for you. Sadly, pancreatic cancer claimed Mrs. Hartzler's life at the age of 39, about one year after our class ended. This book would not exist if I had not been lucky enough to have gotten into her class.

Thanks, Mrs. Hartzler.

When practices aren't productive and positive, the cause is usually an absence of one or more of the basic ingredients of practice. Each section in this chapter outlines one of those basic ingredients.

practice basics

9

34

practice basics

9

Look for Horses, not Zebras

Experienced and caring doctors advise the medical students they supervise to "look for horses, not zebras." In other words, if a patient's symptoms could indicate either a common case of the flu or an exotic illness, it's probably just the flu.

"Look for horses" is also good advice for parents who practice with their children. Difficulties in your practices do not necessarily indicate a bizarre problem that requires something out of the ordinary, such as switching to a different instrument, starting a "challenging" piece, deciding that the instrument is simply too difficult for you and/or your child, concluding that your youngster lacks interest and discipline, switching teachers, quitting all together, or turning yourself in as one of the world's ten most inadequate parents. These kinds of drastic actions are *very* rarely necessary. They are zebras.

Stick with the horses in this section. If you pay attention to these basic elements, your practices will generally be productive–even though they will still be likely to have the usual ups and downs that come with the process of practicing.

Keep the Focus on Making Things Easier

When I'm at a workshop and teaching a group of students beyond *Volume One* of the *Suzuki Violin School,* I often ask them if Suzuki's "Twinkle Variation A," the very first piece they learned in *Volume One,* is easy. Not only do they think it's easy, there are often complaints about it being a "baby" piece. After having them play it–just to be sure it's a cinch for them–I point out that there are young beginners at the workshop who are struggling to play the piece, just as I imagine they themselves once did.

The nodding heads of the observing parents confirm my statement. I point out that the purpose of practice isn't to learn how to try really hard to play a piece, but to repeat things so that they become easier. "Why do people practice?" I'll ask the students several times during the class. By the end, they can all at least parrot back "To make it easier." Perhaps the idea will cross their minds the next time they're practicing.

Whether my lecture sticks with all of the kids or not is somewhat beside the point. What truly matters is that all of those parents were listening. My hope is that my little lecture helps the parents to grasp this concept intellectually. I don't actually expect a few words from me to teach children that the goal of practice is to make things easier–I don't know of a single case in which words alone had much of an impact on a child.

Instead, I count on the students learning this principle through repeated experiences in their daily practices–experiences in which their parents put the concept into action. It is the parents–the adults–who need to understand that merely pointing out corrections to a child doesn't help the playing become fluent and expressive. But repeating things until they become easier and automatic–*that's* the way to make playing grow. Adding easier to easier still requires work, but it's more effective and pleasant than adding challenge to challenge, which ultimately can leave a child in knots.

Things don't get easier just for your child. The work that you, the parent, do during practice will also get easier over time, as *you* "practice practicing." Some or all of the suggestions in this chapter may be difficult for you at first, but as you practice doing them, you'll find them becoming easier, even automatic.

How will you know what, specifically, you and your child need to practice until it gets easier? For starters, your teacher will give you specific assignments. The older and more advanced the student, the more those assignments tend to be about technical and musical points; the younger and less advanced the student, the more frequently they can also be about behavior.

If your child is having difficulty performing a certain behavior, such as keeping his feet in one place, that is the very thing you will need to practice until it becomes easier. If "behavioral difficulties" occur only in the privacy of your own home and your teacher doesn't see them at lessons–and if you don't report them–your teacher will not know to give you assignments that address them. If you inform the teacher, however, you and your teacher can then collaborate to decide whether the most effective course of action is to ignore the undesirable behavior, or whether you need to practice the *preferred* behavior until it is easy for your child to execute it.

Some behaviors are difficult to ignore. Perhaps you want to work on helping the child develop a beautiful sound, but he's running around the room. If that's the case, forget about working on tone. As Kay Collier-Slone (McLaughlin) writes in *They're Rarely Too Young…*, "[the] first task for the student is to develop the ability to focus, in order to find a quietness within himself, and give himself and his will to the lesson situation. The lesson can only begin when the being is centered–when there is a quiet, concentrated mind–a sense of internal calmness." Most adults readily agree, but it is Dr. Collier-Slone (McLaughlin)'s next sentence which is crucial: "Children have a great ability to focus in this manner, *if they are assisted by a proper environment and willing adults*" [emphasis added].

In other places in this book, I give suggestions for developing a child's ability to focus [particularly section 30]. In this section, I merely want to make the point that there aren't really any magic words that can do it. You're going to have to create activities–in other words, as Dr. Collier-Slone (McLaughlin) says, a "proper environment"–in which you give your child repeated opportunities to sense himself being focused. And you usually can't just use those ideas once. Most likely, you'll have to repeat them daily–maybe for weeks–until centering for a practice becomes easier and automatic for your child.

I encourage you to take notice when your child behaves in ways that irritate you. If you can't ignore these behaviors–and only you will know for sure–then you need to help your child develop a different way of behaving. And you have to practice that way until it becomes automatic. For example, if it irritates you that your child doesn't follow your directions very well, keep the focus of your practices on having your child follow directions. Keep doing this until connecting to your directions becomes easier for your child. Of course, you're going to start out making sure that your directions are ones that the child can *easily* follow.

You can even make a game out of it. If your child can both stand still and wiggle on command–and don't assume that all children can–then you know that he can follow directions. After you've worked with these kinds of easy–maybe even silly–directions and seen that the child can follow them just fine, you're ready to move on to more advanced directions. If your child begins to have difficulty following your directions, that's a clear sign that you will need to break these directions into smaller parts. For example, saying "play it again, but make sure it's in tune," may be too complicated. I used to give this kind of direction all the time in my early years of teaching. But then I realized that it can take several months of work until a child has a grasp of what "in tune" actually means. Without this grasp, he's incapable of following the direction. Why does it take so long? Because as soon as a child understands one component of playing in tune, he has to practice it until it gets easier.

It may go without saying, but it's so important I'll say it anyway: If your child needs to practice a behavior until it's so easy that it's automatic, you're probably going to have to give up working on "the new piece" for a while. Or at least you'll have to understand that it will take longer to learn it, because you'll be devoting significant amounts of your practice time to other things.

Say your son has an annoying habit of whacking the bow on the string when you're talking. While you're working to make it an automatic part of his practice time behaviors to leave the bow sitting silently on the string or hanging by his side instead, he won't get many new notes learned. Sure, we teachers–like you–want your child to learn pieces. But it's important that teachers and parents share a vision that is much bigger–big enough to understand that a child will have a much more successful and pleasant experience studying music if we spend time creating the habits that allow learning to happen more easily. We also need to realize that these habits help practices to be more pleasant. It's no fun for you OR your child if you're distracted during practices because you're fretting over whether your child's wild bow is going to do damage.

There's another way to know when your child needs to practice a specific behavior until it's easier. It's when you catch yourself saying something like "Well, it seems to me that he should be able to–*fill-in-the-*

blank–without my having to tell him more than once" but you notice that this expectation of yours isn't working. "Practice slowly," for instance, is one of the most common things that parents have in the blank–and it's the reason that this book has an entire chapter devoted to rhythm. If that's the case for you, read the rhythm chapter carefully. It contains lots of ideas for using your practice time to make it easier for your child to slow down. Generally speaking, when you have an expectation that doesn't match the reality it's paired with, that's your cue that you need to do something other than merely have the expectation. Usually, that something else is creating an activity that helps make it easier for your child to do whatever you put in the blank.

Then, don't expect your child to know how to do something *and do it automatically* just because you mentioned it once in practice and he repeated it a time or two. You will need to repeat it many times until it's an easy and automatic part of how he behaves during practices.

My advice that you pay attention to behaviors that irritate you may sound like encouragement for you to be self-centered, but it's not. It's child-centered advice. I'm encouraging you to pay attention to yourself so that you are then available to help your child. When you're irritated with your child, your response probably irritates your child as well, at least at some level. To be more precise, disappointing you is probably disturbing for your child. Working constructively on the issue is a way to help relieve the load for both of you.

And keep in mind that you can't work on making everything easier all at once. You're going to have to choose judiciously. [For more about this concept, please see section 18, "Shoot One Arrow at a Time."]

The idea that repeating things makes them easier appears at every lesson I teach. Please make sure that the concept shows up at your practices as well.

11

Attending Lessons Really Matters

If you're going to practice with your child, you'll need to participate in *all* of his lessons, including group lessons. At first, you may wonder what good you're doing by just sitting there quietly paying attention and taking notes–which is what parent "participation" in lessons usually comes down to. Still, your presence is crucial, and paves the way for numerous benefits. I'll mention four of them.

The first benefit is that you will gradually be able to develop a clearer idea of what your child does–*and does not*–need to practice. Many parents who practice successfully with their children know little or nothing about music. Some have never even played a musical instrument at all. But they are successful because their presence at lessons gives them firsthand information about the teacher's very specific assignments. These parents know that teachers create assignments to help their children's playing grow. They also know that their presence at lessons ensures that the fine details of these assignments don't get lost somewhere between the door to the teacher's studio and home.

Some parents are tempted to practice more than the teacher assigns–especially the parents who are musicians themselves. But this extra credit work is usually too much, and merely overwhelms the child. A few years ago, I ran into my stand partner from our college orchestra and was very impressed with her awareness of this temptation and the way she worked around it. Though she's a fantastic violinist herself–she has won several competitions and completed a graduate degree in violin performance–when it came time to choose a violin teacher for her daughter, she chose carefully and then *only* practiced what the teacher assigned.

The formula worked like a charm. A well-trained teacher knows that assigning too much can be just as unproductive as assigning too little. Attending your child's lessons gives you the opportunity to get the teacher's assignments firsthand. You also get to discuss those assignments with the teacher. Working together in this way, you and your child's teacher can find an optimal assignment load for your child.

The second advantage of attending lessons with your child is that you will learn, over time, *how* to practice. Frequently, the function of lessons is not to learn new skills or notes, but to learn new ways of practicing the things you already know. By practicing old things in new ways, students fortify and expand their existing skills. When you attend your child's lessons you learn how to support your child's practice in ways that prevent the two of you from spinning your wheels.

A third benefit of your presence in lessons is that it protects your child from an unfair burden–the burden of inappropriate parental expectations. The weight of these expectations inevitably ends up on the child's shoulders–in one way or another–when the parent who practices with the child is not at the lessons.

Before I tell you the two most common of these unfair expectations, I first need to say a bit about expectations in general. Expectations are tricky things when it comes to children. If we didn't expect that they would someday actually be able to play a difficult instrument–or, at a more basic level, learn how to add and subtract, or even to feed themselves–we'd never make them get out of bed. But we need to help them rise to our expectations in small steps, steps that they can manage one at a time. Children whose parents expect them to tackle more than one step at a time can turn into adults who expect to fail at everything, because they grew up experiencing failure in the eyes of the people who mattered the most to them–their parents. On the other hand, if these children exert themselves so much that they are somehow able to accomplish the inappropriately enormous tasks placed in front of them, then there is the risk that they will grow into adults who will never be able to relax. They are so used to making a big deal out of everything that even small chores like taking out the garbage become a major production.

It's not that I don't think each and every one of my students is capable of greatness. I do. I just don't expect to see all of that greatness right now, all of the time. I know that greatness develops in manageable steps and stages. It emerges. Children grow. So I think that it's vitally important that on a day-to-day basis we give children expectations that enrich them, not expectations that overwhelm them.

So here's the first of the two typical overwhelming expectations that parents who don't attend lessons *always* manage to place on their children: expecting that their children will remember the teacher's assignments. While it's perfectly reasonable to insist that your child practice daily, it's *not* reasonable to expect your child to remember all of the intricate–and crucial–details of what the teacher said. *Especially* if that child really pays attention at lessons. That may seem like an odd thing to say, but it's not. Here's why.

A child who is paying attention is involved in the here and now, and not necessarily in the "remembering" of all of the details. Children do not yet have the skill of paying attention *and* taking notes at the same time. While children are, in some senses, like digital video cameras that record everything going on around them, they don't always know how to operate the equipment. In other words, they're often unable to access what they've stored. It's never surprising to me when a child who seemed to understand perfectly how to do something at a lesson, was then unable to remember it during home practices *unless* the parent captured the important details in his or her notes.

Since even the most attentive children are not equipped to remember all of the important details of their lessons, it is unfair to expect your child to tell you–an adult–what needs to be practiced. That doesn't mean you can't ask your child questions about what the teacher said. Of course you can. But asking children questions to see what they remember, or to exercise their brains, is quite different from *expecting* them to remember for you. As the parent at the lesson you are an eyewitness to the details. Since you are not involved in actually playing the instrument, your hands are free to write down those details as best you can.

Here's the second way in which children are commonly overwhelmed with unfair expectations: when the parent who attends lessons with the child is not the parent who practices with the child, the child gets caught in the middle. Much has been written about the dangers of having children be the link between their divorced parents, but even in intact families, children can be used in this inappropriate way. If the parent who practices with the child doesn't also attend the lessons, the practicing parent can sometimes expect the child to remember details–"Now what did your mother mean when she wrote '3' on here?" Asking a question like this to engage a child and encourage thinking can be nourishing. But it becomes a dangerous question if the parent doesn't, in fact, know the answer and is expecting the child to know.

It's not emotionally healthy for kids to be caught in the middle. So if you're planning to practice with your child, you really do need to attend the lessons. You may be one of the parents who thinks you won't fall into this trap. But in my experience, everyone does in this setup, even if only in the most subtle of ways. But the subtleties matter. We're talking about minute details here, after all.

Children who feel trapped between their parents are not going to have happy practices. At best, it becomes like the game "telephone"–there are misunderstandings when the messages become mangled after passing from teacher, to lesson-attending parent, to practicing parent.

On a temporary basis, however, it is sometimes necessary that the parent who practices with the child does not attend the lessons (though I advise against it in the strongest possible terms during the first year). This set-up can sometimes work better than no lessons at all, as long as it is temporary, and all the adults involved are aware of its pitfalls. The "other" parent may very well be "the musical one"–as I've often heard the lesson-attending parent say–and can be very helpful in keeping a student on track when it comes to getting the notes to a piece.

But if that parent isn't the one at the lesson, then that parent missed learning techniques for helping the child with the *process* of learning those notes. It's true that non-lesson attending parents, even if they're somewhat clumsy about it, are often able to figure out a process that eventually works. But they run the very strong risk of increasing a child's resistance to practicing. The child can feel like a patient of the dental school student who's drilling a tooth for the first time. There's lots of squirming. While not the best scenario, this case isn't tragic. A worst case would be if the parent could tell the child that a note was out of place but was at a loss at to which note it was and what to do about it. The upshot would be that the child now had something to be embarrassed about, but no strategy for changing it. Bummer.

Besides which, the majority of practice time usually needs to be spent on things that are more important than figuring out the notes to the new piece–playing review pieces, for example. Getting the notes accurate is only a very small percentage of what practice actually involves. Furthermore, when parents *tell* children what the next note is, they work against the goal of helping them own their playing. One of the themes throughout this book is that the *process* by which children learn to play enriches them much more than merely getting the correct note does. If the process is rich, accuracy of notes pretty much takes care of itself.

Most parents agree, but are uncertain about exactly how to enrich the process. It's something that parents glean from attending lessons with their children, week after week.

To sum up this third advantage of the practicing parent's attendance at lessons: it helps to avoid having the child emotionally poisoned by the two most common unfair expectations, 1) remembering details and 2) serving as a communication link between parents. When parents overwhelm a child by expecting–or even demanding–that he does more than he is capable of doing at the moment, it can do serious damage to the child's belief in his ability to take on challenges. I'm not talking about situations in which children actually *are* able do more than they think they can do–or, truth be told, sometimes *want* to do, such as pick up their toys or play "May Song" five times. I'm talking about situations in which the reality of the moment is that even though the growing child will someday be able to master the challenge, he's not yet capable of doing so.

There's a fourth important benefit of attending lessons with your child. It gives you an opportunity to grow along with your child. I once asked a parent, when I was trying to determine how I could be helpful in a Saturday morning master class, what her questions were about her son's lessons.

She just looked at me and smiled, saying "Oh, I don't really have any…I'm just the one who brought him today." In my mind I imagined the breakfast table conversation she and her husband had had about the

Saturday chores: "O.K., so you're going to get the oil in the car changed after you drop Waverly off at her skating lesson, and then you can pick up the dry cleaning on your way home...I'll get Branford to his violin lesson and then we'll all do the grocery shopping together."

While every family has necessary errands to be run in order for it to function, attending your child's music lessons is much more than an errand. Lessons are not a place where a teacher performs maintenance on a child's playing. They are opportunities for parents to grow and learn about themselves and their children. A mother once told me that one of the most profound things in her otherwise hectic professional and personal life was just sitting still once a week and watching her child learn. She said she learned a great deal about her child, and in the process, a great deal about herself. Many parents have told me that by attending their children's lesson, they not only learned how to coach their home practices, they also grew as people.

There is much more to practicing than getting the music down. It also involves learning about your child and how to work with him or her. Sure, practicing is about developing musical skills, but it's also about developing the parent-child relationship–the soil in which those skills grow. You need to be present for that practicing relationship to happen in the first place.

Take Useful, Accurate, Reliable Notes

In Disney's *101 Dalmatians*, one of the 101 puppies almost dies. This part of the movie is very compelling and captivating, and the people I know who saw the movie cried–or came close. But, like me, though they were attentive and emotionally involved, most of them can't remember the number of that puppy. Those who can remember the number can't remember the names and numbers of *all* the puppies. If we'd had a notepad with us during the movie, we could have quickly jotted down this information, and checked it when we got home. Thank goodness, our ability to breathe the next day didn't depend on this knowledge.

Something similar happens when parents and students get involved in learning new things at lessons. The intensity of the moment of learning can really draw you in, but someone needs to write down the specifics necessary for practicing it at home.

That someone is you, the parent. You'll need to know if it was finger number three or finger number two, if it was on the third beat, or if it was three beats, or if it was measure five or measure six that needs to be repeated fifteen times a day–or was that fifty?–and whether the thumb needs to move this way or that way...and which hand was it? *Your* left? The *teacher's* left? The student's right? Or was it the other way around? Does the bow need to be at the frog or the center? Does the piano seat need to go up or down?

Does it really matter?

Yes. These details matter. If your teacher assigns something to be practiced on the A-string, it needs to happen on the A-string. True, practicing on a different string may be more useful than not practicing at all. But teachers have reasons for the specifics. As a teacher, I could spend lots of lesson time explaining why, and though this is sometimes useful, it often simply takes time away from other productive pursuits. So, take notes, get details. They'll increase your chances of having productive lessons and practice sessions.

Understand that you will get it wrong a couple of times–especially if you are a beginning parent. I don't expect a parent's notes to be perfect at every lesson. But I do get concerned when I see a parent nodding his head, and not taking notes. As the cello teacher Barbara Wampner so astutely pointed out to me, "human beings are not tape recorders."

You will need more than your memories. Your teacher can help you learn exactly what to write down at lessons. Sometimes I have even given parents carbon paper so that I can get a copy of their notes in order to see what details they're getting at the lesson.

Lessons work best for the child and teacher if the parent remains silent. But parents are often unsure about when they get to ask their questions. It's especially tricky because the appropriate time for parent questions varies from teacher to teacher, from level to level, and from age to age. Particularly for beginning students, I like parents to ask questions at the start of the lesson, at the end, and when I turn to them and invite their questions. When questions come at other times, they usually interrupt the flow of the student's learning. Unfortunately, this arrangement doesn't always accommodate the flow of the *parent's* learning. As adults though, parents get second pick. Sorry. Sometimes teachers can read the subtle clues parents have about wanting to ask a question. But don't count on it. You're best off writing down your question so that if it doesn't get answered during the course of the lesson, you can ask it at the end.

As a general rule, though, parents shouldn't have too many questions if they are writing down details as the teacher gives them. While the two tasks of the student are to learn about the skill and execute it on the instrument, the parent's two tasks are to learn about the skill and to write down the details. Admittedly, the details can be daunting. The mother of one of my students, a brilliant woman with both a PhD and an MD, told me that the entire time she was at MIT she and her classmates were not allowed to take notes because they were supposed to exercise and strengthen their memories. This approach worked for her through graduate school and medical school. For a while it worked at lessons, until it didn't work and she, too, confessed that she needed to take notes at lessons.

Because I want to stay student-focused at lessons, I often try to give parents clues about what to write down. I say things such as "Now the next thing we're going to do is pretty complicated, so your dad will need to write it down." Or "O.K., let's go through this several times. The first time your mom can write down the details and then we'll repeat it several times. You may understand it perfectly the first time, but we'll do it several times so your mom can check and re-check her notes."

If you're not sure what to write down, then–at the *beginning* of your next lesson–be sure to ask your teacher what specific method he or she uses to let you know exactly what you'll need to remember. This would also be a good time for you to ask your teacher when it is most useful for you to ask questions during lessons.

As you develop your ability to take accurate, reliable notes, those notes will help give you the confidence and conviction you need when you and your child practice together. Your child is more likely to work with you if you have a clear sense of what's going on than if you seem to be guessing your way through it. To aid you in developing this clarity, it's important that you write down compliments–what the teacher points out is working and going well–not merely what needs practice. [See also section 17, "Talk About What's Working...And Repeat It."]

On occasion, you may find that you will not understand your notes. When this situation arises, as it inevitably does with every parent, you may want to ask your child what he remembers and see if that helps jog *your* memory. With some parents and children this approach works just fine. Some, however, find that it works now and then, while others find it's a complete disaster.

If you and your child should disagree about how to practice something because your notes are unclear, you're better off practicing it *both* ways, or simply leaving it until you can clarify it at your next lesson, all the while realizing that your note-taking skills will improve with time.

There are some things that children simply have to *feel* when it comes to developing technical proficiency with the instrument. In these cases, it is still useful for parents to take lots of notes. The goal is that your words, based on your notes, will trigger things in your child's physical memory. However, if you find yourself unable to recreate these physical sensations at home, it's important to remember that it's neither your fault nor your child's. You've done as much as you can, but you still don't quite have it. That's why there's another lesson coming up.

Don't penalize yourself–and also don't penalize your child–for not always knowing what to do. Say you don't know the solution to a certain yucky something in the playing. Whether it's small yucky or supersize yucky, one way to work around it is to say, "I know this doesn't sound quite right and I wish I knew what to tell you to do to change it…but I don't know what it is. If we can figure it out together, that would be great. If we can't, it's not your fault." Saying something like that is infinitely better than "Come on, you should know this!" With some kids, you're better off just leaving it alone. But don't stop practicing for the day! Work on something else, making a note to ask the teacher to give you clarification at the next lesson. Even though parents don't have to have all the answers when they get home, this fact does not excuse their failing to take as detailed notes as possible.

The notes that a parent takes for a five year old can be very different from the notes for an eleven year old. The difference comes partly from the level of the student's maturity and partly from the difference in the parental involvement, which will change as the student changes.

Finally, on the subject of note-taking, organize your notes. Your teacher can help you organize them in a way that will allow you to access the information as you need it. I recommend a three-ring binder with dividers. And I would think it's obvious, but so many parents have tried that I'll say it anyway: you can't take useful notes on debris in your purse or wallet. Old receipts, spare deposit slips, and the margins of take-out menus just don't work.

And if you would normally take a pen or pencil to a class you yourself had signed up for, be sure to take one to your lessons. In fact, you should think of lessons as your class as well as your child's, even though you both have very different roles. The average observer who popped his head through the door would say "Some kid's in there having a music lesson" and wouldn't recognize you, the note-taking parent, as an integral part of it. Still, get yourself a pencil and a notebook, and arrive at your class prepared. Your preparation will send your child a strong message about how important the lessons are. That lesson will be much more effective than any lecture you could deliver.

Participate in a Group Class

Early on in my teaching, I didn't have group classes because the parents of my students didn't want them. Other teachers convinced me that I needed to do them anyway, so I did. Many parents complained, but they also showed up. After several weeks of smaller group classes, we had a class in which all of my students played together for the first time. At the end of that class, one of the parents who had complained the most gave me a bottle of champagne. "You should celebrate!" she told me.

Clearly, she was beginning to see the benefits of group classes, and I was glad I had insisted. I certainly go along with the mainstream idea that children need individual, one-on-one instruction in order to really learn an instrument. It has also been my experience that participation in a group class can prevent, lessen and often even solve many of the difficulties that come along with learning an instrument.

Children are not the only ones who get something out of group class. Parents benefit enormously as well. I now know that one of a teacher's jobs is to insist on group class attendance. It can be a very tough job until parents eventually see the benefits as well.

One of the most obvious benefits of group class is that it provides a format for efficient teaching. There are many things that I don't have to cover very extensively in individual lessons because I know that we'll cover them in group class. For example, I think it is essential that all intermediate students learn the basic conducting patterns. Since my students get exposed to these conducting patterns in group classes, I just double-check them at their individual lessons. It's much more efficient to offer basic instruction once in group than to repeat it in every individual lesson.

In spite of the fact that not all students may be working on the same technical or musical challenges, witnessing someone getting instruction on a specific musical point–even if it's only for nine seconds–can serve as either excellent preparation or reinforcement for your own child. For example, Raymond may not yet play "Song of the Wind," but simply being around five other students who play it in class exposes him to the idea that the bow will come off the string and make a circle, an important thing to learn in this piece.

Since Raymond's mother, Elaine, is aware that her son will be learning "Song of the Wind" one of these days–maybe even at his next individual lesson–Elaine will probably be watching closely. She may even try to note where the circles are in her copy of the music. As the group plays through the piece, Dale, Alice, and Billy–students playing "Song of the Wind" for the first time in a group–each forget one of the circles. But when the song repeats, they figure it out the second time through. Their teacher's insistence that parents remain quiet during group class, means that the parents witness their children figuring something out without an adult giving specific instruction.

Another student in the class, Jack, learned "Song of the Wind" a few weeks ago, and isn't noticing what his bow is doing during the circles. But he should be. So I ask him to show the class how to get the tip, hand and elbow working together for the bow circles. I know that he can easily do this when his attention is drawn to it, but not yet easily enough so that it happens without him thinking about it. He starts to pay attention to this aspect of his playing again as he proudly demonstrates the coordination of the tip, hand and elbow for the rest of the class.

After class, Elaine asks Jack's father, Bruce, who was sitting right next to her, to take a quick look at her music and see if she marked the bow circles where they belong. Jack's father quickly erases one of the spots and puts it in a different place, adding "Now you've got it. It seemed like it took me forever until I really knew where those circles go." Elaine is relieved to know that Jack and Bruce once struggled with something. To her, it looks like Jack just plays everything effortlessly.

"Oh no..." Bruce reassures her, rolling his eyes. She leaves with renewed hope about the possibilities for her and her son.

Bruce, who–truth be told–has been worried about not understanding some of the things in Jack's newest piece, heaves a sigh of relief. He remembers how he struggled trying to understand the "Song of the Wind" bow circles, and realizes that what he's struggling with now will someday seem just as easy.

Group participation can, in a useful way, do damage to a false belief parents often have. I'm talking about the belief that they struggle with things others don't. The fact is, parents and students often struggle with the exact same things.

In addition to instilling hope and being an efficient forum for dispersing general information, group class is also a great place to learn the things that can only be learned in a group. To use an analogy, it's possible to learn many of the skills of baseball by practicing alone, but you can't really learn to play the game if you don't actually have others to play it with. It would seem strange to have Little-Leaguers practicing their baseball skills at home all by themselves and then only getting together for the games.

Similarly, young musicians need a group to learn many aspects of music. The most obvious one is that students can't learn how to play with a group unless they have a group to play with. Then, once they have learned how to play with a group, the students can use the group to discover ideas about musical expression.

Many people don't understand how a group experience can help an individual student be musically creative, but it can. It happens in two primary ways. One is by giving a student a safety net. Sometimes a student likes playing a solo in what I think of as an idiosyncratic way, not a creative way. I let this happen, and don't usually mention it to the student directly. However, the student's inability to play the piece any other way is often the cause of the idiosyncrasy. When the group performs the same piece on a later concert, I insist that the idiosyncratic student learns to play it in exactly the same way the rest of the group plays it. This set-up ensures that the student learns musical flexibility without me condemning his or her personal, "artistic" decisions. The whole experience gently prevents the student from wandering down a dead end.

The second way group classes can help a student learn to be musically expressive is something I like to think of as the "Michigan Stadium Phenomenon." The University of Michigan football stadium holds over 100,000 people and at games there, fans yell at the top of their lungs. But ask any one of those fans to stand all alone on a street corner and yell the same way, and he'd likely need a great deal of encouragement to do so. In the safety of a group, students can experiment with how it feels to open up and play with gusto. This experimenting can be a big relief for the parents and teachers of the students who can drive you nuts when you try to get them to do this kind of playing during practices and lessons, but they just won't budge. But some of these students will do it as part of a group. The experience gives them just the encouragement they need to transfer that energy into their solo playing. Without the opportunity to sense themselves playing with gusto in group class, however, they'd miss this important step.

A teacher can also use a group class to give students a workout. It's no secret to teachers that there are some pieces and exercises that students resist practicing on their own. So I often make a point of doing these things in group class. The students may complain, but we do them anyway. It's just like when I–as an adult–swam competitively. When I did workouts on my own, I would put off a drill that was no fun by telling myself "I'll do that one next practice." But when the coach told the whole team to do it, I'd complain along with all of my teammates–and then we'd all get busy and do it.

When I know that a child is giving his parent a tough time in home practice about doing a particular exercise, I deliberately do that exercise in group class. Sometimes the child is happy to do the exercise, and the experience serves as a catalyst for his being able to continue the practice with his parent. On other occasions, group class may provide an opportunity for the child to see that he is the only student who hasn't practiced it and, therefore, can't do it yet. His embarrassment is the natural consequence of his not practicing. If your child finds himself or herself in this situation, the natural consequences are enough–*DO NOT RUB IT IN!* And be sure to talk about how you're sure he can get it...after he has practiced it, of course.

This kind of approach is not where I like to start, however. In general, I like to make group class be a place in which we work towards excellence; and where there is also an environment that allows for mistakes to happen along the way.

With this goal in mind, I like to make a distinction in my thinking between the group functioning as a "workshop" and as a performance ensemble. As a workshop, I tell my students that it doesn't matter how well they know the notes, the group provides an opportunity to play in camouflage, if they wish. This is using–but not abusing–the benefits of group playing. It can often be a good way for students to get the flow of playing a piece. Take the case of a piece that most students find difficult to memorize. When they play it in group, oftentimes each student forgets a different part of the piece but then gets back on track with the rest of the group. The end result is that the whole piece is, more or less, usually there. This kind of group practice eventually helps students get the entire piece. The group ends up doing much of the teaching so that the adults can sit back and watch the learning happen.

As a performing group, however, only the students who know the notes and bowings to a piece at least six weeks before a concert are invited to play along. This policy ensures that the students who are still working on getting the piece reliably in their repertoire will not blemish the performance of the students who already have the piece solidly. It also means that the students who *almost* have the piece learned will get to hear a really solid, musical performance of it at the concert. I like to point out to these students–and their parents–that the next time the piece comes up on a concert, they will be part of the model group.

One thing that students can't practice by themselves is how to feel comfortable performing in front of an audience. The group can serve as an audience, giving the students practice with this skill. In my group classes, there will often be one or two students who play a solo. With this as the norm, getting up and playing in front of a more formal recital audience doesn't seem as big of a deal as it would if the students had never had a group to play for.

One of the main ways students develop security with being in front of an audience is by practicing being in front of an audience. My insistence that all students have something positive to say to each performer also helps the students to develop a positive inner audience, which contributes to confident performances. This kind of work also has the benefit of helping students learn how to teach. When you realize that practicing is nothing more than giving yourself a lesson, you start to see how valuable this aspect of group can be.

Sometimes, instead of actually playing solos, students only practice walking on stage and bowing, since this is one aspect of performing that can sometimes feel awkward for children–especially children who haven't been able to practice it enough for it to be effortless. None of these security-building activities are possible without the group. *Imagining* an audience is no substitute for actually having one.

Group class can also teach students how to be polite members of an audience. Talking about concert manners isn't nearly as effective as giving students frequent opportunities to practice those concert manners routinely, from one group class to the next. Group class is also an excellent place for children to learn socializing aspects–how to give useful feedback to others (for example, when a student plays a solo), and how to be quiet and follow instructions–invaluable experience for later participation in orchestras, string quartets, and other ensembles.

Parents should keep in mind that as they are observing group class, they are modeling concert etiquette for their children. In other words, *be quiet*. It can be terribly disrupting to have parents whispering as I'm attempting to listen very carefully to what students are doing. Noisy parents are also a disruption for the students. I like to point out that if I were to be lucky enough to go to a rehearsal of the New York Philharmonic with some of my friends, the conductor would probably ask us to leave if we were just whispering–let alone *talking*. If the members of one of the world's top orchestras have a difficult time concentrating when there's whispering, then it's probably also true of children. They deserve the same respectful silence as they do their work.

Your remaining silent during group class also helps your child to focus. Most parents have a natural tendency to think that it's helpful if they repeat the teacher's directions to their children, but they're actually making it *more* difficult for their children to focus[as described in section 30, from the bottom of page 117 to the top of page 119]. Your teacher will appreciate your silence because even though a skilled teacher can make it look effortless, group class teaching is tricky. It's even more of a challenge when a child's difficulty focusing is compounded by a parent's unsolicited attempts to "help."

Since group class is so enormously beneficial, you'll get the most out of your musical experience if you and your child plan to attend each and every group class, not just the group classes that are conveniently scheduled to happen on days when there isn't, say, soccer. In my own studio, I have made a point of letting students and parents know that I run a "violin priority" program. This policy means that when there is a scheduling conflict between violin and another activity, violin wins. Usually. The exception is for things like SATs, tournament basketball games, and state mock trial championships.

When events like this come up, I offer students my best wishes and thank them for informing me about their absence prior to the group class. These events become problematic when there are more than two per term. In these cases, I'm quite direct in letting students and parents know that they are missing an important component of their music lessons, and that they should consider finding another teacher. In fifteen years, however, it hasn't been too much of an issue, because people who attend group class can see enough of its enormous benefits to make it a priority. (Some of its other benefits can sometimes take years to appreciate.)

Since parents are often not quite as involved in group class as they are in weekly lessons, watching group class from the sidelines can be a good chance for parents to contemplate exactly why they are taking lessons in the first place. Since I know that enjoying music often tops parents' lists of why they are doing it, I also use group classes as a place to have FUN–to play games that usually have a teaching point, but also just to give students a sense of enjoyment from being together and being involved in music.

Listen to Recordings

If I sang "Twinkle, twinkle, little..." and stopped right there in the song, you could probably sing "star" in your head. Why? Because we have all heard it enough times to be familiar with it.

When a student says "I know how it goes" but is a bit frustrated as to how to get her instrument to sing the notes, I know that she's well on her way to learning the piece. It's much easier to get somewhere if you know where you're going, and a child who has listened to a piece many times has made the trip over and over. She knows the destination; she just has to figure out how to get there.

As the adults in a child's life, our job is not to "teach her how it goes"– the reference recordings do that. Our adult job has two parts: 1) to help her develop the skills she needs to figure out how to execute what she's singing on the inside, and 2) to help her manage her frustration when playing the instrument is not as easy as she wishes it were. Like our trying to tell a child what the sky looks like–when she could just step out the door and see it for herself–attempting to explain how a piece of music goes is not nearly as effective as simply having her listen to the recording, whether that daily listening happens via a car stereo, a personal stereo, or a boombox.

Listening is so important that it's at the top of the practice chart I give my students. Though I always look to see if it's checked off every day, I rarely ask about it–just as I rarely ask them if they have oxygen in their homes. I just assume that it's there. I usually tell them that listening is their "musical oxygen."

Sometimes this musical oxygen is missing. Jeff's playing, for example, had all of the skills necessary to handle the Becker *Gavotte* in *Volume Three* of the *Suzuki Violin School*, but he just wasn't getting the piece. So, I asked if he had been listening. He and his mother looked at each other sheepishly. "Well," his mother said slowly "…um…We haven't been able to find the tape for two weeks."

That explained it! They had been fibbing when they checked-off the listening assignments on their practice charts. I then switched the lesson to developing a point in a review piece, since I knew that this was a better use of our limited time. Once Jeff and his mother got a replacement recording–and began listening to it–the Becker *Gavotte* took care of itself.

If your child starts complaining about being sick of the recording, by all means let your child be sick of the recording–*at the same time that you continue to play it.* I know of no incidences in which children were damaged by hearing the recording too much–it doesn't even create the slightest puncture wound. Nobody needs to go to the hospital. It may be unpleasant, but do it. Just don't give children the extra assignment of pretending to enjoy it.

One way you and your family members can get relief is by following the advice Edward Kreitman offers in *Teaching from the Balance Point.* On the days that you can't bear the thought of listening to the reference recording of pieces from your child's current level, listen to the recording of a few levels up.

You Can't Learn As You Go If You Don't Take The Trip

Children usually seem to enjoy their lessons and spending time with their teachers. They often even seem to take criticism from their teachers quite easily. But when parents don't elicit the same reactions from their child during home practices, parents often wonder if something is wrong. (Did I say "wonder"? I mean they *worry!*)

It would be delightful if every lesson and practice were as cute and touching as an episode of a 1950's family show. I'm thinking of those shows where things always worked out perfectly, even when they didn't quite go as planned. The fact that practices don't always go that way doesn't necessarily indicate that something is terribly wrong. Like those early TV shows, the "less desirable" moments can teach us adults what we need to change. They can help us grow. However, unlike the sugar-coated dilemmas of those fictional TV families, real difficulties are only occasionally cute; and answers to troubles are seldom obvious–and even more rarely solved in the final two minutes, just before the credits. But that's o.k. In the process of figuring out what a useful next step would be, we adults grow along with the child. Some days it will be wonderful and some days we will feel horrible growth pains. Most days it will be somewhere in-between.

The deep lessons of practice are never learned, however, if parents don't simply spend time with the child and with the instrument. Daily practice is crucial. Spending time practicing allows you to experience both the trying times of practice along with the profound riches that accompany the process. It is impossible for a child to learn to play an instrument if the child never touches the instrument, just thinks about it or comes up with one reason after another for not practicing.

Parents generally wish that they had wise, inspiring, and fun guidance to offer at all times. But it's just a wish. They don't. Certainly there's a great deal to be said for getting useful information from a teacher, but teachers don't have all the answers either. It's when they devote time to their children and the instrument that solutions can often reveal themselves to parents, and some difficulties can even magically disappear from one day to the next.

If you want to communicate to your child that music is important, then by all means don't tell him that. Instead, show him that by your actions. You will grow in the process. There are many things a parent can do to communicate to his or her child that music is important. A bare minimum would be listening to a wide variety of music (at home and in the car), attending individual lessons and group lessons, and attending concerts–both concerts the student performs in and occasional other concerts that you attend with your child.

The most powerful way to communicate that we value something is by simply spending time with it. In *The Road Less Traveled*, the psychiatrist M. Scott Peck summed it up beautifully:

> Ultimately love is everything... When we love something it is of value to us, and when something is of value to us we spend time with it, time enjoying it and time taking care of it... So it is when we love children; we spend time admiring them and caring for them. We give them our time.

Review Repertoire to Help the Playing Get Easier

Olympic athletes need exercise even *after* they have won gold medals. If they stop exercising, watch TV, and eat jelly doughnuts all day, well, we all know what will happen. Merely knowing how to do some kind of exercise–swimming, for instance–isn't enough. You still have to do it on a regular basis if you want to get the benefits.

In the same way, it's good for children to spend time playing what they already know how to play, even if they play it really well. *Especially* if they play it well. It's also extremely fortifying for a child when parents and teachers simply acknowledge what the child did well on the instrument. If you notice that your child had a beautiful finger motion in a piece, point it out. Rave over it. And then perhaps request to see it again.

The goal of practicing is to make things easier. The goal is not to get better, and it's not to improve. If things get easier, the playing will improve in many ways, with the improvements being the by-products of ease. The interesting thing about practicing is that there is always something new to learn and to develop: there is an infinite number of things that can become easier. Sometimes, for example, people just need to practice *practicing* so that the daily practicing itself can become easier, less of a strain. At other times students need to practice new notes so that it's the notes that become more automatic. And for both adults and children, resolving conflict is one of the things that everyone hopes will become easier over time.

I recommend that parents and students use the bulk of their practice time reviewing familiar pieces, scales, and exercises. This kind of practice allows the students and parents to use well-known notes to learn new skills when the teacher introduces them. Because "new" also often means "strange," "different," and "challenging," effectively introducing new skills to a student is much easier if the notes are familiar and the only thing that's new is the skill. Just as it's easier to heat a cup of milk in a microwave than it is to heat an entire gallon, breaking down the child's new technical challenge into the smallest portion possible helps him to convert it into easy faster, and with less strain. The only new thing that requires energy from the student, then, is the *way* he plays the notes, not the notes *and* the new skill, so there's less chance of a blown fuse. However, this approach can't happen unless the review happens daily.

There's another advantage to review: if you manage and regulate it in a suitable way, it can make your practice sessions feel more casual at the same time that it can make them much more productive and effective. Since musicians have often been described as "small muscle athletes" it stands to reason that a certain amount of practice time is simply a workout for developing the delicate and subtle skills of those tiny muscles.

As a swimmer, I know the importance of regular workouts. In spite of the fact that I have been doing the same four basic strokes for over 30 years, it is still good for me to go to the pool and swim regularly. But I couldn't get the benefits of swimming if I didn't know how to swim in the first place. Pointers from a coach can help–and I get them sometimes–but there's a great deal of benefit to simply swimming those same strokes workout after workout, year after year.

Your child can't get the deep and lasting benefits of playing a piece if he's struggling to get from one end of it to the other. Spending lots of time working on the new piece usually only teaches a child that "to play" means "to flounder." This is not a helpful situation, especially if you keep in mind what the ski instructor Margaret McIntyre tells her students: "pushing a movement to the limit is reinforcing the limitation." When students spend lots of time playing pieces that they already play well, however, the review doesn't reinforce a limitation, it reinforces *ease*, allowing the limits on their playing to expand gradually. (For more information about Margaret McIntyre, including her work as a Feldenkrais® practitioner, please see page 266 in "Notes and Sources.")

Parents often have two main complaints about consistently reviewing: boredom and sloppy playing. These two have fairly straightforward solutions. While everyone likes the thrill of the new, if students and parents get into the habit of reviewing daily, then it becomes not such a big deal. I advise parents to let the child complain about being bored, and to insist that the review happens anyway. Eventually, playing review just becomes an automatic part of what you do during practice. When it comes to sloppy playing you need to give your child concrete, specific instructions. "That was pretty good, but I'm sure you can make it just a little bit better" is definitely *not* what I'm talking about because it's way too vague and will probably only confuse or anger your child. Maybe both. Your teacher can give you *specific* ideas of *specific* things to focus on in *specific* review pieces. Section 62 of this book, "Stepping and Playing with the Pulse," can be useful in this respect.

You can also choose your battles. Your teacher can give you guidance on this one, but as a general recommendation, I like for parents to know that some pieces need to be stellar during review, but other pieces can fall into the "It's-So-Worth-Doing-It's-Worth-Doing-Badly" category. Later, as playing well becomes easier and easier for your child, and as the child's skill level, awareness and sensitivity rise, playing badly will become more and more difficult.

Finally, in praise of reviewing things the child can already play well, I like to point out that nearly every piece the world's great concert artists play is a review piece. It's true that every season they add a new piece or two to their repertoires, but the majority of what they play is review.

It's only fair that if we expect students to play well, we should at least put them under the same conditions as the world's concert artists, asking them to spend much time playing what is secure for them, and not constantly "dancing at the edge of their incompetence," as the violin teacher Ronda Cole once said. One of the most famous violinists in the world, Itzhak Perlman, for example, has been playing some of the same pieces in concerts for over thirty years.

Few things can develop secure, confident, comfortable, easy, and–most importantly–musically expressive playing the way consistent time spent on review can.

Talk About What's Working...And Repeat It

Unfortunately, many adults feel that they're not helping a child unless they offer "constructive criticism" or in some way change the way a child plays a piece.

But that's not the case. Adults often help a child more by talking about what is working well. Review is a good example. It can be beneficial and go much more smoothly if happens every day and if the parent just sits there and listens to it, commenting now and then on what–specifically–went well in the review, and severely restricting comments that the student experiences as negative.

For parents who find this approach difficult, I sometimes recommend that they hold four cards–any four cards–per practice, laying down a card every time they make a remark that the student feels is negative. In this case, it doesn't matter what the parent's intention was in offering the comment. The child is the sole judge of his own feelings. When the parent has played all four cards, he or she has to be quiet for the rest of the practice.

Give it a whirl. Remember that even doing it just once can give you some valuable insights, because it can force you to be quiet. As Yogi Berra so famously put it, "You can observe a lot by watching."

If you force yourself to refrain from talking about what's not working, if you stop yourself when you are about to mention what "could be just a teeny bit better" or if you bite your tongue before you say that something "needs a little polishing," you're pretty much left with talking about what is working. Your only option will be looking at the positive aspects of what your child is doing.

If your child is playing a review piece and being sloppy with, say, the finesse of the last note, be quiet–but make a mental note of it. Then, the next time you catch the child actually tapering off the last note of a piece beautifully, you can point out how well it worked. The child may be completely unaware that he did it. In fact, he may have done it by accident–but I think of these as "happy accidents." If you witness a happy accident like this one, don't talk about all the times it didn't happen. Just ask the child to repeat the tapered note several times "because it was so *delicious*." You've still talked about–*and the child has practiced*–the same issue, but you've addressed it in a way that helps the child feel added to, rather than taken away from.

This strategy reminds me of the time an Olympic swimmer missed winning the gold medal by a fraction of a second, merely because he didn't reach for the touchpad fast enough at the end of the race. For a while, I used this as a metaphor of how important it was never to give up and to keep track of every single detail. Then someone pointed out to me that the fact that he was at the Olympics indicated that he was at a pretty high level. And while he lost the gold, he *did* win the silver, after all–not too shabby! If you only focus on what your child *could* have done with "just a bit more effort," you'll fail to maintain a useful awareness of everything that the child has already accomplished. You'll also fail to appreciate that the child is still growing. In other words, the child is currently in the process of accomplishing, and that process–also known as learning–is usually messy [as described in the last paragraph on page 22 and the first paragraph on page 23]. But if you force yourself to talk about what's working, you'll begin to notice that there's a lot of it. This realization will give both of you the courage to forage into areas that need effort.

You can even use this positive approach in new pieces. As your child is finding the notes to a piece, instead of pointing out what notes he should have played, you can acknowledge how well he prepared himself before starting…or how he flagged down more notes this time than he did the time before…or how you are happy to see that he's hanging in there with struggling to figure out the notes.

You'll not only be pointing out what's working to the child, you'll be pointing it out to yourself. Your awareness of these things will tilt both of you in the direction of optimism during practice.

Shoot One Arrow at a Time

When I was studying violin with Shin'ichi Suzuki at the Talent Education Institute in Matsumoto, Japan, I often observed Haruko Kataoka's piano teaching. What I particularly enjoyed about her lessons was that she would chat with everyone in the room, listen to a student play, chat some more, have the student do some things on the piano, give the student feedback...and then chat some more. It all seemed incredibly relaxed, and yet she had phenomenal students. In retrospect, I think that she was using all of the chatting and listening time to decide *what* to work on in a student's playing and *how*, specifically, to do that. She was like an archer with only one arrow to shoot. She aimed carefully.

As I have watched parents practice over the years, I notice that one of the primary ways they create nasty practices for themselves and their children is by attempting to shoot several arrows at once. "Johnny, good job getting the bow straight. Play it again and make sure that you also keep the speed even and remember to keep your pinkie round and to let the bow float off the string when the piece is over. And don't be so timid!"

Overload. Just as a bow can only hold one arrow at a time, you'll find that practices will be most productive if you remember that your child can only hold one thing to work on at any time.

If you notice yourself wanting to give your child more than one thing to pay attention to, *stop*. Do some prioritizing. If you could choose only one of those things, what would it be? Ask your child to focus only on that one thing. This is not letting a child off easy. It's asking the child to do appropriate work.

Keep in mind that kids really do want to do a good job. When we give children too much to do we unknowingly and unintentionally sabotage them. We need to do the opposite. We need to chop things into small enough pieces so we create what the violin teacher John Kendall calls the "Can't fail" environment. Sometimes it takes a while to decide *what* specific thing you should address, and even when you have made a decision, it sometimes takes a while to determine *how* to approach it most effectively. You'll be best off if you take your time arriving at a decision, and approach it in a way that you are pretty sure will hit the mark. [See also section 31, "Have Strategies for Buying Yourself Time."] Even the world's best archers aim very carefully with just one arrow–and they miss now and then.

Create a positive practice environment by talking about what's working and asking to see it again. When you find something that needs to change, remember that shooting more than one arrow at a time will do a lot more than overwhelm and irritate your child: it will tend to make *you* feel like an incompetent archer. Your child will likely be feeling he can't do anything right and you'll be well on your way to feeling like a failure as a practicing parent. On top of all of this, there's a strong possibility that your child's reaction to this emotional environment will appear to be resistance. It's not. If it looks like fighting and resistance, you'll be tempted to respond by retaliating. You're best off just starting in a different way. Choose one arrow at a time, and make sure the target's fairly close.

If I had eight hours to chop down a tree, I'd spend six sharpening my ax."

Abraham Lincoln

19

Don't Just Do Something, Stand There

Wallace was reviewing the Gossec *Gavotte*–a tricky piece, but nonetheless one he had played with great confidence and accuracy at previous lessons. But on this day he got stuck. He was visibly irritated, and started experimenting. As he was attempting to get himself back on track, the quiet look on my face betrayed the little conversation inside my head that went like this...

"Well, he played it before, so he'll probably figure it out."

"Yes, but look, he's struggling. *Help him!*"

"Certainly, he is struggling. But struggling isn't necessarily a problem for a student. It develops character. In fact, it's important for children to experience frustration in their lives, so that they learn coping skills and a sense of confidence with being in the world."

"You're absolutely right. Children do need to learn how to tolerate frustration, and that's not the problem. That wise pediatrician Winnicott was right when he talked about how frustration isn't bad as long as it's not overwhelming. The problem is that it seems like he's got an overwhelming amount of frustration. And you know how he can be when he loses it..."

"Having a mother who drinks too much is overwhelming for a child; having a father who is attempting to live his life through you is overwhelming. But *come on*! Finding one note in first position? Listen–he's already figured out what string it's on."

"Yes, but what if he loses it...I can hardly stand to keep watching this."

"O.K., I get your point. I'm a little nervous that he's going to lose it. I'll get my violin out and demonstrate for him."

But by the time I picked up my violin to demonstrate, Wallace had figured it out. Moral of the story? His frustration was getting to be overwhelming to *me*, but not to him. As with much of the general population, students often don't want someone else's solution–because they're busy figuring out their own. It's just like when we as adults feel like we could really use someone to talk to. We don't necessarily want or need advice. We just need someone be with us and acknowledge our struggle.

Sometimes the most effective thing is simply to sit there quietly. In other words, *don't just do something; stand there.* Many parents want to yell out a note name or a finger number to child who is struggling, but I usually prefer to wait for the child's ear to kick in. And even though an adult's just standing there when a child is struggling is often the most useful thing for the child, it can be the most frustrating thing for the adult. If an adult can manage to do this task, however, both the adult and the child end up working diligently, and in absolutely appropriate ways.

I'm not just encouraging you to be lazy. You're not being lazy if you just sit there as your child works. If you weren't there, the child might not even be practicing–and might not even notice that something wasn't working. Your being present and shutting up is very different from your being absent. And the work of remaining silent can be quite difficult. If it looks easy when I do it, I suspect it's because I've had years of practice. It's much easier for me now than it used to be. I still have to work at tolerating my own frustration when things that I think should be easy and automatic aren't. But it's my job, not the child's.

If you notice that a child is getting stuck with a passage, that's not necessarily your clue to jump in and save her. It's your clue to be quiet. Let the child figure it out. Be there for her, but don't help her unless she asks for help. If you attempt to "help" before you're invited, you may be in for trouble. As one mother once told me: "When I try to give her help and tell her what to do, she goes *berserk*!" The adult can then start to feel resentful, further fuelling a practice time struggle.

There are even times when it looks like a child is asking for help, but really isn't. I remember watching an advanced student sight-reading a Mozart piano sonata and saying "I can't get this trill," though she was working on figuring it out even as she was complaining about its difficulty. When she started to say "I just can't…" her teacher immediately began offering her encouragement, but the student ignored the teacher as she continued to work away. It never ceases to amaze me when I ask a student to play a piece and the student says "How does that go?" and then proceeds to figure it out as I'm in the process of asking myself whether the student *really* wants me to answer. Not everything that sounds like a question is always a question. Think, for example, about the question "Wasn't that a terrific game?"

But even when a child genuinely wants your assistance, you can often build a child's playing by answering somewhat indirectly, saying things such as..."How about if you..." or "Let's see what happens when you..."

After we have been silent and allowed the child to figure something out, we adults have further work to do. We need to give the child positive feedback about the process he has just gone through, saying things such as "Great job hanging in there!" "Congratulations, you got it!" and "I could see that you were really frustrated, but I'm impressed that you were able to keep at it until it worked!" You might also want to consider saying "Congratulations, you're paying attention to what's happening in your playing," "Great, you're thinking for yourself!" or "I'm glad to see you using information that you learned in other situations."

An alternative to telling the student about what just happened is to ask the student questions: *What just happened here?* or *How did you do that?* or *What did you just figure out?* or *How does it feel to be able to do this?* or *What's it like to have figured that out just now?* If you're impatient and expect answers quickly, or if your child gets antsy with not knowing, see what happens if you privately–ahead of time–assign yourself an amount of time you're willing just to sit there before either you or the child answers. One minute is really not that long, but it can seem like an eternity. It's definitely not a waste of practice time to spend one minute waiting for the child to get engaged. Even if it doesn't happen and you end up giving the answer, it teaches your child that you're willing to give him the time he needs to think through something.

When you see that your child is stuck, wait a few moments to see if he starts to hunt for a solution on his own. If he does, "Don't just do something, stand there" is good advice to keep in mind. If he doesn't, the advice in the next section can come in handy.

People have said, "Don't cry" to other people for years and years, and all it has ever meant is, "I'm too uncomfortable when you show your feelings. Don't cry." I'd rather have them say, "Go ahead and cry. I'm here to be with you."

Fred Rogers
The World According to Mister Rogers

Should we allow name-calling of parents and abusive language? I cannot imagine how it can serve the mental health of any child to be permitted such displays of uncontrolled verbal aggression. This is very close to physical assault and the child who is permitted such license in verbal attack is just as likely to suffer bad effects as the child who is permitted to hit his parents. Of course, we do not need to make the child feel that he is a...sinner and will be struck by a bolt of lightning for his name-calling. It should be enough for a parent to call a halt to this display, "That's enough. I don't care to hear any more of this. You're completely out of control and I don't like this one bit. When you've calmed down we'll discuss this business like two human beings." A child can be permitted to express his anger without resorting to savage name-calling. If he does so, if he loses control, he needs to know from his parents that he has overstepped the line. This doesn't go.

Selma Fraiberg, MSW
The Magic Years

20

Develop the Skill of Acknowledging Feelings

"Choose your battles" is common advice that gets tossed around, but it's a generalization that's not always useful. Since we certainly don't want to engage in battles everyone loses, it's helpful to have more detail about the kinds of battles in which we are likely to triumph. There's no point in wasting our energy on battles that can't be won.

There's a pretty clear guideline that can help: we adults can usually be victorious when placing controls–limits–on children's *actions*, and children will benefit from our doing just that. Making the decision to battle a child's errant behavior, then, is a win-win proposition. Children thrive on a wide playing field with clear, firm, and consistent limits which outline the things they may and may not do.

But there's one battle that parents have no hope of winning: it's impossible to control children's feelings. Since we can't control children's feelings, we need to guide and limit their *behaviors*, but leave their feelings alone. Attempting to control children's feelings leads everyone involved down the path to misery. I know parents have embarked on this journey when they ask me questions such as "How can I make my child slow down and *care* about the details?"–or–"How can I make my child *enthusiastic* about practicing every day?"

These parents can turn around and begin a journey to a happier place when they realize that even though we can eventually teach children how to slow down enough to manage details, we can't control how they *feel* about doing it. We are likely to be successful with making the work a requirement, but there's no guarantee that they'll *care* about those details. (Not to mention that children often do have details they truly care about, they're just not always the same details that are on the adult's list.)

Similarly, we can insist that children practice every day, but we can't make them feel *enthusiastic* about it. Of course we'd prefer that they were, so out come the practice games. Still, there's no guarantee. A child may or may not be enthusiastic about the games. Or he might be enthusiastic for a while–which can get you over a hump–but like most feelings, the enthusiasm will come and go. We often have the ability to influence a child's feelings–games are more likely to help a child enjoy practicing than yelling and screaming, for example–but direct control is a different thing. Some parents may say "Yes, but I'm able to calm down my child when he's upset." Even so, tuning in to your child and giving him the things he needs to calm down is different from *commanding* him to calm down.

If you do attempt to require a feeling, your child is likely to be upset about the additional assignment you have now added to the practice: acting. The younger the child, the more difficult this additional acting assignment can be, since young children are busy trying to figure out what is and isn't real in the world. When their feelings, well, *feel* so real–but an adult tells them that they're not–children can get very confused. There's another thing that can confuse them. Not only are they trying to learn the difference between what's real and what's make-believe, they're also in the middle of learning about being honest. Feeling frustrated and pretending to be fine unsettles a child's sense of integrity.

Take the case of six year old Abby. It's typical of the needless problems that ensue when a parent attempts to control a child's feelings. Like most children, Abby loves music but doesn't like the fact that playing an instrument isn't instantly easy and that she actually has to do some work to make it feel like it is. When her mother tells her to repeat a passage six times, she becomes miffed. "Stop being so upset. It's not that bad," her mother tells her. Now get busy and repeat it!" Though Abby can't explain her feelings with words, she is now royally irritated. At first she was just incensed about having to practice, but now she's *also* angry about her additional acting duties. She's also a little bit worried that she's not up to the role–a part of her fears that she won't be able to do all of these tasks well enough to please the person she cares most about pleasing, her mother.

Like most children in this situation, Abby can't express these feelings in words, so she just huffs and puffs. She stalls, and she sighs. And like many parents who find themselves facing a child like Abby, her mother says, "Now come on! There's no reason for you to be so upset." But, for Abby there is. In addition to having to act like it's fine with her that she has to repeat something to make it easier, now she also has the burden of acting as if her acting assignment were fine with her–but it's not! She's further enraged. Her mother begins to complain about Abby's "attitude problem."

Now you can see the crusty layers of problems that accumulate when attempting to control a child's feelings.

Abby's well-meaning mother isn't alone. These layers that cause so much pain are very common obstacles in many parent-child practice relationships and block an ability to get to the pleasure of making music. Doing the best they can with their lack of knowledge about feelings, many well-intentioned, loving parents find themselves embroiled in similar practice predicaments and rummaging through their minds for a way out.

Instead of attempting to block Abby's feelings–and since we can't control feelings, *attempting* is the most any parent can do–Abby's mother has several other options for acknowledging Abby's upset, all of them productive. She could just describe the feeling: "*It looks like you're really upset about having to repeat this passage.*" She could admit that the world isn't magic, but it would be nice if it were: "*Wouldn't it be great if you could magically just play this easily without practicing*?" Or she could ask a question to get Abby to talk more about her feelings: "*What don't you like about repeating this passage?*"

Any one of these tactics merely notes Abby's feelings–they don't let her off the hook. Her mother will need to spend time listening to Abby talk about her feelings, and Abby will still have to do the work of practice. Being upset does not automatically mean that it's time to quit practicing any more than being happy means a child gets to throw orange paint at the kitchen cupboards in an act of glee. It is possible to have a feeling or "an attitude" and still work productively. The secret is to acknowledge Abby's feelings *before* insisting that she practice. If you try to fight them instead, you end up putting up a barrier that prevents useful work from getting done, or just makes it more difficult than it needs to be.

Acknowledging the feeling is a useful strategy that takes into account two significant aspects of feelings. The first one is that feelings are transient–they may feel overpowering and they may never go away completely, but they don't hold their full charge forever. The second thing about feelings is that they are not easily compartmentalized. We often have several feelings happening all at once. It's like the old joke where the guy finds out that his mother-in-law has driven over a cliff... in *his* Mercedes.

Let's take a look at how these two aspects of feelings apply to Abby. Like most children, Abby is irked about having to repeat something, but acknowledging her upset—just talking about it–helps to drain it of its charge. When her indignation dims because it has less power, she's then able to see that she also has other feelings about practicing: she likes to learn and she likes to master a challenge.

So acknowledging feelings is actually a more efficient use of energy than blocking feelings. Pushing on a feeling tends to make the feeling push back, which then just creates more tension–either pent-up or otherwise. Acknowledging Abby's emotions helps her start to manage them instead of just being a slave to them. Then there's energy left over for continuing the work of practicing.

Even though this strategy is more efficient, it still takes effort.

Acknowledging a child's feelings is *not* easy. In the short run, it's much easier to blurt out something such as "Don't be discouraged" or "'Can't' is a four letter word and you're not allowed to say it." In the long run, however, it is more effective to invest in the tremendous effort it takes to respond with empathy–"*You're discouraged*" and "*Sounds like you're frustrated because you're not getting this as quickly as you'd like to.*" Fortunately, doing the work of acknowledging a child's feelings is a case in which more effort yields more reward.

Of course, it's usually easy for us to acknowledge the happy, cheerful, and positive feelings that children have: "Looks like you're really enjoying that ice cream…" "Sounds like you really like that present Uncle Herb sent you…" and "That was a fun class!" These pretty, clean, and happy feelings are as pleasant to be around as a visit from Mary Poppins. It's when children's feelings take a turn for the other side of the dial that life can start to look and feel a little less like a Disney animation and a bit more like the latest Stephen King concoction.

Still, we need to acknowledge spookier feelings as well. We adults can actually scare children when we react to their murkier feelings by trying to tell them that they don't have them–for instance "Don't worry about playing on the concert" and "Cheer up–even though you forgot the D-sharps on both repeats and fumbled, you should feel proud of the way you played that piece." When we get involved in pretending that their darker feelings don't exist, or attempting to make the feelings go away, we communicate to the child that those feelings are so bad, so terrible, so dangerous, and so awful that even an adult can't stand to talk about them or to have them near. Of course, we don't communicate those things with words. We don't have to. At a profound and deeply emotional level, our avoidance of their feelings says those things for us. Boldly. When you consider how powerful children consider adults to be, them's some mighty strong feelings.

Acknowledging your own feelings is just as important as acknowledging your child's feelings. It's like when the flight attendant says "Secure your own oxygen mask before assisting others" in the safety demonstration prior to take-off. The message is clear. If the caretakers don't take care of themselves, they won't be able to take care of anyone else. If you don't ensure your own oxygen supply first, then there's the strong possibility that you will pass out before the person depending on you gets taken care of. Then we're down two people.

When we start taking a look at our own feelings, we realize why it's so difficult for children to control theirs–we full-grown puppies can't even control ours. What we can and *must* do is control our behaviors, in much the same way that we acknowledge a child's feelings but restrict the child's behavior. The difference is that we have to do it all for ourselves. While children can lean on us for help with managing their feelings, we can't lean on them for help with ours.

An adult's inability to understand the difference between feelings and behaviors can lead to two kinds of problems. At one end of the continuum are people who are aware of their feelings, but are a slave to them. These are the people who shout, yell, and throw things, sometimes for even the smallest of reasons, like a missed rhythm during practice. They are the uptight drivers who tailgate in heavy traffic when they're late. Lateness isn't an excuse for putting one's self and others at risk by engaging in a behavior that isn't going to change anything. But the tailgater is a slave to feelings, unable to use his or her rational mind to think through other options.

At the other extreme are people who operate from a set of rigid rules that prohibit them from acknowledging their feelings, even to themselves. Of course they have feelings anyway, but they are so afraid of what would happen if they acknowledged those feelings that they invest an enormous amount of energy in attempting to block them. They're driving through their lives with their parking brakes on. In the process they create significant problems for themselves and those around them. They themselves eventually burn out, although it may take decades. Such people may force themselves to appear happy and cheerful at all times, for example, but their negative feelings have sneaky means of taking over in ways that catch them off guard. In this respect, they have about as much control as the people who are slaves to their feelings. For example, they may claim that they *always* have fun practicing with their children, but when actually practicing, they find themselves unable to offer positive comments when their children do something well–or they present their comments in a dutiful, inauthentic way or through clenched teeth. Or they may make subtle, yet still painful, put-downs, perhaps sarcastically calling a child "Your Excellency" when he balks at practicing something.

Mature adults realize that the sooner we acknowledge feelings, the sooner they pass–or at least become more manageable. Much like the waves at the beach, feelings come and go throughout the day. Trying to control feelings–our own or anyone else's–is as futile as trying to sweep those waves back into the ocean. At the other extreme, the people who are slaves to their feelings are like pieces of driftwood that can only go where the waves take them. What we all need are the emotional skills that allow us to acknowledge and accept our feelings for nothing more than what they are–merely feelings that we can consciously choose to act on or not. Then we can develop the awareness we need in order to navigate them.

Most of the time, most of us adults are somewhere in between the two extremes of either being completely driven by our feelings or investing energy in blocking and denying them.

For example, several parents have told me about wanting to whack their children with the bow during practice. In an anonymous note to me, one parent actually admitted to breaking a bow over her child's head. She not only had to buy a new bow, she also had to spend a great deal of time working to repair her relationship with her child. Other parents have told me that they knew something was desperately wrong when they found themselves holding the bow over their children's heads, but stopped before striking.

Don't these parents love their children? Well, yes, they do. And they are also very angry. As parenting educator Carol Kaplan-Lyss says, "Every parent can understand child abuse." That doesn't mean that every parent commits child abuse. What it does mean is that every parent has been to the edge. Every parent has come into contact with those intense feelings that can lead some parents to abuse. But like the mother who stopped just before she hit her daughter, most parents have a rational mind that kicks in and makes them halt before they do physical damage. For the parents who don't have that control, we've got protective services. Acting on those angry feelings is absolutely forbidden. But the feelings, themselves, are quite normal. Ideally, what we would like to see happen is that the mother who wants to use the bow as a weapon is able to acknowledge the feeling and manage it before she even reaches out her hand to seize the bow.

These stories about parents and bows are quite dramatic, but I'm telling them to you because I want you to know two things: these feelings during practice are quite common, and blocking yourself from acting on them is absolutely essential. When you do experience these feelings, you need to use your rational mind to figure out what to do about them.

One of the most useful things you can do is to express your frustrations to your spouse, your child's teacher, your clergy, and/or to your parent colleagues. If these resources still don't help, I recommend professional counseling.

If you are able to exercise great caution and self-discipline, so that you are doing it only when you think that it would help your child, there can also be a place for sharing your frustrations with your child. For example, I don't recommend saying "You really need to behave today because I'm not in the mood to practice." The problem with a statement like this one is that while it may help you get something off your chest, it also communicates that you expect your child's actions to take care of your emotional mood.

On the other hand, you could say something that can benefit your child as much as you, such as "*I sure wish we didn't have to practice today–I have so many other things I'd rather do–but I'm going to make myself sit down and practice with you anyway because I know that it's important and that if we don't get it done now, it won't get done.*" Statements like this one model several important things for your child. They demonstrate acceptance of your own feelings and your ability to use your rational mind to make a decision about what to do about them. At the same time they demonstrate how much you value music and the process of practicing. Your comments also show the mixed nature of feelings–you both do and don't want to practice. If your child would also like to skip practice for the day, your comments even provide a kind of empathy. (In case it's not totally obvious, I also want to add that "not being in the mood" to practice is not a reason for you to skip practice for the day any more than it's an excuse for your child.)

I usually acknowledge my feelings silently, to myself, since I can't expect children to listen to my emotional needs, let alone help me manage them [see also section 7]. When I am working with a frustrated child, for example, it is not uncommon for me to feel embarrassed and anxious because I didn't construct the situation in a way that would have avoided the frustration. I then need to acknowledge the feelings and take them as a signal. They're a signal to ask myself whether I could have done something differently. I usually realize that I actually am doing a good job of teaching. But I am grateful for the signal because I think it keeps me kind. It helps me to remember that the frustrated child needs empathy from me as he toils. My empathy won't take away his struggle, but it will give him an extra boost as he works through–as all children must–the many little tutorials of childhood, the ones that teach that life doesn't always happen as we wish it.

Children also need to learn that they're not allowed to express their feelings just any way that they wish. Once again, we're back to the idea that while we can't and shouldn't control children's feelings, we can and should control their actions. In other words, it's the *ways* in which children express their feelings that we can and should control. As Selma Fraiberg writes in her excellent book *The Magic Years*, "the 'right' to have a feeling is not the same as a license to inflict it on others, and in the matters of license we appear to have erred gravely in the education of today's child." She later adds "The principle needs to be this: Whatever the reasons for your feelings you will have to find civilized solutions."

One of my students, Robert, used to have a tendency to explode during his lessons, no matter how gently I approached his playing. If I would ask him simply to repeat a section, he would sometimes do it and "adjust" what he had played the first time. For example, the second time around he might remember that it was a G-sharp. Saying nothing about its absence the first time, I would be sure to congratulate him for getting the G-sharp on the second go-through. Then I'd have him reinforce his success with a few more repetitions.

This strategy usually worked well. Except on the days that it didn't. Sometimes I would ask Robert to repeat a section and he would *yell* at me: "It was fine! I don't need to repeat it!"

So, one day I began his lesson by setting clear guidelines for expressing his feelings–or as Selma Fraiberg might say, I gave him a "civilized solution" for expressing his feelings. I drew several circles on a piece of paper. Knowing that Robert was a little bit embarrassed to admit that he sometimes had feelings that weren't the most attractive, I told him that I understood that sometimes he was "angry," "upset," "frustrated," and "mad" during lessons and that it was o.k. to have those feelings. I added that it was absolutely *not* o.k. to yell, but that he could use one of the circles to draw a face that showed how he felt. In the middle of working away at his playing, at a point where he would normally have erupted, he stopped and drew a face, then got back to work. I expected that the face would have an angry look, with a wide open mouth, depicting yelling. But it didn't. It had a frown and tears.

A few lessons later, I scribbled something on a piece of paper and asked Robert what it said. He had no idea–it was deliberately my most atrocious handwriting. I told him that if he got upset or frustrated he could write down what he was feeling, either in a way that I could read it or in a way that I couldn't. He enjoyed doing this as well, and sometimes his handwriting was legible, and sometimes it was intentionally indecipherable!

All of this activity with a pencil and paper may seem like too much time off-task in a music lesson or a home practice, but in reality, as with Robert, it doesn't take very long and it actually salvages time that otherwise might be devoted to a tantrum, an explosion, or just continued icky feelings that get in the way of learning.

Kids need to be able to express their feelings, and we not only fortify their mental health, we offer them valuable lessons in socialization when we give them acceptable options for expressing them. Yelling at a teacher is not acceptable, but the feeling behind it is. It wasn't helpful for Robert to yell at me–being so out of control scared him, which didn't help him manage his frustration.

It might be easy to misconstrue my actions as teaching Robert respect, but I shy away from that interpretation. It's difficult to define "respect" in a concrete way for children. Mostly, they learn respect when we adults respect them and outline clear limits and options for their behavior. A child's respectful *feelings* for a parent or a teacher are not something the adult has direct control over. Regardless of their feelings, they must express them in respectful–and civilized–ways.

In addition to learning that violent outbursts don't go, children also need to learn the difference between stating their feelings and routine whining. Adults who complain to children about whining–are usually whining themselves! To get out of this bind, you can use one of three strategies for dealing with whining.

The first one is to say "*You're whining and I can't listen to that now. You can't whine during practice. But at the end of practice you can tell me about what you don't like, you can write me a note about what you don't like, or you can draw me a picture about it. Or you can tell me before we start practice next time. I won't listen to it right now.*" Using this strategy, you haven't said "Don't have that feeling," but you have helped the child to contain it. You are putting the child in a situation in which she can function effectively AND have the feeling.

Another strategy for dealing with whining is to say "*I can't listen to the way you're saying that. You'll have to say it to me in a normal tone of voice.*"

A third strategy is to ask your child to whine and complain at the beginning of practice for one minute–use a timer–and then forbid any further whining until practice is over. Or you might schedule a "whining break" in the middle of practice.

Whining usually happens when a child–or an adult, for that matter–finds that it is the only option available for expressing a feeling. Using these strategies gives your child better options for being heard because they communicate that you are willing to pay attention to the things that upset your child. They also communicate that you are only willing to do it in a way that works for both of you, not just your child. Like anything else that bugs you, if your child's whining bugs you, it's going to infect your practice. Having a strategy for coping with it can do wonders for both of you. [See also section 34, "Find Ways to Enjoy the Trip."]

Whether it's dealing with whining or temperamental outbursts, acknowledging feelings in productive ways isn't always easy. I'd be lying if I said it is. Chances are, there will be times when you will find yourself irritated because acknowledging your child's feelings doesn't seem to help as quickly and conveniently as you might wish. What can be even more maddening is that it can take even longer if your child isn't used to your responding to his feelings this way. He'll need time before his insides will trust that you are merely acknowledging his feelings, not asking him to change them. At some level, this reaction will make sense to you because you were once a child. But your child doesn't have a basis for understanding your struggles as a parent, because he has never been one.

Like any other skill, acknowledging feelings takes time and practice to do effectively. And just like remembering the C-sharps gets easier with repetition, acknowledging a child's feelings–and your own, for that matter–does get easier as you practice it, even if there are tricky spots that remain.

Still, since we can't control a child's feelings and usually just make things worse if we attempt to, acknowledging feelings and controlling behaviors is the most useful way to proceed. When an upset child has calmed down (which may take from a few seconds to a day or two, depending on the child and the issue), move on to the next step of practice…doing the work of making it easier. Then, in addition to working through the frustrations of practicing, you can eventually have the pleasure of seeing your child encounter the joy of making music.

Recommended Reading: *How to Talk So Kids Will Listen and Listen So Kids Will Talk*, by Adele Faber and Elaine Mazlish. The title of this popular book attracts many parents and teachers who think that they will learn tricks that will magically make children listen to what they say. But the book actually focuses on the second half of the title–listening so that kids will talk. In other words, the secret lies in learning to acknowledge children's feelings. It's one of the most useful books I've ever encountered.

The true opposite of depression is not gaiety or absence of pain, but vitality: the freedom to experience spontaneous feelings. It is part of the kaleidoscope of life that these feelings are not only cheerful, "beautiful," and "good;" they also can display the whole scale of human experience, including envy, jealousy, rage, disgust, greed, despair, and mourning...

Alice Miller
The Drama of
the Gifted Child

21

Choose Reasonable Times to Practice

If you don't choose reasonable times to practice, be prepared to deal with the consequences!

This is an idea that may seem almost painfully obvious, but, unfortunately, isn't always.

In a drastic example, I once had a seven year old student whose mother could only practice with him from 9 to 9:30 at night. He could function, and he could be polite–a rare feat for a tired child–but his progress was not nearly as fast as the progress for my other students who were practicing at child-appropriate times. Under these conditions, his skills with the instrument didn't grow, and as a consequence he wasn't able to learn many pieces. In his mind–the mind of a child–he couldn't see that he was working under very difficult conditions. Like most children, he thought he himself was the problem, and eventually quit.

Theoretically, if the parent can adopt the attitude that "anything worth doing is worth doing badly," a set-up such as this one can work–especially if it is for just a short period of time due to temporary circumstances. But if the parent expects the child to perform as well as children who are practicing at more appropriate times, it won't be a positive situation for the child–especially if the parent wants the child to progress in order to make him or her look like a good parent. This kind of situation is completely unfair for the child and it's one of the trickiest to deal with as a teacher.

Practicing is challenging enough. Don't let the time of day you practice work against you.

Monitor the Emotional Vital Signs

For some of us, cooking means removing frozen food from a freezer, peeling back a corner of the box, and placing it in a microwave, with our most elaborate culinary technique being stirring the contents halfway through the cooking cycle. For others, cooking means preparing elaborate meals involving items as difficult to pronounce as they are to find in the local supermarket. Most of us are somewhere in the middle.

Regardless of your definition of "cooking" and your feelings about doing it, imagine that the neighbor kid stops by and politely asks if he can watch. He asks you simple questions about what you're doing and sometimes moves to get a closer look, but generally he just stands to the side and watches, offering only the occasional "Wow."

Now imagine that instead of the neighbor kid watching you, it's Martha Stewart. Like the neighbor kid, she doesn't say a word, but just stands there and watches. You probably have a different feeling having Martha Stewart there than you did when it was just the seven year old with the backwards baseball cap.

With Martha quietly off to the side, you would hardly even know she was there if it weren't for the fact that you can't get out of your mind that *Martha Stewart* is watching you make dinner.

Then imagine that she comes a little closer for a more detailed inspection of what you're doing. She may even offer a compliment about something you do, perhaps "Turning up the corner of a frozen dinner neatly. It's a good thing." Then as you continue, she says "hmmm" under her breath as she knits her eyebrows.

And maybe Martha makes some suggestions, or even simply asks if you would like some advice. But your feelings would almost certainly be different, depending on whether it was Martha or the neighbor kid talking–even though they were both *doing* pretty much the same thing: being interested in your cooking and asking harmless questions.

The point is this: just as it mattered to you which of the two was watching–either the neighbor kid minus his two front teeth, or perfect Martha Stewart–it matters a great deal to a child who is watching him or her play a piece.

Parents often wonder why a child will explode when they give him the exact same words the teacher did–for example "Play it again and keep your feet in one spot." But even though the words are the same, they generate different responses in the child, because the people saying them play different roles in the child's life.

A child's upset about a parent addressing flaws in his playing can come from a concern that the child can't put into words–and it doesn't even matter how gingerly the parent offers the instruction. The child's concern is the unasked question, "Do you still love me anyway?" So, unconsciously–meaning the child is *feeling* the question but doesn't have words to ask it–a child may be thinking "If I can't get my feet to stay in one spot, or if I forget, will you still love me anyway?" No one would care about the unconscious if it stayed unconscious. But it often expresses itself through actions rather than words. Expressing itself in actions is especially true for younger children who do not yet know all the words for what they're feeling, much less have the ability to *access* those words.

A child's unconscious is a fascinating thing. Unconsciously, a child may remember what he had for dinner three weeks ago, but it's not a big deal to him. However, because children have a strong basic need to know that their parents love them, the unconscious question "Do you love me anyway?" often fuels children's emotions and behaviors. Biologically, children are dependent on their parents for basic survival. If your parents don't love you, not only is it a bummer on the emotional front, it is also difficult on the physical front. Children are prone to feeling that if their parents don't love them, then they won't take care of them. Not to be overly dramatic, but a fear of death is part of the mix.

When I have spoken to groups of parents about this phenomenon–which the mother of one of my students once referred to as the "I-Love-You-Line"–there's usually at least one parent who tells me afterwards that his or her child actually asked the question out loud. I tell these parents that they are the lucky ones, because their children are able to put the feeling into words, which means that the two of them can deal with the emotions with words, rather than through frustrating and confusing actions.

I definitely don't advocate that parents fire off a curt "Yes-I-love-you-now-shut-up-and-remember-to-get-the-D-sharp-this-time." I also don't think it's a good idea to offer the child a rational explanation such as "Now, I'm aware that unconsciously you are probably wondering whether or not I still love you because the D-sharp was out of tune that time, so I just want to reassure you that, indeed, I do love you and that whether or not your D-sharp is out of tune has absolutely no bearing on the kind of enduring love I feel for you and..."

There are many other effective approaches to take. One is talking about the problem and its solution, instead of talking about the child and what he did wrong–or, even worse, what's wrong with him as a person. You say "The third finger wasn't high enough that time, so the next time it needs to be closer to the bridge" instead of "You were out of tune–the D-sharp was really sour! Don't be so careless." Another effective approach is noticing your voice as you give instructions–paying particular attention to using a pitch and speed that sounds both natural and loving. And then there's simply offering your child a reassuring hug now and then–not particularly connected to anything, just a hug.

Is remembering these options difficult for parents? You bet–but so is getting a D-sharp! "Cooperation" means "working together," and, in this case, while your child's work is to remember the D-sharp, your adult work is to monitor yourself and to search for words and strategies that are sensitive to the child's basic fear of losing your love. Just as the child won't always hit that D-sharp, you won't always be able to do your work. As you practice it, though, the work gets easier for both of you, and you hit your target more often.

The biggest thing a parent can probably do about the I-Love-You-Line is simply to know that it exists. Keep in mind that even though you may use the strategies I've suggested, and you may say things as carefully as possible, your child will sometimes feel that you have crossed the line and that he or she is in danger of losing your love–just like us adults, children feel more vulnerable some days than others. After thinking about what you have said and done during practice, you may realize that you have done everything possible to help your child feel your love. This realization can help you proceed, knowing that you have actually done nothing wrong and that your child will eventually learn through the experience that you still love him. At other moments you may realize that it's time to stop what you're doing and give your child a hug.

Like every other child in the world, your child has a much greater need for a parent who offers love than for a parent who plays the part of a music teacher who fixes things all the time. When I teach, there is always an invisible sign hanging over the student. Written on this imaginary sign is the question "What can I do next that will help the most?" Parents who practice with their children every day, who are "home teachers," will benefit from expanding that question to "What can I do next that will help the most, *given that I'm the parent, the one person in the world my child is counting on for love and support?*" [See also section 4, "Listen to the Actions First."]

Ask–Don't Tell

The first thing I learned the first day of Marvin Blickenstaff's "Introduction to Piano Pedagogy" class was a principle so useful that over twenty years later, it continues to drive my actions in every lesson I teach: "Questions open the mind; statements close it."

This principle of asking, not telling, works itself out in a myriad of ways. For example, asking a student "Which notes need to be short?" instead of blurting out "Remember to make the two G-naturals short this time"–an instruction which usually indicates that the adult remembers that the G-naturals need to be short, but we still haven't found out about the child. Our goal, of course, is that the *child* remembers. Asking questions engages children. They get involved in the learning, rather than simply going along for the ride.

We humans generally tend to listen to ourselves more than to others, so we're best off asking children questions that get them to say the things we were going to say anyway. In other words, if we ask the right questions the child will be more likely to pay attention to the person talking–himself!

To get a child to talk more, be sure to ask questions that start with *Wh-* or *How*, such as "*Wh*at did you notice that time?" "*Wh*ere was your wrist?" and "*How* did that go?" Questions like these beg a descriptive answer. Avoid questions such as "Was your wrist straight that time?" or "Did you remember the repeat?" Questions that start with a form of the verb "to be" or "to do" allow children to legitimately answer with an unadorned "Yes" or "No." When faced with a yes-or-no question, children have a 50-50 chance of getting the "correct" answer–meaning that they may give you the answer you were hoping to hear, but not really learning anything in the process.

If you give a child an instruction just before she does something, one of the most important times to ask a question is immediately after she has completed it. Say you tell a student to play all the repeats, and then she tears into the piece. When she finishes, you ask "What happened with the repeats that time?" If her report does not accurately reflect what happened, before labeling her a "liar"–either out loud, or in your own mind–get a little bit more information. Check to make sure that she understood the question. It's amazing how often I think students know what I'm talking about only to discover that they don't. Yes, sometimes children do lie–for a variety of reasons–but it usually seems to me that a polite and graceful place to start is the assumption that they have faulty information. Innocent until proven guilty.

For example, I once told a young student to bounce his third finger on the A-string. This was something he had had down pat for more than a year–or so I thought. But he kept bouncing his second finger. As he bounced his second finger with great gusto, I reached for an often useful tool, the question "How do you know?"

"Douglas," I began, "how do you know that's finger number three?

"Because it's the biggest!" he proudly replied.

The logic was lost on me. I wasn't sure why three needed to be the biggest. But I was relieved to know that he was thinking. It let me know that he was involved in the lesson and not just spacing out, even if he was a bit confused. If we adults don't ask questions, there is always the danger that we might assume, as in the case with Douglas, that the child is ignoring us and that we have to try harder to make him work. These kinds of assumptions send a day's practice–and our relationship–down an unhappy detour.

"I'm so glad to know that you're thinking!" I told Douglas.

I also realized that I needed to review finger numbers with him. Douglas was more than willing to do this review, but had I scolded him for not paying attention, he would not only have been confused, he would probably not have been too invested in the review of the finger numbers.

As the Danish philosopher Søren Kierkegaard once wrote,

> ...to be a teacher in the right sense is to be a learner. Instruction begins when you, the teacher, learn from the learner, put yourself in his place so that you may understand what he understands and in the way he understands it...

In other words, the first thing a teacher must understand is what the student understands. The primary way we adults discover what the student understands is by asking questions.

It is possible to ask these discovery questions indirectly. For example, if I think a student knows the difference between the words staccato and legato–but I'm not sure–I might say "Play this piece staccato and legato. When it's legato, open your mouth. When it's staccato, close your mouth." Keep in mind that this kind of inquiry only works on a piece that the student plays quite easily–you're not checking the child's concentration skills, you're on a hunt to understand what the student understands.

Sometimes children find my questions irritating and want them to go away. When I note this happening, I sometimes switch the activity, or offer answers. But before doing this switching, I usually monitor the child's tolerance level. While my questions might be as bothersome for him as washing his hands before dinner, I know that they're important. There's a part of every child–every adult too–that wants life to be easy. You can tell your child that you *wish* you could make everything easy for him, but that you can't actually do it. When a child finds my questions aggravating, I'll usually push him to what he thinks his limit is, and then go one baby step further. *Then* I stop.

Children sometimes get bothered by questions, because in addition to thinking that they should always have an answer ready, they also think they were supposed to have thought of the question in the first place. I tell students that the questions I ask are batteries, and it's my job to supply them. It's not their job to have all of the batteries–we work together to light up their brains.

Besides, it's important for children and parents to know that the answer often doesn't matter–it's the process of having to think that ultimately serves the student in real life. The brain benefits from the workout it gets as it grasps for a response. It's like going to the gym and using the Stairmaster. No matter how fast and how great your endurance, you will never be able to enter the Stairmaster finals at the Olympics. The benefit of hopping on the Stairmaster is something other than the specific skill it develops. And just as you can't hire someone to exercise for you, when parents answer a teacher's questions for their children, they deprive them of the very exercises that strengthen them.

Give Your Child Lots of Healthy Choices

Control is like hunger–it's a natural human need that longs to be satisfied. God forbid you should stop feeding your child, but if you did, your child would probably grab whatever food was available.

Children do something similar when we deprive them of the opportunity to satisfy their craving for control. In an attempt to feed this need, they will gnaw at whatever is at hand–including your last good nerve, which at times can seem like a highly prized delicacy of the Child Tribe.

A child's subversive controlling behavior can often be unattractive, unpleasant, and perhaps even dangerous. To make matters even more complicated, the child may not be consciously choosing to act in these ways, just reacting to a gut-level emotional hunger. While some tantrums are a natural part of the growing up process, other tantrums and upsets come about because the child is so starved for control that he takes it in any way it's available.

In the same way that the adults in a hungry child's life need to make decisions about what the child gets to eat–instead of allowing, say, a steady diet of jelly doughnuts and bubble gum ice cream–they also need to make decisions about what the child will get to control. Giving children healthy choices is one important way in which adults can help children satisfy their basic need for control. Producing these nourishing choices requires some thought, however. There is much more to it than simply asking, "What do you want to do?"

The most important thing about giving children choices is that the choices are genuine. Don't make children guess at what you want them to do. For instance, if you ask the young guitarist "Do you want to practice guitar now?" and the child says "No" then you have to live with it, because it was one of the genuine choices that your question offered.

One way to avoid the predicament is by remembering to start choice questions with "*Wh-*" or "*How...*". For example, you could say "*Wh*en do you want to practice guitar–right now, or do you want me to set the timer for ten minutes and then start practice when it goes off?" In other words, avoiding questions that are easily answered with a simple "yes" or "no" will help you give a child the kind of control you are prepared for him to have. Instead of asking "Do you want to work on 'Go Tell Aunt Rhody' today?"–a question which offers the choice of "yes" or "no"–you can ask the child "*What* do you want to work on in 'Go Tell Aunt Rhody'?" or "How many times do you want to play 'Go Tell Aunt Rhody' today?"

For some children, these questions are too broad. They need a question which narrows down the options, such as "Which of these do you want to work on when you play 'Go Tell Aunt Rhody'–keeping the bow hairs in one spot on the string, or making sure everything is ready before you play the first note?"–or–"How many times do you want to play 'Go Tell Aunt Rhody' today–three, four, or five times?"

Starting choices with "Do..." and "Is..." will likely derail your practice, as the rules of language will allow your child to quickly choose "No!" to these questions and you'll find yourself stuck.

There are always children who respond with things like "Never" to questions such as "When do you want to practice today?" In these cases, you have to point out that "Never" isn't an option. It wasn't about *whether* to practice or not, it was about *when* to practice. A child may not like your firmness in offering some choices but not others. However, you can relax, knowing that you really are offering reasonable choices and flexibility–especially about something that is ultimately in the child's own interest.

When a parent makes a rock solid decision about what choices to give a child and the child then attempts to pound on that decision, the parent is not injuring the child. Being hard doesn't make a rock mean. Children eventually figure out that they're better off just taking one of the choices a parent presents. While in the short term a child may resent a parent for having the ultimate power and control, in the long run, children appreciate it when parents are as firm–and therefore, as *reliable* and *dependable*–as bedrock.

If you don't apologize for the choices you offer and if you craft your questions in such a way that the child can have a real choice, you'll be on the right track. If *you* think that your choices were too limited, then let that feeling inform how you construct the *next* set of choices. Only rarely, however, should you actually back down. You may want to offer three or more choices instead of just two–perhaps you know a child needs to practice an A Major scale, so instead of asking "Do you want to practice the A Major scale?" you could say "When do you want to practice the A Major scale–now, before 'Lightly Row' after 'Lightly Row,' or after we practice 'Long, Long Ago'?"

The importance of having choices became very clear to me over ten years ago, when my mother had bypass surgery. After surgery, she was given a device that would allow her to push a button to give herself more pain medication. The computer that was part of the set-up prevented her from over-dosing. A nurse told my family that when patients are given more control like this, they actually end up using less medication than if they have to ask a nurse for doses.

Something similar happens with children. If we give them safe and healthy amounts of control before they are desperate for it, they'll usually need less of it; and they'll be easier to work with. However, just as well-fed children still snitch the occasional cookie, children who are given control through healthy choices will occasionally attempt to take control in ways that you'd rather they didn't.

When you give children choices and are flexible at every opportunity you possibly can be, it makes it easier *not* to give them choices when you can't. That's because they won't be so desperately starved for control.

In general, however, practices are more pleasant when children have lots of genuine, nourishing choices. Like most people, children tend to feel happier the more they feel that they are in control of what happens to them.

When parents are direct and honest in their expectations for a child, she has the experience of being entrusted and empowered. Honest communication is the most powerful system a parent can establish. A child can then make her own choice, can realize "this is my choice," and can feel the reward of achievement when she can live up to it. At the same time, parents are modeling for the child an alternative to emotional manipulation.

T. Berry Brazelton, MD
Touchpoints: Your Child's Emotional and Behavioral Development

25

Make Demands that are Clear, Gentle, and Firm

In the movie *The Karate Kid*, an instructor promises to teach a boy karate, but then turns around and has him wax cars the day of his first lesson. The kid is puzzled, but since he really does want to learn karate from this teacher, he waxes the cars anyway, hoping that they'll get to the karate soon. He later discovers that in the process of waxing the cars and doing the other mundane chores the teacher gave him, he developed physical skills–habits–that are extremely valuable in karate.

I like to recommend this movie because it drives home the message that repeating things–practicing–makes them easier. Through all that waxing and the other chores, the boy's skills became so automatic that he didn't even have to think about them. The movie also teaches that even though repetition can sometimes be very dull, it's your ticket to the good stuff.

There's yet another important message in this movie: doing what the teacher says–or what your parent says, for that matter–is usually to your benefit. Although you may not always understand, your teachers and parents normally work with your best interests at heart. (As with any movie, I encourage parents to review it first for appropriateness of content before they watch it with their children.)

Children need to learn–through experiences, not lectures–that there are times in which they benefit from giving up immediate control. In these situations they end up getting not just a little control in the long run, but *lots* of control. Waxing the cars gave the boy in *The Karate Kid* the power to do what he really wanted to do.

Don't get me wrong. I'm not advocating that practices should be all about parents telling children what to do at every turn. In fact, quite the opposite. Children learn more and are more willing to work when they are given choices at every point they possibly can be. Giving them choices and appropriate control helps develop their trust that we adults are working with their best interests in mind. That trust is crucial. It's what usually allows a child to feel safe enough to give in and follow directions.

When it's not possible to give children choices, parents and teachers need to make clear, gentle, and firm demands. We need to say "Today we have to start with scales,"–or–"Play this again and make sure that all of the notes have a full sound,"–or–"Tap your pinkie 10 times." In cases such as these, demands are appropriate, but they don't need to be as dramatic or traumatic as a "demand for payment" from a credit card company.

But they are clearly demands, nonetheless. In spite of the fact that we make them in the best interests of the child, they are not choices or requests. The fact is, life doesn't always offer choices. It would be absurd, for example, for an anesthesiologist to ask a patient "Would you mind a little anesthesia today before the surgeon removes your spleen?"

When we give children real demands, they may hate having to give up momentary freedom in order to get other things they want–such as information about how to play the instrument, time with the teacher, or a chance to play a game. Giving children practice with the fact that life sometimes makes demands doesn't make adults mean. Much of growing up is learning to tolerate the demands that life itself makes of us. In some ways, even making choices is a demand–life insists that we do *something*. Choosing *not* to make a choice is, in fact, making a choice. There's just no way out.

When adults are uncomfortable with taking control, they can confuse children by softening and blurring–and, thereby *weakening*–their demands. For example, while some children are ready to go when a parent or teacher says "Would it be o.k. if we do some bow exercises now?" other children hear it as what it really is–a choice. They say "No," either verbally or by the way they react, and with good reason.

The younger they are, the more children thrive on instructions and choices that are clear, concrete, and *genuine*–and demands that are straightforward. In other words, in this case, saying "Bow exercises are next." Young children need this clarity because they are not yet able to handle the subtleties of language. But it's even good advice for adolescents. No matter what age the developing child, adults serve that child best when they are clear and up-front.

Parents may feel that they are being polite when they use fuzzy language with their children, such as "Would you like to have a lesson now?"

instead of "Time for your lesson." I understand this concern. I also understand that some of these ways of being "polite" confuse a child, and in a subtle way actually *encourage* a child to behave rudely. I'll explain...

While it's true that kids may be upset about not having a choice in some matters, they will be even *more* upset if they are given the additional assignment of having to read the adult's mind. The original task a parent hinted at may have seemed exhausting but do-able–perhaps the parent asked "How about if you play that five times?" But the child finds that the additional task of reading the parent's mind is impossible and completely overwhelming. He can easily become very uncomfortable because he's not sure if his parent–the most important person in his world–is really making a demand or not. So he's not sure if he really has to play it five times or not.

A child whose mother expects her to read her mind is often overwhelmed by a combination of conflicting feelings. They're feelings she doesn't have words for. But if the feelings could talk, they would say something like "I don't want to play this five times, but my mom doesn't want to tell me I have to do it. That's because she doesn't want to look like a mean person. So she's hoping I will pretend that I *want* to do this so that she doesn't feel uncomfortable. Now I have to do this, I have to pretend to like it, *and* I have to take on the burden of managing *her* discomfort because she can't manage it herself. I have to be mean to myself to take care of her! And I hate having to do all of those things! AAAAAaaaahhhh!"

Remember that the child doesn't usually have the words to express these frustrations, she can only express them through actions. *Voilá* rude behavior.

So if you hope a child will say "Yes" when you ask "Do you want to work on that left hand exercise your teacher gave you?" but he says "No" instead, he will likely be justifiably angry if you say "Well, do it anyway." There are many ways in which he comes out the loser in this situation. In addition to the emotional angst of having to guess what you want, you have taken away his control over the choice you gave him, *and* he also really has to *do* the exercise he doesn't want to do.

You can avoid all of this agitation and distress by being clear about demands and choices. Remember that you are giving your child a choice every time you start out with "How about if we..." "Would it be o.k. if..." "Do you want to..." or "Do you mind..."

If your intention is to give the child a choice, then these are great ways to start out. But if you *don't* intend to give your child a choice, then keep these phrases in their drawer until you really need them. You're better off using these phrases, which come out of the drawer labeled "polite ways to start a reasonable demand:" *Time to... Next is...* or some action word, such as *Lift* (as in "*Lift* your arm at the end") or *Play* (as in "*Play* the A scale..."). As long as you are deliberate about the drawer you get your words from, your practices will go smoother because your child will be clear about what's on your mind.

There's another common snag that can complicate the adult's work. It's when the adult looks to the child to approve and go along with something the child really doesn't have a choice about. For example, a parent might start out with a very clear and effective demand, such as "I know that you want to sit in my lap, but that's not allowed right now, so I'm just going to sit right here and you can sit next to me." In and of itself, this kind of statement has some wonderful emotional nutrients for children–it's empathetic and states clearly what the child must do. But a parent can diminish its effectiveness by adding "...O.K.?" at the end of it. I'm not talking about parents who are asking "O.K.?" to see if the child understood what they said. I'm talking about the parents who want the child to *endorse* what they just said. Tacking "O.K?" to the end of an appropriate and clear demand can turn it into a choice and a request for approval. [For more about the perils of seeking of approval from a child, see section 7.]

There are other cabooses that parents sometimes attach to the end of commands, transforming a clear and reasonable direction into a choice. For example, when a teacher instructs the student to play something on the E string, it's a reasonable demand for the parent to turn to the child and say "The teacher said you need to play it on the E string, so here we go!" But I've heard parents say, instead, "The teacher said you need to play it on the E string, *do you want to try doing that?*" Of course, you may be one of those parents who find that these kinds of tags work at the end of demands. But I've seen them backfire more often than not. The important thing is to pay attention to your results. If you find that your child is difficult to work with, keep this in mind: parents and teachers who look to children for approval will often end up with very angry children.

There's one other common way that failing to make clear demands can get us into situations we'd rather not be in. It's when we use the words "can" and "try" in inappropriate ways. For instance, if you're placing the viola for a young beginner and he needs to lift his chin in order to get the job done, it's most effective simply to say, "Lift your chin." If you ask the child "Can you lift your chin?" or if you say, "Try to lift your chin" you've weakened your demand unnecessarily–it would be really unusual if the child couldn't lift his chin. If you're truly not sure if he can do it or not, however, then by all means, go ahead and check.

But if a child is in a puddle on the floor and you say "Can you stand up?" or "Try to stand up" you're probably not going to get the result you're looking for. The question "Can you…" and the word "Try…" indicate some doubt that the child can do it. He's likely to attach himself to that doubt and stay right where he is. But if he can, in fact, stand up, then just say "Stand up." Don't make him guess what he's supposed to do. Be clear. And state your reasonable demand in a way that lets him know that he's more than capable of doing it.

Because reasonable demands are fine. Adults sometimes need to take control the way the instructor of an aerobics class does. You'd never get the benefits of the class if the teacher let you constantly ask questions–"I know you just said four times on the right side, but can I do it on the left side instead? And can I do it later?"

Just like an aerobics instructor–or a baseball coach, or a karate teacher–there are times when a music teacher or a parent needs to make appropriate demands of a child, not give choices. That's because as the more knowledgeable and mature person in the relationship, the adult holds the most responsibility for determining the course of events. Part of this responsibility involves looking for ways to construct situations in which the child has lots of genuine choices, and noticing which choices work for the child [as outlined in section 24]. The other part is making reasonable demands.

Giving clear, gentle, and firm demands can be an enormous amount of work. At first you may be so overwhelmed with the technical intricacies of the instrument your child is studying that you won't have the resources to pay attention to how you're creating choices for your child in home practices. But the sooner you're able to pay attention to your words–maybe not always, but at least enough to make a difference–the sooner you'll be able to have happier practices.

In the long run, children will appreciate your clarity between demands and choices. Avoid falling into the trap of substituting a wishy-washy approach for a positive one.

26

Look for Opportunities to be Flexible

"I blew it!" Kathleen told herself, realizing what had just happened in practice with her son.

"Want to try that again?" she had cheerily asked five-year-old Joseph.

"Naw," he replied.

Their violin teacher, Mr. Reynolds, had given them the assignment of working together to make ten bow hands a day. So far, she and Joseph had only managed to make one. And now Kathleen felt trapped. Mr. Reynolds had also told her that if she gave her son a choice, then she had to live with his choice. She was kicking herself for having given Joseph a choice about making another bow hand. She wished she had simply said "Mr. Reynolds said that we need to do ten of these a day, and you've already done one!"

Then, thinking quickly, Kathleen instructed Joseph to sit on his foot chart, and the two of them practiced some clapping exercises. When they finished, Kathleen said "O.K., time to make five bow hands." She wasn't sure that this maneuver would work, but was surprised to find that Joseph not only stood still, he was actively involved in doing his part to make five beautiful bow hands. They still hadn't gotten ten in, but Kathleen decided that they would keep coming back to them after they did other things. It worked.

But if it wasn't one thing it was another. When they got to the bow exercises, Joseph kept wanting to make his own version. Instead of saying "Up like a rocket," the first line of a little ditty that goes with the bow exercises, Joseph kept wanting to change it. "Up like a turkey..." he would say, laughing. The next time it was "Up like an eagle."

And on it went. This irritated Kathleen until they got to their next lesson. Mr. Reynolds pointed out that the words didn't matter as much as what was happening with the motions.

"Does he still manage to control the tip of the bow and keep it above his hand when he says it?" Mr. Reynolds asked.

"Well, yes–I just wish he would take it more seriously!" Kathleen said.

"Not to worry. If he's controlling the tip as he moves the bow around, then it really doesn't matter what words he says–he's getting the essence out of the exercise," Mr. Reynolds reassured her. "Of course," he added, "you could insist that he does the precise words. But that's a battle that's probably not worth it, at least right now."

At this point, Mr. Reynolds' main concern was that Joseph develop the physical control necessary to maneuver the bow. Certainly he was also interested in Joseph learning how to follow directions. At the same time, however, he admired Joseph's creativity and saw this as a reasonable opportunity to let Joseph express it.

What it all came down to was that often-repeated advice for parents and teachers: choose your battles. It's good advice, especially if you can realize that your child may not necessarily be battling you. Joseph's creativity in coming up with different birds was probably not about wanting to disobey his mother or his teacher. It was most likely about wanting to have *fun*. In other words, the battle is not Joseph against his mother, it's the alliance of Joseph and his mother against *boredom*. If his mother misinterprets his actions as being about fighting her, then she's likely to retaliate rather than set a reasonable limit. By allowing Joseph to make up his own words, she and her son work as a team to battle his boredom.

In some cases, insisting on the words the teacher originally assigned might be a battle worth waging. I'm certainly not advocating that parents pretend to be flexible when they really can't be.

At their next home practice, having talked to Mr. Reynolds and thinking things through, Kathleen decided that she would not only tolerate Joseph's changing the first line of "Up Like a Rocket," she would *encourage* it. If she made changing the first line part of the assignment, she would feel less like they were wasting time. "Pick a bird," she told her son.

But Joseph wasn't interested.

"I wanna say up like a bear," he told his mother. Kathleen decided that there was no point in fighting it–*as long as Joseph kept control of the tip of the bow.* Which he did. The whole thing puzzled her until she went to a parent-teacher conference with Joseph's kindergarten teacher the following week.

"Joseph is just a delightful student," Mrs. Dunstable said. "He's so eager to learn–like two weeks ago when we watched the video about birds. He kept talking about birds and drawing birds for the rest of the week. Now he's into bears. I'm not sure what sparked that, but he's sure been busy playing "bears.""

Like the light from distant stars that takes thousands of years to reach our planet, Kathleen realized that it may take her a long time until she could really see all the ways in which her son's fascinating mind worked. In the meantime, she knew that she had to be sure to get enough sleep so she wouldn't completely collapse from exhaustion.

Although it takes a great deal of effort to be as flexible as Kathleen was, it sometimes takes even *more* effort to be rigid. Rigidity sometimes sets in when a parent sees a teacher do something with a child and is then unable to do that same thing at home with her child. There is the danger that the parent will begin to feel incompetent because she's not able to pull off the same thing. There is also the danger that she will begin to resent her child for not working with her as well as the child worked with the teacher. Whether the parent says these things out loud or not–and whether she is actually aware of these feelings or not–they will contaminate the practice relationship with the child. And the practices can begin to swirl the drain. Too much work!

The other way in which rigidity makes you work harder is that your child will resist you more. If you are flexible at every turn that you possibly can be, your child will be more likely to go along with the program when you can't be flexible–which is o.k. Please notice that I say your child will be *more* likely to go along with the program. You'll still get some huffing and puffing, but it will be much more manageable than if the child always had to do everything by your decree.

When you absolutely can not be flexible, do not be flexible. You can always just say "No." In fact, it's important for parents–teachers, too–to help children learn the meaning of "No," a simple, straightforward, two-letter word. It would have been perfectly reasonable for Kathleen not to have been flexible and to have insisted that everything be done exactly as she instructed. But in her case, this approach wasn't necessary, and her flexibility saved herself and her son a lot of trouble.

Just as there are sometimes parents who don't teach their children the meaning of the word "no," there are also some parents who don't let their children have enough choices. Ultimately, children need a balance of "yes's" and "no's." It's really healthy for children to learn to recognize limits.

But beware of absolutes. When you are practicing, you will need to make adjustments. You'll notice that I rarely use absolutes–words like "always" and "never"–in this book. Instead, I like to use words like "perhaps," "usually," and "often." The problem with absolutes is that there really are very few of them in the world. As the writer Anne Lamott says, "it is so much easier to embrace absolutes than to suffer reality...Reality is unforgivingly complex."

There is good news: handling the fascinating complexities of practice becomes easier with the passing of time, through doing it daily, and by attending lessons. As you go, you begin to discover what helps and what hurts; what works and what does *not* work. Looking for opportunities to be flexible will make you more nimble. You will also learn to manage the up and down cycles. Some days you'll have absolutely awful practices. Other days you'll feel like the heavens opened up and divine inspiration came your way. Most practices will be somewhere in between, but consistent daily practice is most likely to give you the upbeat ones.

27

Guardrails, not Handcuffs

If you're a parent, you probably recognize at least one of these ways that children test the limits an adult has put in place:

"No, only three times..."
"In a minute..."
"It's not fair..."

Parents and teachers can get confused, because children aren't always limit-testing when they say these things. For example, there are times that it might be reasonable to wait a minute before starting the day's practice. But a promise of "In a minute" is not reasonable if twenty minutes have passed and it's the third time the child is making the promise.

Every so often I hear someone say that "kids like limits." I've even said it myself. But it's not completely true. What's more accurate is that kids like having limits better than the alternative–*not* having limits. Limits on their behavior are like the guardrails on a steep, winding mountain road. The protection they offer helps us relax and enjoy the trip. At the same time, however children also wish that the guardrails were not there, so that they were free to fly over the edge. Although children like the guardrails because they help them to feel safe, they also hate them because they remind them that they don't have magical powers. They really *can't* fly.

Since even young children know that flying isn't an option, you and your child will have much more pleasant practices if you think of limits as being guardrails that prevent your child from going over the edge. That doesn't mean that your child won't complain. But it does mean that your child is likely to feel safer. And children who feel safe tend to be better behaved.

Children test limits all the time, and it can be very irritating and exasperating when they do. Say, for example, you ask your child "Do you want to do this rhythm exercise six times, seven times, or eight times today?" (all choices with which you are comfortable, by the way), and your child says "I want to do it *ZERO* times."

When children respond in these kinds of ways, deep down, they're not testing limits to upset us; they're testing the limits to see if we're really reliable and dependable. They want to know if they can trust what we say. They don't necessarily want the limit to change. It's a bit like when you close your front door, then turn the knob to check to see if it's truly locked. You're not wanting to open the door. But knowing that the door is secured, you feel safer. In the same way, children don't really want their parents to give in. They want to know that they're reliable.

When you realize how much children flourish when they feel that they can trust what the adults around them say, you can realize that testing limits is the job of a growing child. And enforcing those limits–insisting that it's time to start practice, for example–is the job of the adults in that child's life.

That doesn't mean that we don't worry about limits. It's often a struggle to know if the limits we place on a child are too stringent and need to be modified or if we're giving a child so much freedom that we're failing to provide that ever important guardrail. We want to provide safety, but not handcuffs. Parents who insist on putting the truck away and starting practice worry that they're interrupting important play for the child; on the other hand, if they let the play continue after the child has promised to stop, they worry that they're too lenient. Generally speaking, children tend to thrive when the boundaries are as wide as possible. When we restrain children too much, they rebel against the restraint by behaving in ways we really don't like. For instance, they may become belligerent, or–even worse, in my opinion–stop thinking for themselves and turn into little automatons.

The most effective approach is not to think of it as an issue of either or, but as one of finding a balance between the two. You'll be like a gymnast walking the balance beam for the first time. Of course, she could just sit down and give up. But when it comes to working with a child, giving up simply isn't an option. So, know that even though you seek a balance between total freedom and rigid limits, you may not always be as poised as you'd like to be. Things will either get wobbly or come crashing down. Whatever happens, your skill with finding the balance, like anything else, will get easier as you practice doing it.

It's usually possible to give kids the consistency and reliability they crave along with the freedom they need by paying attention to the way we construct limits in the first place.

There are a few important guidelines for creating limits that are generally fair, firm, and productive. The first one is to focus on limiting the child's behaviors, but not emotions. Trying to control a child's feelings is a bit like trying to sweep waves back into the ocean–you don't get anywhere. It might look like it though, because the tide goes in and out. But in reality, this ebb and flow had nothing to do with your efforts. When you try to control a child's feelings, the most you can do is get the child to *act* like your efforts had an effect. Having to act like they feel a certain way in order to please their parents creates nasty, long-lasting toxins that children carry into adult life. Probably not something you want for your child.

Directly controlling a child's feelings is impossible. The most effective way you can influence your child's ability to manage his or her feelings is by empathizing with those feelings–which helps your child process and work through them–and by placing limits on your child's behavior. [For tips on how to help your child work through feelings, please see section 20, "Develop the Skill of Acknowledging Feelings."]

Take the case of a child who is afraid to make mistakes. This is a fairly common and normal fear with children. But we don't help them by our attempts to limit what they feel. In other words, saying things such as "don't worry about it, it will be fine" isn't really helpful. It's much more productive when we empathize instead, saying something such as "You're afraid you're going to blow it, right?" Mistakes–and fear of making them–are part of the process. Children start to relax as we ourselves become comfortable with their not being immediately perfect all the time. And if we're already comfortable with the fact that it may take a while for the paint on their playing to dry, children will gradually relax as we become comfortable listening to their *fear* of not being perfect.

So, you don't try to control–or limit–the child's feelings, but you *do* insist that the child behave in certain ways. You might say something such as "I believe you when you say you're scared you're going to make a mistake. And your assignment is to play this passage eight times every day, so here you go...Do you want to do all eight at once or do you want to do a few times now and come back to it later?" You've offered the child empathy and flexibility, while also enforcing a limit. But it's a reasonable limit–one about what the child *does*, not about what the child *feels*.

Here's another example of controlling a child's behavior while not controlling his feelings. The child wishes that playing came automatically, and is discouraged and upset that practicing is necessary to make it easier. If those are a child's feelings, our attempts to control them will only create problems down the road. However, practicing is an action–a behavior–and children need to learn that feelings don't have to control our behaviors. We need to help them develop the part of their minds that can both acknowledge their feelings and take the demands of life into account.

You practice anyway. Your sensitivity and empathy towards a child's feelings shapes the way in which that practice happens. Nevertheless, practice still happens, because you insist on it. By practicing and realizing that practicing does get you somewhere, a child's feelings may change, but that is because of the child's experience, not because you made the child change his feelings. Children develop maturity–the ability to acknowledge their feelings and, at the same to act in productive ways–through repeated experiences like these. Another way of thinking about it is that they develop discipline.

While attempting to control a child's feelings can complicate a practice in unexpected ways, children who only get empathy–and not the responsible behavior that adults insist on–can end up feeling lost and insecure. For example, if you're placing the violin of a young beginner and she keeps plucking away at the string when she's not supposed to, you need to do more than merely say "I know you like to pluck." Make sure that you also add a simple consequence that you then enforce, perhaps "If you pluck, we have to start all over." Failing to enforce the limits with reasonable consequences usually has the unpleasant result of creating children who are scared and angry–not only do others find them unpleasant to be around, they find *themselves* unpleasant to be around. Not good. Firmly insisting that a child control something she's genuinely capable of controlling teaches that child about her ability to control herself. Without your enforcement of that limit, she doesn't get to discover the positive ways in which she has powers–albeit not magical ones. Your consequences help her sense her genuine personal power in the world. The trick, of course, is not to overwhelm her with responsibility. So...

A second important guideline that will help you create reasonably balanced limits for your child is to make sure that you require your child to do things that you know he can do. In other words, establish reasonable goals. For example, instead of saying "We're going to keep working on this piece today until you've got the whole thing memorized," you say "We're going to divide the piece into sections and spend fifteen minutes repeating each section seven times–we'll see how many sections you get through in fifteen minutes." Your child doesn't really have direct control over how quickly he memorizes a piece, and neither do you. But you both have control over spending fifteen minutes working on it.

Or–better yet–maybe you don't say anything at all about memorizing the piece. You just work at it for a while, keeping on the lookout for any small change from the way it started out. That may be enough. When you come back to it the next day you'll be coming back to something that felt doable, not something that become a HUGE JOB. It's usually surprising how much *more* you can get accomplished with this casual, yet consistent approach.

Yet another consideration in practicing is to cycle between activities. For example, instead of playing a scale over and over, making sure that the bow gets back to the frog, your child may find it easier to play it that way just one time. The next time through the scale, focus on the rhythm; and the next time on the ringing in the sound. Then go through the cycle all over again. Finding the practice strategy that is most productive for your child is part of that balancing act I was talking about earlier.

One of the most creative limit-setting practice strategies I've ever heard of came from a mother with an extremely energetic young son. His practice task one day was to play three notes on the piano with his hand working just the way she showed him. After he had completed those three notes (demonstrating that he actually understood how his hand needed to work) she had him get off the piano bench, run out the door of the house, run all the way around the house, and come back to repeat those three notes exactly the same way. If he didn't play the three notes the way they were assigned, he had to repeat them again before he could run around the house. He loved it.

It may go without saying, but a third important guideline for setting limits–and it's often overlooked, which is why I'm mentioning it–is checking to see that your child understands the limits. This principle is especially important if you are playing a game (such as cards in section A2, page 256). You'll probably be better off if you are the one who states the rules. Don't let your child make up the rules–or, worse, change them–as you go along. I've seen it happen. Disaster.

Even if you're not playing a game, you still need to be clear about the "rule" of whatever you're practicing. For example, having determined that your child really can get the bow to the frog if she thinks about it, you tell her "The next thing to practice is the G scale. Play it three times, and if every single up-bow doesn't get to the frog, it doesn't count." And you stick to it. It won't work, however, if your child doesn't know what the frog is–as I'm sure many of you non string-playing readers don't. It also won't work if you just tell your child that the rule is that she must "do a good job," which is way too vague. You need to get much more specific about the criteria for a "good job." In this case, it means moving the bow to the frog. (And for any of you who don't know what a frog is, it's the part of the bow closest to the player's hand.)

There's a fourth principle when it comes to creating limits: avoid painting yourself into a corner by issuing ultimatums. It can be tempting to threaten things like "If you don't turn off the TV and get ready to practice when the timer goes off, then we're *not* playing that dice game during practice today!" While it's true that your child loves the dice game and it makes practice go easier, it may also be true that banning it for a day will make the practice miserable for *you*–or that your child will complain to such a large extent that you won't get much done during practice anyway. You may be better of just turning off the TV yourself for a consequence. (Or if you're really sneaky, you might want to consider using the breaker box, if you can figure it out how to do it safely and you don't end up also turning off a full freezer or having to reset too many clocks and VCRs.)

We're not really being nice when we change a limit a child is testing. Our inconsistency, in fact, is mean because it confuses the child: what we at first say is a limit turns out not to be a limit after all. At some level, the puzzled child doesn't know if he can trust us, which is a very difficult and dangerous position for a child to be in. If he can't count on what's important to him–the reliability of those he needs–he can end up worrying about his very survival in the world. But when we hold steadfast about keeping limits "lovingly in place"–as I once heard the British violin teacher Helen Brunner put it–we're working in the child's best interests, even though the child may balk at the moment.

As long as the limit is clear and is not damaging the child, stick with it. If you think the limit was too severe, you can always change it when you re-create the situation at tomorrow's practice.

Look for Opportunities to Play Games and Have Fun

Over the years I have run into many parents and teachers who feel that if they can just find a cute set of words, or the right fun game, then their children will always enjoy practicing and their practices will always go smoothly. This approach, it seems to me, doesn't respect the natural curiosity that children have. Children want to learn. We adults need to work with them in ways that tap that natural curiosity. One of the primary ways we do that is by helping them develop comfortable, fluent physical skills with the instrument, which grow through a combination of small manageable steps, and daily practice. We also help by doing everything we can to create a positive relationship with the child. I find that learning can often be its own reward, its own good feeling.

A game or trick isn't always required for everything. It's o.k. when you can't figure out how to make something "fun." If you're moving in small enough steps and practicing consistently, the child will get to the other side of the struggle, the side where the pleasure kicks in. It's also the side where the skills he has developed through practicing make it possible for his natural curiosity to be the driver.

Having said that, I also think it's important to look for opportunities to have fun during practice. This recommendation is especially important for beginners. These students can't really get the joy and the rewards of playing because they can't really play yet. Having a game or a silly–yet productive–way to practice something can help them tolerate the dry period that comes before their playing is up and running and the musical juices can help sustain them.

Most of the students I work with attend lessons because at some point they expressed an interest in playing violin, an interest on which their parents followed up. But these children were interested in making music, or perhaps in playing by the fountain at the mall–just like they saw the "big kids" doing. Most of the time they were not interested in learning to stand in rest position or bending their right thumb. While I'm always on the lookout for ways to make these beginning stages musically fulfilling, it's also true that some of the essentials can be dry.

For ideas of games you can play to make practice interesting, please see the appendix, which begins on page 249. Your own teacher can likely be of tremendous help in giving you ideas for games as well.

Let the fun begin!

Give Concrete, Pertinent Information

Sometimes–and I, myself, have usually done it in a moment of desperation–teachers and parents make the mistake of using finger-shaking explanations that start with "Someday you're going to need to know this because..."

I've learned that these explanations don't work. I still give my students information about how something they're working on now will help their playing grow big enough to do fancier things later on, but I'm more surprised when these explanations motivate a student than I am disappointed when they don't. I offer these explanations because I know that even though there's only a slight chance they will motivate the student, the *parent's* adult brain will usually find the explanation helpful.

I've come to realize that children generally don't want or need explanations about the future benefits as much as they want and need real concrete information about what, exactly, to do in the here and now. They usually respond quite well to information that is concrete and pertinent to the moment.

Take the example of Adam.

Bonnie was practicing with her four-year-old son, Adam, and she was getting irked…

"What happened to the nice Adam?" she finally asked him.

"I'm the nice Adam," he told her, absorbed in the fun he had discovered in jumping on and off his footchart, and not seeming to take the question too seriously.

"Tell the nice Adam to come back, please," she gently said.

"But, mommy, I *am* the nice Adam! I'm right here!"

"Well, let's make a bow hand again and see if the nice Adam is really here or not," Bonnie said.

As she began to move Adam's fingers around the bow, she said "You're going to have to learn how to be nice or your teachers won't be able to teach you the pieces the older children are playing…"

Adam just wiggled his hips, didn't watch what his mother was doing, and tensed up his hand.

"That's it!" Bonnie said angrily "We' not going to practice any more today until you can be *nice*!"

Adam, in tears, shouted, "I *am* nice!"

In spite of their good intentions, Bonnie and Adam ended their practice in misery. Bonnie was trying her best to be gentle and firm. And "nice." But she was unaware that even though Adam was wanting to be "nice," *he didn't really know what the word meant.* As I spoke with his mother, it became clear that she didn't really know either…

"If I watched you practicing and Adam was being 'nice,' I asked her, "what would I see him doing?"

"Well...just being...you know...*nice*," she replied.

"How would I know he was being nice?"

"Well, he wouldn't be wiggling so much, and wandering around the room all the time."

I continued to question Bonnie until we got to a clear, concrete definition of what "nice" meant: Adam would stand on his foot chart–and stand still–while she helped him make a bow hand. And he would look at what she was doing.

During their practices the following week, Bonnie gave Adam these clear directions. He knew what she meant and–more importantly–he was genuinely able to do what he was asked. I had suggested a game for them to play, but when Bonnie arrived for their next lesson, she said that they didn't even need it. Adam merely needed concrete directions. They had had a pleasant week of "nice" practices because there was no longer a secret about what "nice" meant.

Because children want to look good in the eyes of their parents [for more, please see section 4], they will often do a great deal of hard work as long as they are clear about what, specifically, that work is and as long as they can accomplish that work in the here and now, not at some vague date in the future. Like this story of Adam and Bonnie, I have witnessed a lot of practices going off track because the parent is using language that is vague–"be nice," in this case–instead of the concrete "stand still". A child who isn't exactly sure of what to do often fumbles around, usually upsetting the parent. In turn, the parent can end up feeling hurt because she thinks the child was not paying attention to her at best; defying her at worst. Clear and concrete directions in the here and now tend to save everyone involved a lot of misery.

Another example...

Six year old Lena casually picked up her bow and got ready to play "May Song." Her bow hand was a mess.

"How's your bow hand?" I asked her.

"Good," she casually replied.

I then asked a very useful question: "How do you know?"

Lena looked at me with a blank stare. Her usual criteria for whether or or not she had a good bow hand was that her mother or her regular teacher told her "good job." Or they said nothing, which to Lena meant her bow hand was fine. Most children are the same way. When asked about something in their playing, confused children will often say that it's fine because they really and truly hope it is. But they're not actually sure. It's just wishful thinking.

"Well…um…is your pinkie round?" I asked.

Lena rounded her pinkie.

"Is your thumb bent?"

Lena bent her thumb.

"Are the middle fingers hanging over?"

Lena dropped the tips of her middle fingers from their perch on the top of the bow, so that they hung over the bow the way your feet dangle in the water when you sit on the edge of a pool.

We repeated this sequence of preparing to play over and over, with me asking Lena the same questions each time. As we repeated this interchange throughout her entire lesson, I thought of what someone once told me about goldfish. They never get bored in their little bowls because their memories are only few seconds long. So, they swim to one end of the bowl and say, in their dippy little goldfish voices, "Hey what's behind that castle?" By the time they make it behind the castle, they say "Hey, I wonder what's on the other side of the bowl."

I realized that my adult brain was going to have to keep holding the details of a bow hand until Lena could hold them all by herself. One pass wasn't going to be enough. By the end of Lena's lesson, she proved that she wasn't, in fact, a goldfish. She was a typical child. I once again asked her how her bow hand was and she said, "It's good." Then, once again, I asked her "How do you know?"

"My thumb's bent…um, my pinkie is round! And the middle fingers are hanging over," she said.

I was pleased that Lena had concrete information that let *her* know whether or not her bow hand was what it needed to be. By her practice session the next day, she may have forgotten it, which is why her mother was there taking notes. Her mother's reinforcement during their home practices helped Lena develop a memory *much* longer than that of a goldfish.

Like Adam, Lena was not only *willing* to do a good job, she *wanted* to do a good job. She just needed concrete information about what "a good job" was.

Young children don't have the sophisticated language skills we adults have, so words that seem to be clear to us are often confusing for them. You'll be most effective with children if you use language that is as concrete as possible. Of course, as an adult who uses language freely, you'll mess up on this left and right. Don't penalize yourself or your child when misunderstandings arise. Just silently acknowledge them to yourself and move on. On a good day, you'll laugh. On a not-so-good day, you'll be irritated. Communication is hard work. The miracle is that it ever happens at all.

Though Lena and Adam are pretty young children, the same communication difficulties happen with older students. I once asked a master class student what her teacher would like to see change in her playing. The student told me "She wants me to get more tone." When I asked her what "tone" meant–and I asked in various ways–it became clear to me that she wasn't quite sure. No wonder her teacher kept complaining. They weren't speaking the same language!

You can save yourself a lot of trouble and confusion if you remember to beware of words that don't fit into a grocery cart. Had the teen's teacher had asked her to get more apples, or stereos, or books, or gummy worms–all things that fit in a grocery cart–the student probably would have understood. But "tone" doesn't fit in a grocery cart. Neither do words like "intonation," "articulation," "crescendo" ...or "nice," and "effort," and "focus." Yet we use these words all the time. These are not illegal words, but we need to be aware that students may have difficulty understanding them and will probably need for us to explain them several times.

So, the next time you're working with a student and you're tempted to start your comments with something such as "Do it again, but try a little harder..." or "I know you can make this better..." or "Make sure you don't start until you're ready," keep in mind that the child is going to need a lot more specific, concrete information about what constitutes "try a little harder" or "better" or "ready."

If you, the parent, don't know exactly what that specific, concrete information is, wait until your next lesson and then ask your teacher. That's what she's there for, and also why the lines of communication with the teacher must remain open. It's also why you must pay very close attention at lessons, take excellent notes, and learn as much as you can.

Don't Talk About Focus, Develop It

It was bad enough that Vera had spent the morning dealing with two difficult clients, but in the afternoon her assistant announced that her husband had received a promotion and they would be moving across the country…and she was pregnant. Vera, who had a good relationship with her assistant, was happy for her. At the same time, she had come to rely on Sharon's attention to detail and her ability to pacify their often irrational and irate director. She was worried.

Now, here it was, 6:30 in the evening, and Vera was finally getting a moment to practice with her four year old daughter, Kate. Vera had taken detailed notes at Kate's lesson with Mrs. Shaw, and she knew exactly what was supposed to happen in her daughter's practice. But it wasn't happening, even though Kate had seemed to understand it completely at the lesson.

After several failed attempts, Vera started getting frustrated and disappointed. Not knowing what else to do, she angrily told Kate "Can you *focus* here?" Kate, sensing that something was wrong–but not sure what–started to cry. Her mother had asked her a question she didn't understand, only it didn't really sound like a question, it sounded more like she was supposed to do something. But she didn't know what. All Kate could sense at the moment was that the most important person in her life was upset, and she didn't know what to do to satisfy her.

Vera could easily have been you–with the exception that perhaps your child reacts to a scenario like this by arguing or shutting you out. In a day in the life of a parent who practices with his or her child, practicing is but one event. Residue from other areas of life is bound to find its way into the practice arena.

The challenge isn't to learn how to eliminate all frustration from your life so that you can avoid getting overwhelmed during practices–as if that were even possible. The challenge is to learn skills and strategies that allow the job of practicing to go as smoothly as possible, even when you're frustrated. These focusing strategies become like tools–hammers, pencils, whisks–that will be handy, regardless of your mood. You can use them to help your child develop focus even on those days when you're stressed.

With the three focusing strategies I'm going to give you here, it's important to remember that in spite of the way things sometimes appear, what stays constant during practices is the need children have to look good in the eyes of their parents, the people that matter the most to them [for more about this need of children, please see section 4]. Remembering this crucial element of the parent-child relationship will help you help your child focus. Be looking for it and noticing it as you read through these strategies.

The first strategy for helping a child focus is to keep the word "focus" on your mind, but to refuse to let it cross your lips. While you're at it, you may as well do the same for the words "concentrate" and "pay attention," because they don't work either.

Here's why these words don't work: they're too vague. Put yourself in four-year-old Kate's position. Given what I've told you–which is really all Kate was told at that practice with Vera–what, *specifically*, was Kate supposed to do? Stand in one spot? Relax her arm? Hold her hand a certain way? Jump up and down five, not six, times? Play a concerto?

Children get frustrated–and usually express it in their behavior–when they are confused about what, specifically, they're supposed to do. Sometimes they manage to guess what the adult wants and it ends up working out. But if the guessing doesn't work and if they don't *really* know what they need to do in order to look good in the eyes of their parents, you can usually kiss focus goodbye.

So, you need to give your child clear directions. One trick to help you do that is imagining what, exactly, you would see the child doing if you were to watch a video of the child practicing, *and focusing*. Ask yourself "What do I *see* the child doing in this video that shows me she is focusing?" You can also ask "In this imaginary video in my mind, what do I *hear* the child doing that tells me she is focusing?"

When you then start talking to your child, "focus" is very much on your mind, but you don't say it. Instead, you talk about the answer to those questions. You describe what you saw and heard in your imagination.

Now I'll tell you more about the case of Vera. When she imagined the video in her mind, she saw Kate watching the tip of her bow as she moved it back and forth. She was also keeping the tip of the bow above her hand. What Vera heard in her mind's videotape was silence.

Kate had been silent when doing the exercise before, but she hadn't been looking at the tip of the bow. So Vera took a cap from a water bottle and put it on the tip of the bow, telling Kate "Do this again, and be sure to watch the tip. Move the bow slowly enough so that the cap stays on." As my mother used to say, now Vera was "cooking with gas." She wasn't telling Kate to focus, but she was giving her something very specific to focus *on*.

Another thing that worked in Vera's favor was that she avoided the tripping over the temptation that's always there–using confusing judgmental words–such as "good," "bad," "super," "wonderful," "terrible," etc. Had she said "Do it again and do a *good job* with the tip of the bow," she would have just been substituting the vagueness of "focus" with the vagueness of "good job." Neither one really tells a four-year old what, exactly, to do. But Vera was successful because instead of these vague words, she used a concrete *description* of what constituted a "good" job–watching the tip of the bow, and moving the bow slowly so that the tip stayed above the hand.

The younger the child, the more necessary it is for parents to use tricks like imagining a videotape of the child focusing. It's a good idea for parents who work with older children as well. Vague abstractions are difficult for *adults* to deal with, let alone children. Merely barking a stern "Concentrate!" is no guarantee that a child will notice the specific thing you want him to notice. But there's a pretty strong guarantee that he'll respond to the emotional content that he senses in the tone of your voice. And *that* response will probably not be the one you had in mind.

Another way to keep focus on your mind but off of your lips is to remember that words like "focus," "concentrate," and "pay attention" are incomplete sentences. So, instead of the fragment "Pay attention!" you'll end up with something more effective: "Pay attention...to how clear the notes are." Instead of just "Focus!" you'll end up with "Focus...on keeping your thumb bent." You can clarify your directions even further by lopping off the words "Pay attention..." and "Focus..." which leaves you with simply saying "Play this again and listen for clear notes" or "This time, make sure your thumb is bent."

The second strategy for developing a child's focus is to gradually increase the amount of focusing the child has to do. You may find it helpful to think of it as the weight training approach to focusing. Instead of having the child play an entire piece keeping his head floating up, for example, you have the child play just one phrase–what I often call a "musical sentence" [see page 155]–with a floating head. Then you repeat that success many times before moving on to the next phrase. Eventually, maybe in a few days, you have the child do *two* phrases at once, until he can gradually handle the entire piece. When you avoid straining your child's "focusing muscles," you're avoiding the frustrations of failed attempts, and you're going to find you have slow, but steady progress. And brighter practices.

Or think of practice as starting like a motorcycle. I'm talking about the older model motorcycles where you have to slam down the kick-start several times before the engine eventually cranks and fires up. After a few short bursts of focus–which are followed by short bursts of spacing out–you may find that your child is up and running for the rest of the practice. You may also find that getting the focus engine turned over takes longer on some days than it does on others.

The third strategy that helps your child develop focus is crucial: *your* refraining from talking during individual and group lessons. And I don't just mean refraining from talking with words. I've often seen parents talk to children with their hands–one of the most common maneuvers being the parent who looks directly at the child, gestures wildly to get the child to stand up straight, and mouths the words "Get your violin up!" as if auditioning for the role of a large mouth bass. Other parents are more discreet, but their coaching from the sidelines is still problematic.

Before I tell you why these kinds of parent interventions don't work–and, in fact, make things worse–I need to acknowledge that parents do them with the best of intentions. Parents tell me that they don't want their children to develop bad habits. They also tell me that they not only want their children to behave politely, they want them to get everything they possibly can out of the class. I can't imagine a teacher in the world who would argue with that list of concerns. They're *excellent* concerns to have.

In order to address these concerns in a genuine way, however, the first priority has to be getting the child focused. Teachers recognize this need and go to great lengths to draw students in. It's difficult work, even though it often appears effortless. It's only made more difficult when a parent repeats the teacher's directions or–worse–*adds* another direction for the child. What ends up happening is that a child's focus gets diluted as he attempts to pay attention to the teacher *and* the parent, which is way too much for a child to coordinate. It's not like rubbing your belly and tapping your head, it's more like playing flute and writing Chinese characters. When a child's focus is diluted in this way, it's as difficult to get his focus back to full strength as it is to take out the two extra cans of water you mistakenly added to the frozen orange juice.

There's another problem. A child who is getting directions from both a teacher and his parent is in a double bind. He knows he's supposed to pay attention to the teacher, but because children are hardwired to care tremendously about what their parents think, anything a parent says during class will always trump what the teacher says. If his parent keeps telling him "Pay attention to the teacher," he will divide his attention between trying to pay attention to the teacher and checking to see if he's satisfying his parent.

It's very common, especially the younger they are, for children to look at their parents. When this happens, you can smile back at your child, or just keep looking at the teacher yourself. Scolding the child will only cause him to be preoccupied with your evaluation of his behavior, and his anxiety will cause him to want to look at you *even more* for reassurance.

The best thing, then, is to sit quietly as you watch your child interact with a teacher at a lesson. Your child will appreciate it, and it will help him focus. Sitting quietly gives you a chance to learn even more about how to help your child focus, because you get to watch how the teacher continues to draw a child in. It will also give you a chance to see when and how a teacher ignores a child's lack of focus. Children sometimes "check out" for a moment, but teachers usually ignore it because they know that the focus will soon return, and that highlighting the temporary lapse will just throw the lesson off course. In other cases, when the child's lack of focus has thrown things off course all by itself, the teacher will often address it. The key is to observe the child and see how he works. Sitting quietly will help you do this.

Merely telling a child to focus doesn't work, so "focus"–along with its kin, such as "concentrate" and "pay attention"–are words that need to be invisible. Think of these words as your secret genies. Let them guide your actions so that you can give your child what he *really* needs in order to learn focus: zillions of opportunities in which he can experience himself *being* focused. Through these experiences, children not only develop their instrumental skills, they also develop the emotional fortitude they need in order to take on challenges.

Have Strategies for Buying Yourself Time

It's o.k. not to know what to do next. In fact, if you don't always know what to do next, join the club. Teachers are often stumped as well.

In order for your instructions to hit their target, it's often necessary to buy time so you can aim carefully. I've seen some parents and teachers frantically shoot lots of information in a child's direction, but not get any of it to hit the mark. In other words, they're talking but not saying anything at all. Which is to say that they're wasting motion.

I prefer to work a different way. Even if I'm close to the target, I don't really want to let the arrow leave the bow until I'm pretty confident I'm going to hit the mark. Here are some examples of situations in which you need to buy yourself time:

- Your child has just finished playing a piece and you're not entirely sure what to do. You are aware that something didn't quite work the way it was supposed to, but you're not really sure what, exactly, wasn't working-let alone what to do about it. You just know that something seemed a little...well, off...and you need more time to check it out.
- You're really irritated with something that the child did while playing, but a little voice in your head tells you that mentioning your upset will only deteriorate the practice. You realize that practice will go better if you buy yourself time simply to let yourself think through the reasons you are so upset and to give yourself some time to think through what you're going to do next. You have come to realize that there's no point in pretending you're not upset–which would only make your child worry–and you want time to think about how to talk about it constructively with your child.
- Your child is having the exact same difficulty with the piece that she had yesterday, when you thought you had it all worked out. Now, however, you're not quite sure that what you did yesterday was effective. You need some time to think about how you should proceed today.

There are several productive ways to buy yourself time. Here's what I most commonly do: I honestly point out everything that went well–which may be limited to "The first note was really in tune!"–and then I say "Play it again" or "Give yourself seconds on that." This strategy usually works, as children are much more likely to repeat something because it went well than if they're repeating it because it was inadequate. [Also see section 17, "Talk About What's Working...and Repeat It."] As the child repeats it, I use the time to think.

The funny thing is, when a kid plays the piece the second time through, what was a problem the first time often isn't a problem the second time. This tells me that he may just need practice, not instruction. The repetition of it taught him more than any specific instruction I could have given him. That doesn't mean I haven't done any valuable work, though, and it doesn't mean that my work is finished. The next thing I do is to say something genuine to the child such as "When you went back and repeated that section a bit slower, the notes evened out," or "I'm so glad you noticed that it's a C-sharp and changed it" or "I know it's not all turning out the way you want it to, but you are working on it in a way that's really going to help your playing grow."

My job is to highlight what's productive in the way the child is going about growing his playing. Everything may not be working perfectly, so I don't want to lie and say that it is. But I can provide an upbeat comment on how the child is focusing his energy–"It was good to see you slow down when you repeated it; that's going to help you figure it out." I talk about what is positive in the process: "You're listening and adjusting! Fantastic!" In other words, I talk about how I see the student working, learning, and progressing. Putting that kind of stuff into words is work, but it's much easier for you and your child than saying "You forgot the G-sharp again."

You can also buy yourself time through playing some of the games I outline in the appendix. I find that I use these games more with younger and less advanced children.

When you're practicing and in doubt–and you will be at times–don't just start poking at things, giving vague instructions such as "Fix this," "Change that," and "No, not like that." When a parent can't clearly see what to do, but starts batting at things anyway, a child can start to feel like a piñata being swung at by a blindfolded contestant. A child who feels this way will start to dodge you, and it won't be pleasant for either one of you. And just like the piñata, while some goodies may come out, other things get destroyed in the process.

Having ways to buy yourself time allows you to strategize in order to figure out a gentler and more effective plan for you and your child. The upshot is that both of you are more likely to be at the top of your game.

Quit While You're Ahead

If a child plays through a piece and we say "Hey, great job keeping the bow hairs in one spot!" a reasonable next step is to say "…so do it again!" Sometimes, however, you're just as well off leaving it alone and moving on to something else. In general, though, I recommend repeating the success several times.

But say your child can only play the first line of the piece with the bow hairs in one spot. Instead of pointing out that inconsistency, you'll probably be better off if you remember to quit while you're ahead; and then repeat the success.

In other words, have the child start the piece again and play just half of the first line, before you surprise him by yanking the bow hairs off the string and saying "Wonderful! The bow hairs are still in one spot! Do it again!" Your child then repeats the piece again from the beginning, but you again interrupt him with your positive comments–*before* the child's endurance fails. The next time, you wait just one or two notes more–you still need to be sure that you quit while it's still working–before you interrupt. When something is working and the child repeats it, you are working towards helping that skill become easier and easier. Eventually the skill will be easy enough so that the child can sustain it through the entire piece. But the child doesn't necessarily need to play the entire piece in order for it to be a useful day's work.

For today, you're just working on getting through a few notes. Tomorrow, you can add a few more.

In my experience, children don't usually mind being interrupted for this kind of genuine good news about their playing. But some children get impatient about not getting to play the entire piece. Actually, I don't think that they get impatient as much as anxious. They're not sure when they're going to get the entire piece learned if they never get a chance to play it. If they already know the piece, they're afraid they'll forget it. Either way, the fear is that they'll somehow get penalized. So I get explicit about the importance of the process, saying "The goal today isn't to play the entire piece, it's to get a good sound on every note. I'm setting the timer for three minutes, and we're going to go at this until it goes off. If you get the whole way through the piece, fine. If not, that's o.k. too, as long as there's a clear ringing sound on every note."

The child may still be frustrated not to get through the entire piece. Children do like to start at the beginning of a piece and run with it. I generally want to avoid having that happen, but if this urge is really strong, then after working on it in the way I have outlined above, I might let a child play the entire piece. But I wouldn't comment on the result if it's a mess.

Our adult duty is to understand that for the time being, it's not getting though the piece that's important. It's getting a clear sound on each and every note that counts. You can sleep well, knowing that even if the entire piece wasn't consistent, you worked diligently toward that end. You can also know that the "quit while you're ahead" strategy made the practice cheerier. You stopped your child over and over to offer upbeat information, to give a genuine "Yes, just like that!"

And in the process, your child consistently experienced himself playing really well.

Imagine Practicing with *Your* Parent

Take a moment to switch roles. If *your* parent had said to you what you just said to your child, what would your reaction have been? Forget about the kind of reaction you might have been taught you were *supposed* to have. Instead, think about what your gut-level emotional response would have been.

When I mention this idea to groups of parents, I realize from their reactions that all I need to suggest is that you think about it. It's a rich field to mine!

Another idea is to do one of the bravest things a parent can do: videotape a practice *and then watch it*. Actually sharing the video–especially the first one–with your teacher is about as courageous as canoeing through the rapids of a stream full of piranhas just after you've cut your leg.

What do you notice on the videotape? If anyone–especially your parent–had treated you the way you treated your child, what would your reaction have been?

34

Find Ways to Enjoy the Trip

Find ways to make practices pleasant for *you*, the parent. Of course, I'm not advocating that you are selfish at the expense of your child–for example, don't expect your child to do the work of making you happy [For more on this concept, please see section 7]. But it really is o.k. for you to be thinking about things you can do that will help you enjoy practicing. As you and your child practice, imagine that you're wearing one of those t-shirts that says, "If mama ain't happy, ain't nobody happy."

There's a lot of truth in that t-shirt. If mama is addicted to crack cocaine, the nastiness that comes along with that addiction is *obviously* going to cause problems for the child. But the flip side of it is that if mama is in a good mood during practice, it's going to have a positive impact on the child. Always remember that since practicing happens in a relationship, a change in the parent will make a change in the relationship, even though it might be a subtle one. But many times, subtle and small is where it's at. Think about how moving a finger just slightly on a viola makes all the difference between a sour note and a sweet one.

So, if you're in a bad mood, take a few minutes to calm down before you practice. If you've only got fifteen minutes to practice that day and you're tense about fitting it in, your taking five minutes to calm yourself can produce 10 minutes of productive practice versus 15 minutes of struggle. Even taking ten minutes and then only practicing five minutes would be better than fifteen minutes of strain.

Or maybe you're in a bad mood, and you *do* have the time for a full practice, but you steer clear of pieces and exercises that you know will irritate you. You can't avoid that work forever, though. So maybe you just put it off until you can get yourself to a place where you're not necessarily thrilled about doing the work, but you are able to take on the challenges it presents the two of you. In other words, you start with pleasant and easy work and gradually make your way to the bigger challenges. (If you elect to skip some things all together, be sure to tell your teacher…)

Since your child will sense it if you're irritated, here are some other suggestions for making practice more enjoyable for yourself:

•Sit in a comfortable chair.
•Have some good coffee.
•Wear comfortable clothes.
•Instruct your child to play something simply because you enjoy hearing it and/or because your child enjoys playing it, which is still useful for the child. [For more about the value of this strategy, see section 17, "Talk About What's Working...And Repeat It."]
•Use a strategy for managing irritating whining. [As found on page 79 in section 20, "Develop the Skill of Acknowledging Feelings."]
•Practice at a time of day when *you're* fresh.

One of the most creative approaches I know came from a brilliant and intense father who took up knitting during his daughter's practices. The father did this because he would get bored and anxious during practices and find himself telling his daughter things she neither wanted nor needed to hear. His daughter, a delightfully curious girl who was as intense as her father, hated it when he would pester her. It was as if she were saying "When you tell me and don't let me discover it for myself, you rob me of the thrill of learning and discovery…like giving away the ending of the book I'm reading." The father's attempts at knitting became something they both laughed at, but it gave him a way to channel energy that might have otherwise gone into attempts to over-control his child. Their practices became more and more productive, and in spite of the dropped stitches, someone had a warmer neck when the weather turned cold. It wasn't a desire to knit that made the father turn to the needles. It was a desire to calm himself so that he was available to support his daughter in the ways she needed his support.

The result? The trip became more enjoyable for both of them.

> [A] great deal of the elegance and dignity of the Japanese garden is not the result of the designer's brilliance nor the garden builder's skill, but is developed over the course of time by the caring hand that nurtures it. This patina evolves from years of care, like the wooden floors of temples, polished smooth from daily wiping…caring for the garden is not a chore, but the very point of having the garden in the first place.
>
> **Marc P. Keane**
> *Japanese Garden Design*

How can I get my child to loosen up and play with more freedom and expression?

When do they start to feel it?

musicianship
35
53

musicianship

35

All Students Have Something to Say

At the center of my teaching is a belief that all students have something to say musically. This belief drives every action I make as a teacher, although it might not always appear that way to the naked eye. For example, I have my students leave their shoes at the door not just to satisfy the more mundane concern that the carpet stays clean, but so I can see their toes. Curled toes can ripple tension right up the body. Shoes often hide this tension. Tension usually leads to discomfort at best; pain at worst. Like trying to speak right after having dental work, pain and discomfort make it difficult for a young musician to say what it is she has to say.

The job of the adults in a child's musical life, then, is like the job of language teachers. We help students develop the fluency they need to say what it is that they have to say. For example, teaching a loving child to say, "I love you" in six different languages gives her six different outfits for dressing a feeling she already possesses.

I think students already possess musical feelings. We merely teach them how to express them. "The first obligation of a teacher," the piano instructor Seymour Fink once told me, "is not to inadvertently teach unmusicality, anything–particularly notation or technical regimentation–that gets in the way of a student's innate musicality."

I don't need to make my students be musical. What I do need to do is make sure that I'm doing all I can to create a learning environment that coaxes the music out of them. As part of that work, for example, I monitor the exposure they get to the musical language through both live and recorded performances. Creating that kind of environment is an ongoing challenge–there isn't just one way to do it, and most students need for us to do many things for them in this regard.

While I don't think that I need to teach my students *what* to say, I do need to spend a great deal of lesson time helping them learn *how* to say it. For this reason, at nearly every lesson I remind students that the reason people practice should be to make it easier. Parents often understand this concept by thinking about how carefully they diapered a baby the first time, compared to the 500th time. Going for easier makes movements more reliable, predictable, consistent, and fluent. By the time you get to the 500th time, you're pretty much at ease. It's ease that makes it possible for musicians to say what they have to say.

Too often, it seems that students evaluate a performance based on criteria such as whether the performer kept his feet in a certain place or held his pinkie just so, instead of basing their evaluation on what the student had to say musically. These evaluations usually say a great deal about what the adults in the child's life have addressed and valued in lessons and practices. Of course, physical issues certainly need attention.

But a musical performance is more than a demonstration that all of your body parts are in the right place. We also need to help students focus on what the performer communicated musically. The two are not mutually exclusive. It is often possible to teach technique in ways that communicate the importance of *music*. One way we adults can do that is by focusing *ourselves* on music and not merely the execution of notes. This focus will keep us on the lookout for opportunities to weave *music* into lessons and practices.

Here's an example of what I mean...

36

Let a Desire for Musical Playing Permeate All of Your Actions

Eleven year old Tina ran her fingers up the keys, landed on the top G, and once again collapsed her wrist. Though neither illegal nor immoral, a collapsing wrist is cause for some alarm. It's one of those physical motions that seems easy at the time but ultimately stunts a student's growth towards greater fluency with the instrument. Her teacher for the week, Nehama Patkin, noticed it during Tina's lesson, a lesson I was observing during a free hour while teaching at a summer Suzuki institute several years ago.

Nehama knows how to use her personality to great effect when teaching–I think it's partly that delightful Australian accent and partly the sparkling, lipsticked smile. If that were all there were to her work, there would be no point in my observing her, as I lack both the accent and the lipstick. Since I have known Nehama for years, I know that there is much, much more to her. Having silently observed Tina's collapsing wrist, I was curious to see what Nehama would do next. She went for the wrist.

As with any ordinary, solid teaching, Nehama clearly explained what needed to happen, checked to make sure that Tina understood it–and could actually physically do it–before going on to the crucial next step, which was to repeat the action until it was fluent.

"Now, you play 20 G's just like that," Nehama said. As Tina repeated her G's, the teaching dazzled unlike anything I have ever seen. Nehama, on a second piano, improvised a harmonized melody around the girl's repetitions, managing to musically round off her ad lib composition as Tina finished her 20 G's. That, to me, was stunning teaching, because even the repetition of a physical motion was put into a musical context.

Though it is difficult for most of us to pull off the kind of dream teaching Nehama seems to whip up at every lesson, it's a good idea for us to constantly be on the lookout for ways to present technique-building vegetables in a musically appetizing way. We need to teach music musically, not just talk about chores, fixing mistakes, or playing and moving things in certain ways. Students do need to develop fluency and comfort in their playing–goals which take much of lesson and practice time. And while moving toward these goals, we constantly need to remind ourselves that the *way* in which we teach those skills can help students say what it is they have to say. Or it can shut them up.

Musicianship is something we have to blend into the process of helping a student mix his or her basic technical batter. Violin teacher Ronda Cole points out that musicality is "not the sugar you add to the cake after it's baked."

We need to help children practice musically. Sometimes, we'll miss the mark–I know I often do. But we're more likely to hit the target if we're aiming. And not only do we need to be on the lookout for opportunities to teach music *musically*, we need to be vigilant about finding moments when we can *create* opportunities to teach music musically.

Even though the subject needs continual and ongoing exploration–and I am always searching myself–that is not to say that I don't have strong opinions. I once heard the psychoanalyst Robert Stolorow say "We believe that we should hold to our theories lightly rather than tightly...*even though we feel passionately about them and will fight for them to the bitter end.*" In the following sections, I share ideas that I am passionate about.

Clear the Path; Then Stay Out of the Way

About the only song I remembered from her recital was "Smoke Gets in Your Eyes." I was too excited thinking about the small party I had been invited to afterwards in honor of the singer, the legendary mezzo-soprano Marilyn Horne. Partly it was the thrill of meeting such a giant of the musical world. And partly it was because I was on a mission.

Her pianist, Martin Katz–a good friend of mine–formally introduced us. I started babbling, something that's easy for me to do when I'm nervous and excited.

"Miss Horne, what a thrill to meet you. You know, I finally got cable TV a few months ago, and I was flipping through the channels one night and I came across that special about you on Bravo, and I understood from that special–and Martin told me it's true–that, um, when you were first starting out you made ends meet by doing lots of recordings in Hollywood because you could make yourself sound like lots of different singers, but the show never really answered the question that I was dying to know the answer to–I think it was, uh, kind of an obvious question–but, anyway, um...With all that flexibility to sing like so many different people, how did you know how *you* sang?"

Her response was both simple and profound: "I just always knew."

And for me, that is the goal of teaching in a nutshell. I want to help my students develop ease, fluency, and flexibility. I also want to provide them with an environment in which they can discover how *they* sing. My goal is not that they use their skills to sing things the way I would sing them. I'm not a ventriloquist; and they're not dummies.

We adults need to resist the temptation to use the child to play the instrument for us. Our job–and it is a huge one, indeed–is to provide the structure and the nurturing that children need in order to become skilled with their instruments. In other words, we need to make sure that their practice is consistent and that we're kind. But we always need to remember that when a student plays a piece, it is the student playing, not us.

There is a tremendously satisfying reward in this for me. If all goes well, when I have finished my job I hear musical things from a student's playing that I haven't heard before. I'm always thrilled when it happens. I hear the soul of the student in the playing. I see art.

Musicianship is the Ability to be Expressive

We've all encountered people whose pronunciation and grammar mark them as native speakers of our language, but who say little that's interesting, important–or even, sometimes, honest. Take the guy on TV who hawks steak knives, for example. I don't really believe that even when one of his knives has just been used to saw through a steel cable, top chefs of the world's finest restaurants still prefer his brand to all others.

On the other hand, we've also encountered non-native speakers who may not have the pronunciation and grammar of our language down pat, but who still manage to communicate in a way that allows us to understand their meaning and to hear their sincerity. If the language we're talking about is English, a few names quickly come to mind: The Dalai Lama, Maria Von Trapp, and Jacques Torres–the French guy on the food channel who's thrilled about working with chocolate. (If English isn't your first language, I'm sure you can think of examples of people who speak *your* native language as a second language.)

As a violin teacher, I aim to do my part to help my students become honest, native speakers of the musical language. In other words, my goal is to develop their techniques to a very high level.

For me, however, musical playing results from sounds that express beyond the perfect pronunciation of correct notes and rhythms. That expression may be conveyed through the way the artist changes volume, uses various rhythmic inflections, or begins and ends notes. Or the expression may simply come from the quality of the tone the artist produces. Most of the time, however, musical playing is created through subtle manipulations of various combinations of these and other variables. The possibilities are infinite. It's the performer's unique personality that determines how these elements get combined. In essence, what we're hearing in a musical performance is a relationship between the composer–whose personality greatly influenced what notes ended up in the piece–and the performer, whose entire being contributes to decisions about how those notes get played.

Even students who aren't very advanced in their technical skills can be expressive. We adults need to create an environment that encourages and allows them to use what they've got. Recordings of the great jazz singer Louis Armstrong can be quite instructive in this respect. Armstrong didn't really have much of a voice, but man could he sing!

Just as some people may sound sincere to some and phony to others, so will some people find a musician's playing musical and others won't. As Chuck Fisher, former Professor of Piano at the University of Michigan, used to tell his students over and over "That's why there's chocolate and vanilla." Most people–like me and his former students who have fond memories of our interactions with him–find his motto amusing. But some don't.

Which brings me to the other comparison. What one person finds *humorous* will sometimes bore someone else. Think of the glee children sometimes get from playing with words about bodily functions, but their parents demand that they "stop this instant!" Likewise, a musical performance may really send one person, yet leave another cold. Indeed, that's why there's chocolate and vanilla. And poop jokes.

We certainly hope that students develop a high level of technical skill, or "native speaker fluency" in their playing, but a higher priority is musical expressivity and sincerity. It certainly is possible to teach technique and not to teach music. Boring. It is even possible to teach technique and to *block* musical expression. Criminal.

39

Teach Flexibility, not Correctness

There are currently over 100 recordings available of Mozart's ever-popular *Eine Kleine Nachtmusik*. Is that because they're still trying to get it right? It can't be, because there's no "right" to get. While musicians and music enthusiasts may disagree about which version of *Eine Kleine Nachtmusik* tastes best, it is important to keep in mind that the disagreement is a question of *taste*, not a question of right and wrong.

In the big world of musical expression there doesn't exist a "correct" or a "right" way to play a piece of music, so we shouldn't confuse children by telling them that there is. Just for the record, I do believe there is such a thing as right and wrong in the world–as in it is wrong to murder, it is right to turn your head so you don't sneeze in the teacher's face. But I don't think that the words "right' and "wrong" have a place in describing various approaches to musical expression. When it comes to musical expression, the real goal is to train the student to be flexible, not to be "correct."

Take the case of 15-year-old Ian. He is just discovering how to be passionate in his playing, and at his lesson he slows down in the middle of a piece in a way that I think isn't really musical and doesn't really make sense. As his teacher, I am at a point where I have to make some choices.

I could tell Ian that slowing down in that spot is wrong and that he should keep the speed even. But I don't, because I don't think that way.

I could say to him "If you slow down in that middle section, it sounds too sentimental and contrived. Keep the speed even. But I'm glad you're at least doing something to be expressive because your playing has been pretty wooden for the past two years."

Since I'm delighted that he's at least attempting to do *something* musical, I don't say either of these things because words like "sentimental," "contrived," and "wooden," are really nothing more than sophisticated put-downs. And a put-down runs the risk of shutting down the exploring and experimenting he's starting to do with the expressive possibilities in his playing.

So, instead of those options, I silently heave a huge sigh of relief that Ian's playing is finally beginning to open up. I also remind myself that my reaction to Ian's playing may not be another musician's reaction. I can think of concert artists who would do something similar to what Ian just did with the piece. At the same time, I am also aware that those artists are controversial and that I don't particularly enjoy their playing. I'm also aware that I have had much more musical exposure and training than Ian. I need to look for opportunities to share my expertise.

What I end up doing is telling Ian something that is also true–that the bowing in the section isn't quite working and that metronome practice will clear it up. I address his technical approach, but steer clear of making any sort of pronouncement about his musical intentions. His assignment for the week is to practice the section with the metronome. That will keep the tempo even. Bringing up the question of musical taste comes later.

At this point, the goal is not for Ian to play the piece "the right way," or even "*my* way." The goal is for him to have a choice about how *he* wants to play it. I suspect that his attempts to be "musical" may in fact be more like a mask to cover the fact that the bowing isn't working. If he can *only* play the section by slowing down, he hasn't developed the flexibility he needs in order to make a choice. I gave him the metronome assignment because my job as a teacher is to craft assignments that help students develop flexibility.

You can often save a lesson or a practice session by getting away from making the child do it "the right way," and moving, instead, towards having him practice the section a variety of ways. In other words, what you're doing is helping the child create choices and options. You're also making sure he isn't stuck. When a student is doing something that I think is a bit odd, I have to silently ask myself "Is he doing it because it's the way he *wants* to play it, or because it's the only way he *can* play it?" We adults need to make sure that children are not locked into playing a piece a certain way–especially if that way seems a little bit loopy to us.

The job of a teacher and a parent–musically speaking–is to make sure that children can play a variety of ways, on demand. That demand can come from a parent, a teacher, a conductor, or the consensus of colleagues in a chamber music group. Ultimately, what we're doing is giving the student flexibility so that the demand comes from the wishes of the student himself or herself.

You might be one of those parents who have concerns that they lack enough flexibility and knowledge to be comfortable with this approach. You may not know what specific limits and options to give your child in terms of musical expression. Still, you can use this information about taste to know where you can safely back off and let go. When in doubt, go for helping your child create a variety of options, and then let the teacher deal with the details of narrowing them down. When it comes to musical expression, backing off and letting go are exactly what all parents must do.

Back to Ian. The following week he says that he hasn't practiced his assignment because he was sick for three days and had finals at school. The assignment stands. If he weren't such a serious student, I'd watch him practice the assignment at his lesson. Knowing he's serious, we work on something else in another piece.

The following week, he has clearly done the work. At this point, seeing that he has developed a bit more flexibility with the piece, I share with him what I know about musical style. "Mozart was a classical composer, and during the classical period people were a bit more restrained. Yes, they might slow down or speed up a bit, but not to the extremes you were doing with this section. But, we're not living in the Classical period, and now that you can clearly do it both ways, the choice is up to you. Most musicians would expect to hear more of an even pulse, but they might bend it slightly in this part. Notice how artists do it as you listen to recordings of it this week."

I'm not trying to convince Ian about what is right, just inform him about what I know. The mezzo-soprano Joan Morris once told me that she talks to her students about "selling" a song, which I think is a terrific way to think about it. Ultimately, Ian is going to have to sell something he believes in.

But my work is done. I've helped Ian stock his warehouse with options. Now he has to choose the one that rings true for him.

40

Give the Recipe for Vanilla

Sometimes I go around the group and have each child tell the class his or her favorite flavor of ice cream. There's usually quite a variety. Of course, chocolate and vanilla get votes, but so do peppermint, cookies and cream, cookie dough, strawberry, and rocky road. I throw in that I'm a big fan of butter pecan. Then I ask them what would happen if we mixed all of those flavors together. The predictable reaction is a group groan sprinkled with "*Yich!*"s.

"Even though you might have a favorite," I tell them, "there are probably *lots* of flavors you would enjoy. And there are lots of tasty ways to flavor the pieces we're playing. But in group class, it's important to watch the leader so that we're all making the same flavor. Otherwise, we get a yucky mess."

While that group lesson is primarily about the importance of watching the group leader, it does hint at another important aspect of our job. Although adults need to help students find their musical voices so they can play in a way that is sincere for them, we also need to teach them what are generally considered to be "standard" interpretations of pieces. In other words, they need to learn to make "vanilla."

The way I educate students about musical conventions depends, for the most part, on their ages. When younger students perform on a concert, I generally let them play their solo pieces as they wish. If a young soloist is really excited about the way she is playing a piece, but I think it makes the needle on the taste meter dip into the red zone, I don't mention it. But I definitely make a mental note of it.

When it comes to group playing, however, I insist that everyone interprets the piece the same way–meaning that they play it the way the leader is playing it. The young soloist who played what I thought was a wacko interpretation may find that on the next concert I have programmed the piece as a group piece. And I might have done that just to make sure that she has an occasion to learn to play it in a more "standard" way. While the student may have offered a Pregnancy Special–the orange-sherbet/

dill-pickle version of the piece–at the following concert, she cranks out "vanilla" with the group.

With an older student who is already confidently expressive in her playing, I might just say it straight: "One of my jobs is to let you know when I think that your musical interpretations are outside the range of what most artist-performers would do. This is one of those times." I will quickly add "Ultimately it's your choice, but first we need to make sure you can do something more standard."

If I have shared this opinion with the student–and checked to make sure that she can play it in what I know to be the more "vanilla" way–then I have done my job. The job of the parent (if the parent is still involved in the student's practicing) is to structure practices so that the student develops the ability to play the piece in both ways.

When the student then performs the piece, it is *her* performance. She gets to do what she wants. If it turns out that it's not the interpretation that her parent and/or I would have offered the audience, then at that point our job is to marvel at her technical flexibility as well as her ability to make decisions for herself.

If you're having a difficult time getting your child to play things "the vanilla way" you can often leave the job to the teacher, especially if you are able to find other constructive things to do during practice. A parent doesn't need the burden of knowing all about musical interpretation. It's the teacher–an experienced, educated musician–who's most qualified to tell the child how most musicians would approach various aspects of musical interpretation. I've heard many more recordings and concerts, sat through more classes, and read more things than my students have. These experiences gave me a fair amount of information, and it's my *duty* is to pass that information on to my students. Parents, often lacking this kind of background–and clout–are usually at a disadvantage when it comes to coaching a child's musical interpretations.

And then there's the whole parent/child relationship complication [for more about this complication, see section 4, "Listen to the Actions First"]. Even professional musicians usually have a difficult time convincing their children of what a standard musical interpretation is. They're best off leaving that aspect of the job to an outsider. It's like the time my brother, himself a physician, went to the emergency room when his face swelled up after eating a mango. He was pretty sure what the problem was, but he also knew that it's sometimes best to get an outsider involved. So, even if you're a musician yourself, let the teacher help with musical interpretation issues when serving as your child's parent makes it difficult for your child to take coaching from you. Children need parents much more than they need music teachers, and a child who senses that a parent is transforming into a music teacher can become very difficult to work with.

Although most musicians would more or less agree on what makes for basic, vanilla musical expression, they don't always agree on what makes for extraordinary musicianship. We adults need to share this fact with students. Amy Oshiro, a violinist with the St. Louis Symphony and a member of its audition committee, told me "Sometimes one person on the committee will choose a candidate because of certain aspects of his or her playing, while another person on the committee will reject the playing *for the very same reasons!*" We may as well put students under the same conditions that we put the pros under, and let them make their own decisions about interpretation. It's best, however, if they make that decision after we have helped them to develop the ability to make vanilla.

41

Dreaming and Practicing

This is what I read on an adolescent's t-shirt as I walked to teach my first lesson of the day: "If you don't practice, you don't deserve to dream." I immediately wrote it on the board in my classroom, because it seemed to sum up what I had been encountering all week at the institute: parents and students who only wanted lessons and practices to be fun, creative, and artistic. I certainly appreciate the sparkle of these kinds of practices and lessons, and I constantly search for ways to create it more often. I also recognize the necessity of practicing even when it seems a little bit like polishing the silver. Eternal optimist that I am, I'm grateful to have silver to polish. And I think the students and parents should be as well.

But this week, they weren't. They had a completely different mindset. It was as if they wanted to play in the Super Bowl but only wanted to go to the team workouts once a week. And only if they felt like it. Sadly, their parents thought that by being positive and cheering them on, they would still be able to score. The parents equated telling a child he needed to practice with "being negative." I had been struggling to find a way to broach the subject, and that kid's t-shirt seemed to provide a way to start talking about their painful distortion of reality.

As I finished up writing "If you don't practice, you don't deserve to dream," twelve-year-old Ahmed walked in for his lesson, looked at the board, and immediately asked "If you don't dream, how will you know what to practice?" He was right, of course, I realized as he unpacked his violin. It does work both ways.

I am constantly searching for ways to have a student's dreams drive his playing. The basic dream sequence goes this way: he hears something–wishes it–inside himself, makes physical motions to produce what he's hearing on the inside. The result is the expression of a musical dream. These three steps may seem to occur simultaneously, but I don't think they really do. It takes a great deal of practice for them to *feel* like they do.

It's common to encounter students who have been trained to pay so much attention to what they are doing physically–keeping their feet flat, moving their arm this way or that, making sure their bow stays in one spot–that they have been blocked from having much awareness of the sounds they are making, let alone awareness of their musical dreams.

I think of them as having been taught the "Pin the Tail on the Donkey," approach to making music. In the usual version of this party game, as you recall, a blindfolded player is given a paper "tail" and spun around in a circle a few times before he walks over to the wall where a picture of a donkey hangs. There he attaches the paper tail to his best guess of the location of the donkey's rear. He then takes his blindfold off to see how he did. In the musical corruption of this game, instead of the student's *vision* being blocked with a blindfold, it's the student's inside *hearing* that is blocked–most often because of the way he has been taught, not through any fault of his own. He moves body parts and manipulates the instrument, and *then* listens to what happened. (If he listens at all.)

It doesn't work. A musician has to hear where he's going to go before he gets there. It's like walking. If you only look at your feet–where you are–you'll bump into things. You have to see where you're going *and* be aware of where you are.

My usual way of talking about this "pre-hearing" comes from the violin teacher Ronda Cole, who refers to it as "inside singing," a concept that's typical of her gift for using a minimum number of words to make the maximum impact.

When a child actually sings out loud what he's working on playing on his instrument–even if he doesn't sing all that well–we adults can more easily see the child's dream of the piece. Then we can use practice to help make that dream a reality. When we do this, practice becomes more about helping children dream their dreams and then realize them, instead of only practicing the things adults tell them to. For a mature player, after all, it is the dreams that drive the work of practice. While we can and should control whether a child practices or not, we need to let go when children are dreaming. Their dreams are theirs.

Treat the Printed Music like e-mail

I was at a newsstand in Europe one summer, leafing through a *New Yorker*, when the scruffy old guy behind the counter glared at me and growled something that sounded like the exact opposite of "Make yourself at home and feel free to have a look around." Not speaking his language, I simply put down the magazine, *pretended* to be interested in some other things by looking at–but not touching them, of course–and then left. Recounting this story later, my friend said I should have just looked at him and barked.

For all I know, it might have worked as well as anything else because even when both people involved in an interchange understand the words, language is not nearly as precise a tool as we pretend it is. "Do you think my new pants make my hips look big?" may *technically* be a question, but in reality, the person uttering those words may be using them as a substitute for the statement "Please tell me I did the right thing when I bought these pants." Not being quite sure what the appropriate response is, the head of the queried person often wobbles like a puzzled dog, perhaps emitting a sympathetic "hmmmm..." [Note: kids are often similarly puzzled when "Do you want to play that again?" comes out of an adult's mouth. For more about constructing genuine choices for children, see sections 24 and 25.]

It's easiest to guess at the hoped for response when these kinds of puzzling exchanges occur in person. It's much more difficult when they happen over e-mail, a medium lacking the ingredients that give live communication its flavor. Over e-mail, punctuation and those cute little "emoticons," like the winks–;)–that some people use to pepper their e-mail, can sometimes fill in for the sender's body language, facial expressions, intonation, and pacing. But these markings are as much like the real thing as a toy dog, which may be cute, but doesn't ever really growl or wag its tail in a genuine way.

So clear communication is challenging in person, and it's even more difficult via e-mail–but try communicating with a composer who has been dead for over 100 years. I'm talking about the composers who penned most of the music that budding musicians study. It's a messy communication problem.

Thinking of the composer's musical scores as e-mail can help. Just as it's easier to transmit personality over e-mail if the two people involved in the communication volley know each other, it's much easier to get a sense of what a composer hopes his score will tell us if we know something about him–where he lived, what he wore, how he smelled, who he gossiped about.

In the case of e-mail, everything from minor embarrassment to unemployment can occur when messages containing sarcasm and irony accidentally get shot to unintended recipients who misconstrue their original meaning. With composers, the consequences of our misunderstandings aren't so dire. However, if we don't have much of an understanding of the composer, we can miss out on the musical juices a composition has to offer.

People writing e-mail are often in a hurry, so someone may write one thing but inadvertently imply the exact opposite. Guess what...composers were also busy people. Lacking computers and printers, many composers in previous centuries were forced to write out copies of their music as quickly as possible. The lucky ones sometimes had money to pay someone else to do the copying. In any case, people didn't always have time to put in all the little markings that might give us an idea of where to start with the music today. Sometimes they didn't put in many markings because they understood each other so well that they didn't need to. In fact, some of the manuscripts may have been so messy it was difficult for the performers of the time to make out exactly what the notes were supposed to be. Nevertheless, they got the job done.

Over the years, composers have gotten more and more precise about the kinds of markings they put in their scores. But a composer such as Händel, who lived during the Baroque period (1685-1750), really didn't mark much in his scores. When my students study Händel Violin Sonatas, I make a point of showing them the Henle edition, which is really just a neat printed version of Henle's best guess of the original sources. Because other editions are much cheaper, students don't usually buy the Henle edition. The editions they do end up buying are somewhat misleading because most of them have lots of markings telling the performer to slow down here, get louder there, play quietly, etc. By showing students the Henle editions, which have virtually zero markings, students can understand that the markings in their editions are only ideas, not "the truth" about the way the piece is "supposed to go." If a student is playing from a gussied up edition and we adults point to a "p" and say "this is supposed to be *piano*," we're really engaging in a lie. (There's another catch to all of this as well. There is a raging controversy about which of the "Händel Sonatas" Händel actually wrote....)

Just because the most authentic edition of the Händel Violin Sonatas has virtually no dynamic markings in it doesn't mean that the works don't deserve dynamic performances. So, the focus of lessons and practices needs to be on developing flexibility, which allows the performer to discover a way to play the piece that seems the most dynamic to him or her.

Two things happen when we focus the teaching of musicianship on flexibility rather than correctness–"play it the way I said." First of all, if a piece of music is open to interpretation, the possibilities can become so wide that studying the written music is necessary in order to narrow the options. Having too many choices can actually make things difficult. I think of it this way: you could repaint your living room every weekend and it would look great in lots of different colors, but who has that kind of time? We need to use scores to narrow our decisions and help nail down an interpretation. Whether age 5 or 95, it's true that the longer a musician lives with a piece, the more he or she learns about that piece of music. We may choose to remodel our interpretations once they're done, and fortunately the process doesn't involve harsh chemical fumes. Studying the score helps musicians make enough decisions so that they can at least move in the furniture.

The second thing that happens with a teaching approach that values flexibility over correctness, is that you find yourself facing the stark realization that studying the score can be confusing. For example, while a marking may have meant one thing at certain period in music history, it means another thing at a later one. The confusion leads us to a need for some understanding of music history. Studying a score from this perspective puts the work of the music history where it belongs–in getting at resources to create a living art, and not in memorizing lifeless facts.

General Principles of Musical Expression

Even though "the right way" to play a piece of music doesn't exist, there are some general principles that can help parents and students develop a sense of why a performance may or may not seem musically expressive.

A basic departure point is the famous quote of the legendary Spanish cellist Pablo Casals: "Monotony is the enemy of music." Shin'ichi Suzuki was quite fond of this quote and used it often in lessons. It's a handy tool that works nicely to begin shaping a musical performance. Keep it in the top tray of your tool chest.

To assist you with getting the playing away from monotony, you can follow three general principles from my college piano professor, Marvin Blickenstaff, a giant in the piano-teaching world whose clarity about these issues has been extremely helpful over the years. These principles are as follows:

1. Low notes lead to high notes.
   for example, "Twinkle, twinkle, LITtle star"
2. Short notes lead to long notes.
   for example, Beethoven's Fifth: "dut-dut-dut-DUM"
3. When in doubt, swell.

"Lead to," as you can probably see, means to get louder. Language provides a good way to think about it. It's like the accents of words:

la-SA-gna
Mis-sis-SIP-pi
Pep-er-O-ni

While the ideas of Casals and Blickenstaff have been useful for getting countless numbers of musicians out of musical mazes, even these guidelines have limited use. I remember hearing wonderful performances by the French violinist Virginie Robilliard, in which she would completely eliminate vibrato in certain passages–giving her playing an eerie, sterile quality. When she then re-introduced the vibrato, the contrast was breathtaking, but would not have existed had not some passages been almost monotonous. And then there is certainly the example of Phillip Glass, a composer whose musical expression thrives on what can seem an interminable sameness.

Though there isn't a right way to play any piece of music, general principles of musical expression can give you ideas of things you might be able to do to help your child's playing become expressive rather than monotonous. Please keep in mind, however, that these are merely principles.

Rules carry handcuffs; principles are free, acting only as walking sticks to be used when necessary, and ever adaptable to the territory. [When Ivan Galamian wrote] his book...he chose as its title, *Principles of Violin Playing and Teaching.*

Elizabeth A. H. Green
Miraculous Teacher:
Ivan Galamian and the
Meadowmount Experience

44

Check to See if They Mean It

Parents and teachers have a lot to monitor. For one thing, we have to make sure that children learn important factual information–that two plus two equals four and that Paris is the capital of France, for example. Students also need to learn how their instruments and their bodies work. So, it's important to give them assignments that help them develop genuine technical skill. In other words, they need to develop the ability to be physically comfortable producing a wide variety of sounds on their instruments.

But there's even more important work we have to do. Since a performance of a piece of music should give us a glimpse of the soul of the performer, we need to help students feel comfortable showing us their souls–who they are.

One of the most significant ways we can do that is by listening to the feelings they express with words. Faber and Mazlish's book *How to Talk So Kids Will Listen and Listen So Kids Will Talk* is an excellent primer for learning these skills away from the instrument. Section 20 in the "Practice Basics" chapter, "Develop the Skill of Acknowledging Feelings," can also help.

Another substantial way we can help children feel comfortable with who they are is by listening to the feelings they express with their music.

Sometimes, however, we will find ourselves confused about what a student is telling us with the music. Then we need to respond in a way that helps him feel comfortable revealing his soul during performance. Instead of simply telling him how he *should* have played it, we can ask him what he wants to say with the music.

Our work becomes like that of English teachers who need to help their students rearrange sentences to accurately convey what they mean. In an eighth grade essay, for example, I wrote something like:

"My mother bakes apple pie in a brown paper bag."

Mrs. Ash looked at me over her half-glasses–on a chain, of course–and asked: "Do you mean that your mother wears a brown paper bag when she bakes pie?"

"Well, no," I said. "I mean that my mother, well, she puts the pie in a brown paper bag and then puts it into the oven to bake–but only the apple pies." It still sounded odd, but at least I was accurately representing what my mother did. (Since none of my siblings remember where she told us she learned this quirky technique, its origin is just one of those things she took to her grave.)

What I remembered from this experience was that I might not always be communicating what I think I'm communicating.

I'd like to say that Mrs. Ash helped me rearrange that sentence so that it said what I wanted it to say. But she didn't. She was a terrible teacher. She was good at snidely pointing out our flaws, but not with teaching us how to change them. She was like a plumber who shows up to your house and says "The drain's clogged," then leaves.

I aim to be different. I work from a belief that every child I teach is one-of-a-kind who has something unique to say musically. I also believe that the *enormous* job of teachers and parents is to assist students with saying what they have to say. We can do this in many ways. One useful and respectful way to do it is by using ourselves as mirrors, reflecting back to students what we heard in their playing, then asking them if it's what they *meant* to say.

For example, Wendy was playing the opening movement of the Händel D Major violin sonata quite beautifully. The ending of the piece was smooth and delicate, until the beginning of the last note.

"Wow, wonderful job with all those shifts and the sound," I told her. "And this is what I heard in the last phrase…"

I then played the last phrase for her, and I really made a point of clobbering the very last note.

"That's not *exactly* what I heard–I'm really exaggerating," I said, "But I think you get the idea. You didn't sock the last note nearly as much as I did, but what I got was a feeling that you were putting the baby down for his nap very gently, then when you got him to about an inch above the mattress, you dropped him and ran out of the room. Is that the feeling you meant to convey?"

Wendy laughed and said "No!" Then she played it again with the last note tapering off, creating the gentle mood she intended to create the first time.

"I like that much better, do you?" I asked. "It seemed like it all fit together with what you wanted to do with the piece."

Of course, a much faster and more direct approach would have been to say: "Don't punch the last note. Make sure it's as tender as the way you're playing the rest of the phrase." However, I think that students can develop their powers of expression much more if they are given feedback about the effect of their playing *and* given the option of deciding if they want to have that effect or not. Had Wendy decided that she really did want to explode on the last note, I would have made sure she could have played the phrase in a more conventional way, with a final note that evaporated.

If she had been able to do it both ways, my job would have been done. And her job would have been to make a choice. Developing this flexibility means that she will have ensemble skills. When a conductor insists that the last note of a similar phrase tapers, she will be qualified to do precisely that. More importantly, when she encounters a piece of music in which she herself wants to do it, she will have the skill. I have also pointed her in the direction of thinking about various parts of a phrase and the ways in which they fit together.

These kinds of lessons and practices help to make students be mindful of what they're doing instead of just cranking out the notes. Working this way also moves in the direction of helping students clarify their own musical ideas; ideas which they can then express in performance.

Make Sure Students Have Technical Facility

Winifred Crock and I describe ourselves as "String Nerds." The volume on our animated conversations usually goes way up, and we inevitably transform restaurant cutlery into makeshift bows when the topic lands where it always does: the fine points of violin technique. Our enthusiasm about these issues usually gets some heads turning.

While I am constantly on the hunt for ways to teach technique musically, when I can't find a musical way to do it, I teach it anyway. I also insist that students practice it at home, because I know that skills on an instrument give students the capacity to express themselves musically. I don't like to think of increased technique as "improving" a student's playing, just as expanding its musical possibilities.

After teaching thousands of young violinists in workshops and master classes over the past twenty years, my observation is that the number one ingredient missing from student playing is adequate technique to execute what they *already* have to express. (Number two on my list would be learning too much new repertoire too soon, and number three is violins that are too big.) I want to hasten to add that the most important piece of music is musicianship. But having the skills with which to be musical is crucial.

It always breaks my heart when a parent or teacher describes a student's playing as "stiff." Or "not very creative." Or "inhibited." Or "unmusical." Even sadder is that these students aren't usually given the option of rejecting these descriptions; they end up using them to describe themselves. What's generally going on is that they simply have not been taught and practiced with in a way that allows them to develop their ease and fluency with technical skills. Lacking this fluency, children are unable to dig their way to the musical treasures buried inside of them.

It's not that these students don't *want* to be musical. They do. But like mittens on a board-certified thoracic surgeon, an obstacle–the lack of instrumental technique–gets in the way and frustrates what they actually can do.

Telling them "play-from-your-heart" can put students in a terrible dilemma. Using their limited technical skills, they do what they can, but still often end up not being able to do enough for the parent or teacher who asked them to play from their heart. When their heartfelt efforts don't meet with adult approval, an adult can compound the problem by saying–in one way or another–"That wasn't good enough," a sentiment which is WAY too close to "*You're* not good enough."

The adults in a child's musical life need to remember that if something is difficult it's hard to focus on its musical flavor. For people used to eating with a knife and fork, being forced to eat dinner with chopsticks means that a lot of effort goes into getting the food into your mouth, and not necessarily on savoring it. That's why, to be musical, it's important to focus practice on making things easier.

There is no substitute for a fluent, functional, flowing technique. It takes years to eliminate technical concerns–if, indeed, they ever are totally eliminated–but focusing practice on developing skill and ease helps to minimize technical concerns as much as possible. Your practices will be much happier and more productive if you keep this idea in mind. In other words, always remember that the reason you practice is to make it easier.

Sometimes I run into parents who think that I'm being too easy on students because I don't expect them to try their hardest at all times. Often, these parents don't have experience with music, but they do have experience with sporting events in which the players are–quite appropriately–admonished to give their all, and then some. It's not that I don't expect students to work, it's just that I think that a musical performance should be an experience of expressing music, not surviving the notes by trying your best–which can make a student overheat and burn out like a blender trying to purée forks.

The concept of "trying your best" is kind of a myth anyway. Life, in general, demands a great deal of us. We mess up all the time because there is just so much to do and keep track of. You remember to pick your daughter up from her Girl Scout meeting 15 minutes earlier this week because of a one-time change in the schedule, but then get home and discover that you grabbed the wrong kind of batteries at the store.

I generally use review pieces to help my students develop their technical skills. I don't insist that they pretend to "love" doing review. In fact, many of them hate reviewing repertoire, but I still insist that they do it because I know that it helps to develop the facility and ease they need in order to say what it is they have to say musically. Fortunately, it's often possible to work on review in a musical way, and students find that much more interesting.

It's useful to remember that "a spoonful of sugar" does, indeed, "help the medicine go down." The more the work of review can be joyful and playful, the easier it is to tolerate. While I'm always looking for ways to make review musical and enjoyable, an inability to make the medicine taste good doesn't mean that it isn't necessary.

46

Group Section-Practice Musically, not Rationally

Take a look at the following and decide if it's English:

l a r g e e l e p h a n t

–or–

larg eele phan t

–or–

l arge elep hant

It may not be easy to recognize it right away, but when I tell you that the letters above make the words "large elephant," you can see it immediately. However, the way that I initially spaced the letters makes it trickier to see. In English, letters usually come grouped in words. You're probably so used to these words that you found meaningful groupings–"large elephant"–on your own.

In the musical language, however, notes are not printed on the page in ways that necessarily tell you how they are grouped. When looking at the notes on the page, it's not always obvious where the musical "syllables," "words," "sentences," and "paragraphs" are. For string players, the problem can be even more confusing, because oftentimes the bowings don't even really tell you the groupings.

Teachers need to help the parents they work with understand the musical groupings of the notes that students learn; and the teacher-parent team then needs to work together to help communicate this information to children. One of the primary ways we do that is *not* by showing young children what is on the written page, but by having them practice things in musical groupings.

One example is the folk song "Long, Long Ago," which many string students learn. Most violinists play it with a down-bow at the beginning of each new phrase, or musical sentence. I usually like to teach students the concept of musical sentences by telling them a story in English and asking them to jab their index fingers in the air when they hear a period in the story. Most students get this right away. Though some students hear several short sentences as one big sentence, all students put the periods in places where a period might actually be, depending on the author's choice of punctuation. None of the students put a period in the middle of a word. After telling a bit of a story in English, I then tell it in a foreign language, or in a nonsense language that I make up on the spot. Students are usually able to "find the periods."

From there, I like to tell the student that I am now going to "speak violin" and I ask them to find the periods in what I am saying on the violin. I may play a piece of music they already know, or I may make something up.

The next step is simply to have the student play "Long, Long Ago," putting the bow on top of her head every time she gets to a period. Once she has practiced the piece this way several times, it is possible to tell her that every sentence in "Long, Long Ago" starts down-bow and that she will find a place in the piece where she will need to make a bow circle to get the next sentence to start down-bow. Depending on the student, I might also talk about needing to breathe during the bow circles, though I find that with this approach most students do it naturally.

Teaching the bow circles in "Long, Long Ago" this way makes much more sense than telling the students to remember the "spot with two down-bows," which I find about as useful as telling them to remember where the two "e's" happen in "large elephant." When you run into students who don't yet know what sentences are, you can see if they catch on by having them jump when you get to the end of "a part" when you are speaking and playing. Many non-readers get this right away. If they don't, you can just make a point of practicing one sentence at a time until they sense it as a chunk, a strategy which also demonstrates the idea of practicing in *musical* chunks, not rational ones. Another option for introducing the concept to young children who don't yet read words is to tell them to "jump at the end of a part."

Pianists–as well as string players–can use this concept of sentences and words to teach a variety of things. For instance, the teacher or parent can have the student play through the piece, stopping to shout his name at the end of each phrase. Or stand up, turn around, then sit down again. When a student can do something goofy or even outrageous at the end of a phrase, the next step is to remind him that the reason we practice is to make it easier and then to have him identify the phrases that went easily and the ones that were difficult. The difficult ones can then be repeated, and, using a similar technique, the adult can help the student find the tricky "words"–or even "syllables"–that need to get "worked into easier."

In the case of a student like Dora, who often claims that, "every part is easy," it's crucial to respect her "opinion." Since it's also crucial that she practices those spots, you yourself can just make a mental note of the parts that weren't easy. The next day, you can then start your practice on those spots without giving her a choice and *without* telling her that you are doing it because she blew it yesterday. If you think it's likely that you'll get some resistance you can plan ahead of time to use some kind of "game" (as found in the appendix). You're always more likely to have a happy practice if you can plan ahead for ways to deal with resistance rather than merely react to it when you encounter it.

It is especially important for string players to realize that *consecutive up bows–or consecutive down bows–are not always part of the same musical grouping, even though they may be part of the same musical sentence.* For example, the *Bourrée anglaise,* the fourth movement of Händel's *Flute Sonata in G Major*, HWV 363B, which a typical violinist would bow as follows:

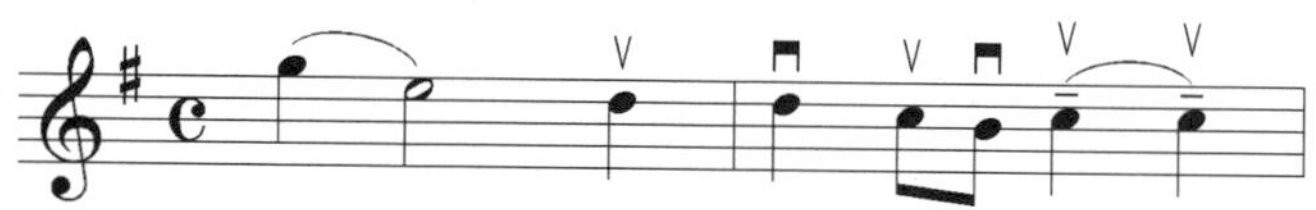

The second measure of this excerpt contains two up bow, quarter note C's in a row. The first one is the last note of one grouping; the second C is the first note of the next. I like to think of these two up bow C's as part of the same sentence, even though they are separated by a "comma."

A typical bowing for the opening of Schumann's "Happy Farmer" is a good example of consecutive down bows that are not part of the same musical grouping:

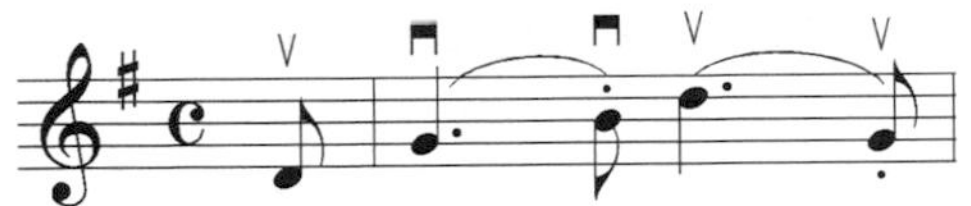

Rather than focus the practice on the fact that the G and B are both down bows, it's easier to think of them as belonging to two different groups, with the double down bows merely being a coincidence. So I have students practice the first two notes–the D and the G–several times as one group. Then I have them practice the next two notes–the B and the D–as another group. The next step is to have them practice all four notes together, perhaps with a pause in the middle to start the second chunk down bow. You could also make up temporary words, such as "the cow" for the D and G; and "the pig" for the B and the D." But having students practice D-G-B over and over in order to "remember the double down bow" would be like saying "the cow the" over and over. Just as it wouldn't make sense in English, it wouldn't make sense in "Music." But "The cow, the pig…" makes sense.

Years ago, Geri Arnold pointed me in the direction of thinking of music as coming in units much like language, when she gave a master class to one of my first students. The piece was "Lightly Row," and the student was having difficulty with the following notes:

A lesser teacher would have taught the student to remember that there were 5-B's, perhaps even having the child sing "One, Two, Three, Four, Five." Not Geri. She made up words–on the spot–that incorporated the student's name: "My name's Sasha."

This sentence only covered the first four B's, but they practiced it until the student really had it. Then they went on to "Here we go!" which covered the remainder of the chunk that was giving Sasha trouble.

I'm not a big fan of teaching words unless they are used as skillfully as Geri used them in this case. By her next lesson with me, Sasha could not only play the spots easily–since she and her father had repeated them several times a day in their home practices–she had also forgotten the words. I really admired the way Geri had used words as a bridge to the land–to the *language*–of Music.

Finally, be sure to keep games musical. While it may make sense to play Suzuki's "Perpetual Motion" leaving out all of the E's, for example, this kind of game works against the musical flow of the piece. A more musical approach would be to have the child play the entire piece, alternating playing four notes on the instrument with playing four notes in his head. This "Four On Four Off" game requires a great deal of concentration, but unlike the "Leave out the E's" game, it groups the notes in rhythmically musical units, which help a student develop a sense of flow and ease.

Experiment with Playing Phrases Different Ways

Sometimes I ignore *minor* mishaps in a child's playing, such as when a child plays a note the composer didn't put in the piece–often referred to as a "wrong note," a phrase I usually avoid.

But please don't get me wrong. Accuracy of notes is important. It's just not the *most* important. Although I hope that the stray note eventually finds a happy home in another composition, swapping that note for the one the composer intended is probably not going to be the most important thing that happens at that lesson.

For example, seven-year-old Monty was working on a *Minuet* by J.S. Bach. At his lesson, he played a C-natural instead of a C-sharp, and–like nearly every moment of teaching–I was faced with having to make a decision. One option, which I often use, is to be straightforward: "Um, this is a C-sharp, not a C-natural." That approach, simple and direct, can be effective. But some students, not knowing what you mean, will look at you intently and, wanting to make you happy, just pretend to understand. Then they'll turn around and miss the note. If you're like most parents and teachers, you're likely to feel ignored, brushed off. This sad scenario frequently happened with Monty and his mother. Not fun.

Since I wanted Monty and his mother to have a way to create more pleasant practices, I approached the C-sharp issue in a different way. I realized that part of the problem was that it was the fall of Monty's first grade year in school, and after school he was a bit like a puppy that had been caged all day. All he wanted to do at his lesson was romp around. He *needed* to play C-sharp. Given that it was a great effort for him just to stand still and play the violin, C-sharps or not, he was likely to feel threatened and become defensive, as children often are when they are overloaded and nobody notices. Children are especially likely to feel overloaded–and sense the work they are doing is taken for granted–when they're practicing with their parents.

So, keeping in mind that playing a C-natural instead of a C-sharp is not the worst thing a person could do (it is slightly more offensive than using the meat fork for the salad, though), I shifted the focus to musical expression.

Monty had already demonstrated a solid understanding of the difference between C-sharp and C-natural in other pieces he had learned, and he had demonstrated that he was capable of playing both. Knowing that he was listening to the reference recording daily, and that he attended group classes and recitals where students played the piece with the notes where they belong, I decided not to say anything to him directly.

I started out by seeing if Monty could play one phrase (sentence) from the middle of the piece all by itself. That was a challenge, so I had him put his violin under his arm and just sing that phrase. When he could do that, I then had him bark the phrase like a dog. He loved it. The next step was to have him *play* the phrase like a barking dog. Then like a mouse...an ape...a mosquito. His kid sister looked up from her coloring and suggested "Barney."

Somewhere in the middle of all of that, Monty played a C-sharp instead of a C-natural. I had a feeling that would happen, what with all the exposure he had been getting through listening and attending group events. And my priority is musical expression, not correctness, so I said, "It's fantastic to hear how you're getting your violin to sound like so many different creatures. And, by the way, I noticed that you figured out that it's really a C-sharp instead of a C-natural." When he forgot it the next time, I said "Play it again and be sure to make it a C-sharp like you discovered the time before." Then when he got it, I said "Sounds like you're really remembering that C-sharp. Play it again!" He repeated it several times, and we then went on to one more animal.

Of course, Monty's getting the C-sharp may have been an accident. Doesn't matter. I treated it like he did it on purpose, which allowed me to talk about it in a positive way. Some children figure out these note changes sooner than Monty did. Some take longer, but I'm willing to wait a pretty long time. The important thing is to *continue the experimenting*, commenting on the desired change *and* pointing out what a variety of expression the child is getting on the instrument.

Outcome? Musical possibilities explored, and the C-sharp reinforced. Nurturing a child's ability to be musically expressive is the most important to me, so when it's possible to kill two birds with one stone–as it often is–I like to aim for the musical one.

The basic formula is this: give the student some examples, and then engage his imagination in order to create choices. In addition to creatures, other possible categories include:

- Kinds of people
  - a football coach yelling from the sidelines
  - a parent singing a lullaby
  - a bored kid at a lecture
- Characters
  - Oscar the Grouch
  - The Wizard of Oz
  - Snow White and the Seven Dwarfs
- Moods
  - happy
  - sad
  - joyful

worried
sleepy
confident

Colors

from a paint sample chart–red, blue, orange, etc.
colors found in the room
markers or crayons
within a group–dark red, bright, red, pink, hot pink, etc.

Textures

corduroy
silk
canvas
wooden floor
carpet
glass

Other possibilities include having a child play one phrase one color, and the next phrase another color. Or you can even say "Play this phrase pale yellow, but have the C-sharp be bright orange." Or "Play this phrase and make it sound like all the notes are really bored, except have the C-sharp be really joyful." Or "Have the chimpanzee be sleepy until he gets to the second phrase, when he suddenly wakes up."

Still other options include:

varying the speed
(start the phrase slowly and then speed up
or start fast and then slow down)

varying the volume
(start out really loudly and then finish quietly
...play like the band is five miles away and coming
closer...like the band is right in front of you but
then marches far away by the end of the phrase...)

You can use these musical ideas with review–which doesn't have to purely consist of the child playing a piece followed by parent or teacher commenting about everything that was wrong and needs to be fixed. Lots of review can be musical experimenting, in which children can discover what they can say with what they already know. Of course, attempting to explore the musical possibilities of each and every review piece means the day's review will take forever. But one or two pieces a day certainly wouldn't hurt.

When Experimenting Doesn't Work

The first week of music camp between my junior and senior years in high school, I was in the cafeteria when I overheard two ornery pianists from the next cabin talk about how they had just snuck into the recital hall to play on the Steinway. Instead of just practicing their audition pieces, though, they started fooling around with them. The head of the piano program walked in just as they were howling over their discovery that if they changed only one note in the opening of Beethoven's Moonlight Sonata, it suddenly became the "Sunlight" Sonata. "Mrs. Rabinoff didn't say a word, but we were really embarrassed," one of them said.

It was just one note. All they had to do was change just *one* of the specific notes Beethoven wrote, and the piece's musical meaning was drastically different. So, obviously, accuracy matters.

But even though it counts for a great deal, accuracy of notes is not always the *most* important thing about a musical performance. And it's certainly not always the most important thing about a practice session either.

Furthermore–as most parents have noticed when they attempt to support the accuracy cause by, for example, telling a child which note comes next–children often ignore these directions completely (which irritates parents) or they get angry, commonly turning practice into a struggle of wills. All of which confuses the parent. After all, a dad who tells his daughter to play the F-natural with a first finger, is only wanting to do what all parents want to do: be as helpful as possible.

The funk that direct instruction creates for parents and children gets in the way of productive work. The bitterness in the relationship is likely to incubate aggressive, battleground playing, rather than generating musically expressive playing. Of course, there will be practice battles to work through. But *indirect* practice strategies can lessen them. *Indirect* practice strategies can prevent you from creating conflicts needlessly, so that the emotional environment will be more conducive to hatching that musical playing we all dream about.

I think twice before blurting out "They're C-sharps not C-naturals." This kind of direct instruction can seem efficient and less monkeying around than the indirect alternatives, but in addition to being a move that that many children find difficult to stomach, a direct instruction often squanders opportunities to help a child develop the high octane skills and conditions that *really* fuel musically expressive playing:

- *independent thinking*
- *ownership of the playing*
- *ownership of the practice process*
- *listening to how your actions affect what comes out of your instrument*
- *an awareness of the creative possibilities*
- *a low level of anxiety*

Gains that a direct strategy produces in note accuracy often cause losses in these other important areas. Which means that indirect ways of developing accurate notes actually teach more about musical expression–which is what it's all about anyway.

Before I go on to make my case for developing indirect methods of leading a child to accurate notes, I want to acknowledge that the older and more advanced the student, the easier it is to toss out information such as "the second section starts up-bow" or "make sure that last note has three beats."

How much older? How much more advanced? The answer doesn't really have to do with a child's chronological age or what piece she's on. *It has more to do with our noticing what happens when we offer direct information.* If it doesn't work, your experiment shows you that the child can't use the information in the form you just gave it and will need to be older and more advanced than the present.

The problem with many direct instructions, as you can probably testify, is that children often can't use them. Which is a fancy way of saying that they simply don't work. Giving a direct instruction can make us adults feel powerful, though, because we know we said something true and important. But a child might not really know the difference between C-sharp and C-natural, so we may as well have been speaking Martian. There are other common cases in which a child clearly knows the difference between C-sharp and C-natural, to give just one example, but is too overwhelmed to take in the information because she's trying to get a couple of other pieces of her technique to work at the same time. The C-sharp/C-natural instruction becomes the straw that breaks the camel's back.

Then parents can worry that their children will never be able to handle direct instruction or, as it's also commonly known, "constructive criticism."

"After all," parents ask, "don't musicians in an orchestra have to do what the conductor says?" Or "Doesn't everyone have to learn how to take criticism?"

Of course, and "constant worry" is a large part of a parent's job description, but these specific worries are like worrying that a nursing child will never be able to handle solid food. Forcing the issue creates more problems than it solves–and militates against achieving your original goal anyway. When we use indirect means to generate things like awareness, accuracy, and fluent skills, we are preparing a child to use and follow directions in the future.

In general, I'm most likely to offer direct instruction when I see that a child is engaged with solving another challenge in her playing and I sense that my words will prevent her from spinning her wheels and assist her with managing her pressing issue. I don't say anything if I think my instruction will just add to her burden.

Please keep in mind that I'm talking about direct instructions as they apply to the accuracy of things like notes and fingerings. I'm not talking about a child's ability to follow simple directions such as "stand up" and "turn your head." But when a child has difficulty following more complicated directions–anything from "Put your second finger on the A string," or "Telemann is a Baroque composer, so start the trill from the upper auxiliary"–the work of practice may need to move away from working on "the piece" and, instead, focus on a child's learning how to follow more complex directions.

Following directions, in fact, is an important skill to help a child develop, and much of lessons and practices is about preparing a child to handle more and more complex directions. If a child can't follow your instruction the first time–I don't mean *chooses* not to follow it, which can be a difficult distinction to decipher–then your instruction was probably too complicated. I often quote the veteran Suzuki teacher Elizabeth Mills, who pointed out a crucial thing she learned as a teacher: "What I once thought was a single step I now realize was twenty."

Pare down your instruction or somehow rearrange the practice conditions so that the child will be successful. For example, before you talk about that trill, you may need to ask a child what a composer is. (Asking instead of telling is an indirect strategy, by the way, but I'm getting ahead of myself…) Then you can move on to making sure that the child knows what the other words mean. He may be clueless.

Teaching musicianship and efficiency are not always mutually exclusive, but if I have to choose I am much more likely to choose teaching music. In the case of dawdlers, however, I may opt to teach efficiency, as I know it will be a useful tool for them as they dig for those musical treasures that I'm convinced are in them. Efficiency becomes a shovel that eliminates the tedium and exhaustion from digging with a teaspoon. So I teach efficiency not only because it helps make it easier for me to work with the child, but because it ultimately makes it easier for the child to work with himself–to do his own digging.

Even if a child is "advanced enough" to use direct information that you lob his way, stop yourself. You may still be giving up opportunities to develop those other virtues, such as his own awareness of what he's doing–not your awareness. In the process of developing that awareness, you'll be leading your child to the land of accuracy, musical creativity and, ta-da, expressive playing.

The remainder of this section outlines four indirect strategies that I've found to be extremely helpful: being quiet, which will give you time to contemplate your options; asking questions; dropping hints; and becoming a mirror for children.

When a child plays an inaccurate note and we make ourselves wait to say anything about it, we're using an indirect strategy that I've found to be one of the most effective and efficient ways to eventually get a student to accuracy. Our adult work in this strategy is to readjust what a wrong note means we have to do. Instead of having it be a signal to say something quickly, we make it be a signal to be quiet. It's one of the most important pieces of work we can do.

I want to emphasize that *saying* nothing doesn't mean *doing* nothing. It doesn't mean keeping your eyes and ears off the accuracy target and–heaven forbid–it doesn't mean leaving the practice session, telling your child "call me when you've figured it out."

It means letting the process do the work. It means staying out of the way so that you don't impede your child's ability to exercise his *own* awareness and his *own* problem-solving skills–the skills that generate musical playing.

Saying nothing means that you're quiet so that you can go on to your next task: contemplating your options. Once you are quiet, you will discover that you have many.

One option is to remind yourself that not everything needs immediate attention. Just because you notice the inaccuracy doesn't mean you need to talk about it that instant. Some issues can linger. Others can't–at least not for long. No matter what the issue's shelf life, we all want to avoid what the viola teacher Dee Martz calls "Three-Part Learning," which she defines as "learn/unlearn/re-learn." Still, you've usually got at least a two-minute window (which is a long time to bite your tongue) before you *really* need to worry that you're in for Three-Part Learning. Being quiet for those two minutes–in some cases you've even got a week or more–can buy you the time you need so that you can determine what you need to do to ensure that the learning sticks the first time. It's very similar to the advice my father used to give me when we were cutting lumber for construction projects: "Measure twice, cut once."

Your being quiet contributes to calmer practices and lowered anxiety because it gives you time to come up with the least confrontational ways to develop accuracy. Of course, in some instances your child may take your comments as confrontational even if you don't mean them that way, but your silence will give you time to, as they say, "pick and choose your battles."

When the parent–the most important person in a child's life–stops barking instructions all the time, a child becomes less anxious because he no longer lives with the constant worry of coming up short in the eyes of the person who matters most to him. The payoff of that lowered anxiety level is that it helps to create the conditions that allow both accurate and musically expressive playing to emerge on its own. So as you're biting down on your tongue, remind yourself that blurting out directions may create more resistance than it's worth.

In some cases, I think there can even be some issues that are appropriate to leave for the teacher to deal with. Again, just because you notice something doesn't mean it needs to be talked about instantly. In addition to setting aside your impulse to say something, you'll also need to set aside your need to be right. Remind yourself that you're the parent and you're bigger–so big that when your teacher does bring up the issue you don't need to gloat with "See, I noticed it too, but I knew you wouldn't listen to me."

Students certainly need to be coachable, but until they've developed the ability to handle adjustments to their playing, I'm a teacher who is willing to be the bearer of bad news if that role helps to create a more pleasant practice environment, which, in turn, allows the parent and child to continue productive work on other issues. I'm *not* suggesting you stop practicing altogether!

Here's another option for you while you're being quiet in the face of a child's inaccuracy: ask yourself if the musical environment–and by that I mean *daily* listening, *daily* review, and regular attendance at group classes and concerts–will be enough to germinate note accuracy in this case. Since a rich environment is usually enough, my next step is not to point out the erroneous note, but to make sure that the necessary environmental factors are in place. If they are, I'm likely to wait for the playing to change on its own.

And it usually does. But if pieces of the musical environment aren't in place, then I address putting them in place rather than fixing the wrong note. Trying to make accuracy grow in unfavorable conditions can be as senseless as tugging on a seedling to make it grow, when what it really needs is light, water, and rich soil. Tugging may make me feel like I'm doing useful work but it merely thwarts what was going to happen anyway if I would have just left it alone. Furthermore, impulsively nipping a problem in the bud can easily result in nipping buds you don't want nipped. One of those buds is Independent Thinking. Musical Expression is another one.

And let the record show that although I'm not so concerned about a stray note for a day or two–or maybe even up to a week or more in some cases–I am *extremely* concerned about students practicing without a fluid and comfortable physical approach to the instrument, an approach that will continue to develop through the routine of daily practice and review. I wouldn't approach a student in the way I have outlined in this section if the student weren't already well on his way towards mastering the basics of efficient body mechanics with his instrument as well as developing a beautiful tone. While I'm not likely to address notes and bowings directly, I am *quite* likely to address physical skills directly. *Take cues from your teacher as to which physical skills to leave alone and which ones to mention.*

Being quiet gives you time to decide if you want to move on to another indirect strategy: asking questions. If you *do* want to venture into this strategy, staying quiet for a while longer will give you time to think about what specific questions you want to ask.

There's a lot to recommend asking questions instead of telling a child something directly. The question-asking strategy is a helpful solution that lays somewhere between telling a child precisely what to do–which a child can experience as an intrusion which he must battle–and leaving the child to struggle unproductively on his own–which a child can experience as abandonment. Questions can support a student by pointing him in the right direction, but they require him to walk to the solution on his own power, making them a great way to engage a student. And because they engage a student, they're a nice catalyst for helping him develop independent thinking, which in turn gives him the skill and freedom to generate his own musical ideas.

The questions you ask can take a variety of forms. Some questions will be easier for a child than others. Instead of a direct instruction, for example, you can ask the child "Does this section start down-bow or up-bow?" With either/or questions like this one, the child has a fifty-fifty chance. Children also have a fifty-fifty chance with yes/no questions such as "Is the first note down-bow or up-bow?" Other questions can be broader, such as "What color do you think the first note of the second part should be?" Questions like this one point a child in the direction of thinking musically, but don't require a specific answer–which is good, because with issues like this one, there's not really a specific answer to get. [For more about constructing questions, see section 23, "Ask–Don't Tell."] For older students who are nearing the point where they will start practicing on their own, it can even be fun–and useful–to ask questions such as "What would be a good question for me to ask you about this?"

Sometimes, questions allow us to scratch the surface of what appears to be a problem, allowing us parents and teachers to realize that things are changing in positive ways, even though we couldn't see the change before we asked the question. The discovery often gives everyone a sense relief. Part of the relief for busy adults comes from an awareness that even though it doesn't look like things are changing, they are. You're not wasting your time. The relief lowers the nervousness for the adults, which, in turn, helps a child to be musically expressive.

Take the case of little seven-year old Rita...

"What color do you want to make the last note?" I asked her.

"Hot pink!" she said.

I wasn't exactly sure how the hot pink note would turn out, but I was expecting that it would be different from the other ones. Some psychotherapists would refer to this kind of instruction as "artfully vague" because even though it is precise enough to point in a specific direction, it is also broad enough to encourage individual effort and creativity. I was thinking that the work we were doing would communicate the general musical principle that not all notes are created equal and would require

Rita to use her own resources–without giving her cause to fret about "getting it right."

But when she actually played, I didn't hear any difference between the last note and the notes that came before it. They all sounded the same color to me. Before leaping to the conclusion that she wasn't doing anything to change her playing, I asked her a question: "Was the last note hot pink?"

"Mmmm-hmmmm!" she said.

Since I don't really know what a hot pink note sounds like, instead of telling her that she just gave me the wrong answer I went on to another question: "How were the notes different?" Rita told me that the difference was that on the hot pink note she made sure her bow thumb was bent, an issue that she and her dad had worked on intensely–three weeks earlier! Maybe after another twenty years of teaching I'll stop being so amazed at the rich information that come from asking students questions like "How were they different?" and "How do you know?" but I doubt it. I will probably still be floored by the things *they* were noticing but simply escaped my antiquated radar.

As the example of Rita illustrates, we work toward the goals of getting children connected to their own playing and lowering their anxiety by finding out what they are aware of and by then helping them connect to their *own* experiences. In some ways, in fact, it doesn't really matter what we adults notice. What matters more is the extent to which the child is engaged and being creative.

The whole experience with Rita reminded me of an old saying I once heard: "We learn to skate in the summer and to swim in the winter." In other words, the child may just need some time to process the information. Consistently zeroing in on an issue from one day to the next, like swimming every day in the summer, can be very productive. Time away from working on an issue can *also* be productive. The important thing is to pay attention to the result. (And, by the way, I'm not suggesting that you stop practicing any more than the original saying was suggesting that you give up exercising.)

Sometimes, when you ask a question–like the time I asked Robert if he made a difference between the carpet sound and the velvet sound–the student will respond with an honest "No." With Robert, when I inquired further I found out that it wasn't that he was spacing out, it's just that–like Rita–he was busy attempting to remember something else he had worked on with his parent earlier. At other times, he would readily admit that he simply "forgot." In both cases, my response was to instruct him to do it again and to re-ask the question when he finished.

Dropping hints is another strategy, one that comes just shy of direct instruction. You might say something like "The B-flat Fairy didn't show up that time–do you think she'll show up the next time you play it?" Sometimes a subtle reminder like this is all that students need. Often when I talk about the B-flat Fairy (...or the C-Natural Fairy ...or the Down-bow Fairy...or the Get-Ready-Before-You-Play Fairy...), the student will bang his palm on his forehead and say, "Oh, ya." That tells me that I have gone far enough. But if the student looks at me like I have just recited the chemical formula for Teflon, I may need to give him a fuller explanation. (By the way...it's important to make sure that you don't get your hints from the sarcasm bin. Sarcasm and children don't mix.)

I like to think that creative hints also help keep a child in touch with his imaginative side, which is where the musically expressive playing comes from.

For children who are really connected to their playing, another indirect strategy is to become a mirror for them. When using this strategy, keep in mind that mirrors don't issue reports about right and wrong. They just reflect what is there. All a mirror tells you is that your hair is sticking up. *You're* the one who adds the judgment "this looks terrible."

So when you're a musical mirror for your child, you say things such as "I heard the B-flat as the loudest note in the phrase." You leave out judgments such as "...and the loudest note should be the A–be sure to get it right the next time," and "it really sounded goofy." If the student's genuine wish is to make the A the loudest note, he's probably already asking *himself* what his options are for making that happen and, chances are, he just needs to give it another whirl.

But maybe not. On rare occasions, your child will feel stuck and need you to step out of your mirror role and go back to your question strategy: "Can you think of ways to make it louder?"–or–"What would happen if you used more arm weight?" But, like I said, it's rare that a student engaged at this level, will need any help from us. I'd prefer to give him the opportunity to exhaust his own resources. *He* needs to be working on the problem so that in the process, he develops his musical muscles.

The problem with all of the strategies I've given you in this section is that they can feel tedious. Sorry. They're no free ride for children either–for them it can feel like musical gruntwork. Still, they're efficient in the long run, because in addition to leading a child to accuracy, they also help to create the conditions that nourish a child's freedom to be musically expressive, something that direct instruction can't do as well.

Accuracy is a worthy goal, and it's important to remember that you have several ways to get there. Another way of thinking about it is that these indirect strategies ignite the oven in which a child's musical skills bake. Direct instruction can snuff it out, leaving your child with nothing but a really well-mixed set of raw ingredients.

In the long run, relying solely on direct instruction is exhausting. And limiting our job description to correcting and undoing bad habits–along with telling students everything that they did wrong and how to fix it–is a depressing way to go about teaching. The child will get very skilled at following directions and waiting for the "correct" answer from a parent or a teacher, but will not become skilled at thinking for himself or being musically creative.

This approach also prevents us from doing the really important part of our work: structuring situations in which a student can grow. We need to create situations in which students develop their skills, which means that they're generating solutions to problems before they even appear. It's a heck of a lot more work, but in the long run it's the most fruitful way of helping them develop their powers of musical expression. The farther you get from engaging children in the work, the farther you get from developing their ability to be musically expressive.

And being musically expressive is what it's all about. The ultimate goal of lessons and practices is to give children the skills–the *freedom*–they need in order to perform music in a way that rings true for them. Every one of the students I teach is unique. I need to work with each one of them in ways that develop independent thinking, because it's the independent thinking that encourages a student's unique and wonderful musical voice to emerge. If our ultimate goal is to train a student to play a piece the way someone else plays it, we may as well just listen to a recording.

When I hear a student performing, I'd rather hear something I haven't heard before. I want to hear what the performer can do with the musical message the composer has given us. I want to hear something that the performer authentically believes in.

49

Memorization can Usually be a By-Product

Like a bull who thinks that the matador's red cape is really the issue, it's easy for us to get distracted and think that memorizing pieces needs a lot of attention and effort. But when a student's daily practice diet includes listening to the recording and reviewing repertoire, the memorization usually takes care of itself. I've only had to help students memorize a piece on the rarest of occasions. Even then, they only needed miniscule amounts of assistance.

There are many things in daily life that people memorize without effort, such as words to pop songs and television commercials, names of people in church, recipes of frequently made dishes, phone numbers of people often called, and baseball statistics. These things get memorized through living with them and working with them. The same is true of music. As my violin-teaching colleague Ed Kreitman once said, "I've never had a student *not* learn the notes." In some ways, he was stating the obvious–in twenty years of teaching, it has certainly been my experience as well. In other ways he was pointing to an important fact that we can overlook as easily as we might continue to hunt for the keys that are lying on the table right in front of us. We don't need to spend lesson and practice time working on something that's going to happen on its own.

It's not that we teachers are lazy, it's just that our job requires us to spend that valuable lesson time on the things that really count–*especially musical expression and the skills that feed it.* It's the old "Give a man a fish and he eats for a day; *teach* him how to fish and he eats for life." Of course, teachers do tweak notes here and there, and we often preview certain spots when a student begins to study a piece. But memorization is not something we have to approach directly because it's usually a by-product of listening to the recording, focusing on skills, and working with–"*playing* with"–a piece of music. So, I'm not lazy, I'd just rather let the process do the work it's going to do anyway.

Besides, no matter how long a lesson, it seems that there's never enough time to fit in all of those meaningful things, especially when you realize that one of the most important things to fit into a lesson is a sense of calm–a sense, perhaps, that nothing much is happening...even though it is.

And that sense of calm, that freedom from worry, is the biggest reason I don't attempt to teach students how to memorize a piece. Since they'll memorize it whether I attempt to teach them how to or not, instructions I might give them would just end up being worry-coated globs of useless information cluttering their minds–obstacles for them to trip over. I'd rather leave a clear path that allows them to go directly to the music and gives them room to dance.

I don't even really talk about memory with students who are just learning to play Suzuki's "Twinkle Variation A." Like many teachers, I teach the "Bread Song" and the "Meat Song," which are the necessary ingredients for making a "Twinkle Sandwich" (i.e. "Variation A," which is a "Bread Song" followed by two "Meat Songs," followed by another "Bread Song.") But I don't tell the students about the sandwich.

I tell their *parents.* Although beginning students can understand the form of the entire sandwich, I prefer to keep that information away from them because as soon as they get it, they almost always want to play the entire variation, *but their physical skills are usually not up to the job.* Their powerful urge to play the whole sandwich makes it difficult for them to spend lesson time working on developing a comfortable approach with the instrument, bowing skills, and SOUND. These are *enormous* projects that usually take several months to become easy.

But I find it useful for parents to know the form. Then they can structure their practices so that the student plays the parts in order. In other words, they practice the "Bread Song"…then the "Meat Song"…then another "Meat Song"…and then the "Bread Song" again. After each song, they take a brief break to re-organize the bow hand, violin balance, body balance, etc. Parents walk their children through the piece every day, but the children don't know they're doing it. Through a combination of this kind of practice, listening to the recording, and attending group classes and concerts, beginning students eventually come to a lesson and delightfully announce, "Mr. Sprunger, I can play what's on the CD!" It happens the same way that they memorize rhymes and stories–not because we tell them to, but just because it does.

Their discovery usually comes right about the time that they are physically ready to play the entire song. For students who don't discover the form on their own, I just wait, and only on rare occasions do I teach them about "The Sandwich." There's still usually plenty of other things to work on that have a higher priority, since the memory will happen whether we work on it or not. It's not a big deal. I definitely want to wait to tell them the form until they've mastered each of the smaller sections. If I tell students the form too early, I rob them of their delight at its discovery. I don't want to steal that delight from them, because it will likely feed their interest in "figuring things out" in other pieces.

From there on out, most students learn their pieces without knowledge of the form of what they're playing. Knowledge of form, however, is a useful thing for advanced players to know about, so I will often talk to the younger students about form *after* they have learned pieces. Then form becomes not something they have to remember, just something they know about…and a concept that they have stored in their toolkits as they approach more advanced pieces.

The Martini *Gavotte*, found in *Volume Three* of the *Suzuki Violin School* isn't one of those "more advanced" pieces, but many people think it is. In workshops and master classes, I've encountered many students whose parents and/or teachers have attempted to teach them the form of the piece–often in rather complicated language–but who still can't really remember the form and only rarely can they actually play the piece musically–probably because they have a mind cluttered with confusing information. They're left with a sense that there's something that they need to do, but they're not really sure what it is.

So I work with these students the way I work with my home students. The first step is the one many people skip: playing the individual sections of the piece, making sure the student has a beautiful sound and is musically expressive. After doing this work–and listening to the recording, etc.–the student is usually close to having the entire piece down anyway.

Then, just a little bit of information tips them into security with the entire piece. I tell them that I like to think of this piece as having a "home section." Throughout the piece, there are various excursions that always end up back home.

When I have approached Martini *Gavotte* this way and they're listening to the reference recording daily, students usually figure out the form on their own. However, they often find it useful to have a few simple tricks to help with the memory. At this point they can really use them. I point out that since D comes before F in the alphabet, the D-sharp section comes before the F-sharp section. I also let them know that a ribbon is whole before it is cut up, so the bowings in the D-sharp section are slurred, and the bowings in the F-sharp sections are cut up.

Keep it simple. The child should be able to use the information instantly. If you find yourself going into a long explanation about the form, chances are you're overdoing it. The idea isn't to give the child so much information that he's left bowled over with a burdensome set of instructions, but to give him just enough useful information to help him keep track of where he is in the piece.

The same idea holds true in pieces in which students have difficulty remembering whether they did or didn't play the repeats. Take Schumann's "Happy Farmer," for example. It's possible to describe the form of the piece in a really complicated way. I prefer to describe it as having only two sections, with each section being repeated. But even that information is too complicated to lead with. When students pretty much have the piece learned but are a bit unreliable with the different sections, I just have them stand in front of a window and play the first section for that window. Then they stand in front of another window and play it again for that window. The second section I have them play for one door, then repeat for another door. After that, it's time to put it all together, with the form of "Happy Farmer" being window/window/door/door. When they've done all of this traveling, they play the piece standing in one spot, *looking* at the various windows and doors. Then it's time for them to do it just *imagining* that they're standing in front of the two architectural objects. (If you don't have two windows and doors, obviously you can substitute things like chairs, walls, rugs, tables, stuffed animals–anything you have two of and can place far enough apart so that the student has to stop playing and walk to them between the various sections.)

These kinds of instructions not only help with the memory, but they also help with the musical expression. Playing a section for two windows–which are of different sizes–sneaks in the idea that even though the notes are the same, they will come out slightly differently.

Especially after students start reading, there are some students who have music memorized much sooner than they realize. I make these students go cold turkey. I take away the printed page and ask them to play the piece from memory. Once they get over their shock that I'm being so demanding, their next jolt comes when they realize how much of the piece they already have memorized. It's usually just one or two notes that they have difficulty with. I like to think of those notes as "clogs" that prevent them from getting to the next huge section they already have memorized. I give them the names of those notes, or let them look at them in the music, and then they continue to play until the next clog. At the end, I point out that they missed only 3 notes out of 175, giving them a *very* high score if it had been a test. The next step is to go back to the clogs and practice the phrase for musical expression and ease in the playing. Then memory of those notes becomes a by-product as well. If it doesn't, then I work with the student to come up with a way to remember it.

And then I like to tell them about the time my college piano professor, Marvin Blickenstaff, passed out a one-page, intermediate level piece of piano music and gave us five minutes to memorize it. We hadn't even heard it! We could all go to the piano and play the bulk of it, but there were a few places where we got stuck. Although awareness of the fairly simple form of the piece helped, I found the exercise extremely difficult. But I did learn an important fact: we can and *do* memorize things much sooner than we think, it's just that there are occasional little obstacles in the path.

After this class, I began practicing everything from memory, because I realized it wasn't such a big deal. Along with listening to recordings of pieces I was playing (when they were available) I looked at the music when I needed to, and, generally speaking, it all would eventually sink in. Of course, I was spending a great deal of time practicing. It's just that I wasn't practicing remembering. It became a by-product of practicing other things in the piece.

The clincher on realizing that memory wasn't a big deal was when I was in Japan, studying with Shin'ichi Suzuki, and heard a story about a Suzuki student who studied with a world-famous violin teacher in the United States. Her teacher told her that in the future she shouldn't bother to memorize her technical studies, and she replied "I'm sorry, I couldn't help it." When students grow up playing from memory, it really isn't a big deal for them.

So you don't have to fret about your child learning the notes. Whether you fret or not, it will happen. If you want to do something productive, make sure that you're covering the practice basics–especially the listening and review. These things make it possible for much of the learning to happen easily and automatically, leaving the child free to be musically expressive.

I'm not impressed when a student figures out the notes to a piece, and I tell parents that they shouldn't be either, because it happens all the time. But I am *enormously* impressed when parents and students can set aside the urge to "work hard to learn the notes" and, instead, put their energy into building their children's fluent skills with the instrument. Then the student is not only playing all the notes to the piece, she's playing them with an ease that really allows her musical soul to express itself. And *that's* something to *really* cheer about!

Sound First, Measurements Second

During my third year of college, we developed a problem with ants in the kitchen. I came home from class one afternoon and discovered that one of my three roommates had decided to take action. The note he left on the kitchen counter read:

> *ANTS: Do not read below this line*
>
> ....
>
> *Hey Guys,*
> *I put ant poison on the counter,*
> *Ted*

Since this section is about bowing, if your child isn't studying violin, viola, cello, or bass, you don't need to read below this line

....

In my experience, nothing kills musical expression quite like the early introduction and over-teaching of bow distribution (also known as bow division). I firmly believe in teaching beginners a great deal about bow control, but I have run into many students who are unable to notice what kind of sound they're making because they're consumed with their struggle to "do the bow division"–to play the "short-short-longs" inside the little stickers on their bows. It seems excruciatingly difficult for many of them. Although most of them can do it, their playing becomes much more musical when I let them out of their little bow division cages. In the folk songs beginners play, such as "Lightly Row," I give them a pretty long leash, merely instructing them to use enough bow to get a beautiful sound. Then, instead of using their eyes to watch where their bows are, they're using their *ears* to *listen* to what their bows are doing.

I do believe in putting tape on beginner's bows, however. The first tape I put on my students' bows is a white one about 4 inches long. The first songs these very beginning students learn use fairly quick notes, which they play under this band of tape.

"The white part is *your* yard and you need to play there," I tell them. "If your ball accidentally goes into the neighbor's yard," I continue, "the neighbors aren't mean or anything–you can go and get it–it's just that they'd rather you stayed in your own yard most of the time."

I introduce longer bows slightly later, with students starting at the balance point in the bow and using enough bow to get a good sound, which means that the bow ends up somewhere in "the yard."

For the first several months, students spend the majority of their lesson and practice time bowing these short and long bow patterns on open strings. You may think that this kind of practice sounds really boring, but we use lots of games to make it tolerable.

The beginning stages are where the violinist's genetic code is set, so it makes sense to ensure that the child is well on his way to developing the basic elements of a gorgeous tone: a straight bow, a beautiful bow hand, and a loose arm. Without this kind of groundwork, students are pretty much equipped to use the bow merely to hear whether their left hand fingers found the notes to the song. They end up missing out on one of the best parts of playing–the idea that the bow is a magic wand that can turn the notes into all kind of things. Instead, they end up turning the frog into a toad. In the process, they develop bad habits, subjecting the parent, teacher, and student to the heartache and struggle that come with nagging a child about them later on. So, I like to keep in mind that we're training for the long run. In the long run, everyone's happier if we take the time at the beginning to get the bow arm really working.

With later pieces, it is simply a case of using the "bowing Legos" that the students have created in these first few months. I instruct students about where to start in the bow and which general areas to use. Since they're not locked in with having to use very specific amounts of bow, they've got the freedom they need to focus on the sound they're making.

They're also free to vary the amount of bow they're using in order to serve their musical urges.

When I do formally teach students "bow distribution" it's much later, when they're mature enough to be able to understand and to use the rationale behind it. And boy do I teach it–scales for days! Their knowledge of bow distribution–along with lots of practice with it–helps these students develop thorough flexibility and control. But we need to give beginners just enough to do the job done. They need to be able to get a pleasant sound. Rather than making them use a prescribed amount of bow for each piece they play, we end up ahead if we keep the beginning students focused on getting a pure sound and doing something musical with it.

51

Demonstrating: Pros and Cons

I often pick up my violin to demonstrate during lessons, but there are two reasons it's not my first option.

First of all, most parents don't play the instrument I teach. When they are practicing with their children at home, they don't have the option of casually demonstrating the way I do. Since I'm convinced that one of the most important functions of a lesson is to teach students and parents how to practice without me, I want to avoid doing things that they are unable to do at home. For many issues, I often work with singing, since most parents can sing–if not like Frank Sinatra, at least like Kermit the Frog, which is good enough. When it comes to physical skills with the instrument, I like to teach parents how to "whisper" with their hands, so that they can gently guide and adjust a student's physical motions.

In fact, before I start students I spend a few weeks with only the parents as I teach them this "language of the hands." I know I need to teach parents this language because when I just told parents to "talk" with their hands they ended up *yelling* with their hands. It was much like the frustrated American man who was living in rural China in the early 1980's and found himself repeating very slowly to the store clerk "DO YOU

HAVE FLOOR WAX?" If you know a language you don't have to yell, you can whisper to get your point across.

The second reason I'm not quick to demonstrate is that I feel it runs the risk of encouraging students to duplicate my playing, an impossible–let alone undesirable–undertaking. At six feet, I'm much larger than even most of my adolescent and adult students. The instrument doesn't fit on me the same way it fits on them. So I'm not convinced that the image of me playing is always the most helpful solution. I also don't think it's very helpful for them to copy my musical ideas. When I demonstrate musical ideas, I like to demonstrate more than one. I'd want them to make their own choices and discover what they have to say with the pieces they are working on.

There is definitely a place for a teacher's demonstrating, and I do it when I think it will be the thing that will help the most. But when it comes to working with students who are still in the process of finding their musical voices, I think it's better if we teachers err on the side of not demonstrating enough, rather than demonstrating too much.

Keep Musical Expression as the Target

Home improvement projects–re-doing hardwood floors, for example–can create some stunning results. But things usually get worse before they get better, what with all the noise and the dust of sanding, not to mention the fumes of the finish that brings out the lovely grains of the wood. It's just the nature of remodeling.

The same thing happens when students make the move from playing a piece by going through the motions to playing it musically: the process is often messy. When students start experimenting with shaping phrases or coloring notes in pieces they seemed to have known quite well, they commonly forget notes and otherwise bungle what had previously seemed so completely secure.

Don't panic. What appears to be a setback is actually progress, it just doesn't always look like it. Or feel like it.

Treat the student the way you would treat a professional contractor, the one taking a sledgehammer to the wall between your dining room and kitchen. Stay out of the way. Tolerate the mess. It's a sign that things are changing. If you stand around and offer advice at every step of the way, or if you try to clean up every particle of dust as it happens, you'll annoy the worker. But when taking breaks, both contractors and students usually appreciate hearing how glad you are to see that change is happening. "Ooooh" and "Aaaaah" once in a while. Talk about what really matters–admire their work and effort. Bake them cookies. [For more about why these gestures are particularly powerful when they come from a parent, see section 4, "Listen to the Actions First," and section 22, "Monitor the Emotional Vital Signs."]

For instance, Ralph knew a Brahms *Waltz* quite well, but when he tried to throw some crescendos into it, the bowings started getting flipped around. He also lost track of where he was in the piece, and the rhythm became uneven. I certainly noticed the mess–I'm about as allergic to uneven rhythms as I am to plaster dust–but I didn't mention it. Instead, I simply said "Sounds like you're really thinking about getting louder in this part...Start on the B again and play through it again." After he did that, I said, "YES! This is really starting to get more and more interesting. Do you like it?" He said he did, and I said "Great! Play it again!"

This time through it, I noticed that the rhythm started to even out and the bowings got back on track, so when he finished, I said "Wonderful–you're getting the expressiveness of this part, the rhythm is evening out and the bowings are working again. Do it a couple more times until the whole thing starts to flow."

In a similar lesson, Margaret, a much more advanced student who was otherwise secure with the Vivaldi concerto she was studying, started to stumble when she tried to make a section of it sound like two different people talking. After she had played it once, I said "I noticed that it started to get out of tune a bit and that you weren't quite sure of the notes any more. And I'm guessing you noticed that too–but I'm not too concerned about that. What's really important is that you're thinking musically." Then I added "Sometimes things get messy when you're remodeling, but I'm glad to see that you're making changes."

When you're pretty sure that the student herself is aware that something isn't working, it's generally helpful to briefly acknowledge it *along with* pointing out that it's *o.k.*, because something else of value is happening. These kinds of comments can often help to relieve a child's jitters over his or her unasked question "Am I going to get in trouble for messing up?" Since that anxiety can be a barrier to being musically expressive, I like to do what I can to get it out of the way. Reassuring the student that she's on the right track usually helps.

Now, fasten your seatbelts. After all this metaphoric talk about remodeling I need to abruptly switch metaphors on you. Bottom line: if a child is playing a piece accurately but not musically, the target is too near and too big. In the process of moving the target farther away and narrowing the focus to musical expression, there will be some arrows that don't hit the target. The goal of practice is to make it easier. With time, more and more arrows will hit the target. In the meantime, the student needs support for aiming and firing, not penalties for missing the target. Eventually they'll all hit again.

Nourish Growth

Parents often ask me questions such as "Can musicianship be taught?" and "Is there an age when it kicks in?"

In responding to these concerns, I think it's useful to think about the way in which children grow physically. We can't actually do the physical growing for them, but we can provide children with the nourishment they need in order for their bodies grow. Emotional and musical development are similar. Just as we can't *make* a student feel a certain way, we can't make a student be genuinely musically expressive in a certain way. But we can provide him with the nourishment he needs in order to do that growing on his own.

There are two main ways we give children this nourishment. One is by creating practices that help them develop a comfortable and efficient physical approach to the instrument. The other is by providing an emotional environment that allows them to feel comfortable expressing who they are and feeling the way they feel, though not necessarily behaving as they wish, which is something altogether different. [For more about the distinction between feelings and behaviors, see section 20, "Develop the Skill of Acknowledging Feelings."]

When we parents and teachers provide students with a consistent environment that helps them develop in these two areas, we need to appreciate the fact that changes may happen in small increments–so small, in fact, that it's difficult to notice the changes accumulate. So I like to look for–and point out–even the slightest shifts. Earthshaking breakthroughs are wonderful, but they don't happen every day. Big breakthroughs are usually preceded by a series of small but important ones. They're often not larger than the amount of earth that moves when a blade of grass shoots out.

I also find that it's helpful to look at a child's personality. A timid child, for example, will not likely sing out right away. Forcing him to do so often only makes him retreat. I like to remember the line from the *Talmud*: "Every blade of grass has its angel that whispers 'grow.'" While *whispering* "grow" might seem to take more time, it usually ends up being the shortcut. With more outgoing children, you can be more animated.

No matter what the personality of the child, there's another helpful saying: "A mind stretched can never return to its original shape." If there's a small change in the sound, which means a small change in the musical expression, it's still a change. Tell the child when you notice it, no matter how small.

My daughter is the Bulldozer Queen–why does she act as though she can't wait to be finished? Doesn't she enjoy playing?

My child loves going to his lesson with his teacher but at home he doesn't slow down enough to give himself a chance to remember all the technical details he needs to–what am I doing wrong?

How do you get them to play slowly and accurately–to a "standard of excellence"–instead of quickly and sloppily, especially in review pieces?

Why does the metronome just seem to confuse my child?

How do you help them develop a firm steady internal beat, yet still play musically rather than mechanically?

Rhythm–especially slowing down–is one of the biggest challenges parents and children face. The good news is that working on rhythm skills can be both fun and productive.

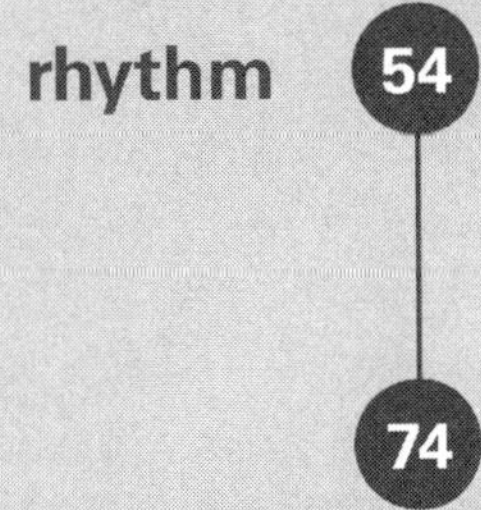
rhythm
54
74

rhythm

54

Two Things to Keep in Mind when Teaching Rhythm

"I did it! I did it! I did it!" four year old Lindsey chirped, jumping up and down with glee. She was right, she had. This was a wonderful lesson to be teaching. It's delightful to see a student excited about learning and making discoveries. I've often said that the thrill of teaching is like playing pinball–you shoot ideas out and then you get to watch things light up. It's especially exciting when I get evidence that a student is well along the path towards being able to play with an even rhythm.

Contrast the story of Lindsey with the story of Henry. It was his umpteenth lesson on the same concept: playing Suzuki's "Perpetual Motion" with a steady rhythm, a decent sound, an acceptable form, and a speed that was slow enough so that it could all be in tune. Too much to ask? I didn't think so, because in various ways I kept asking for it over and over again.

I told him it was really important. I played it in order to demonstrate exactly how to do it. I pounded out a slow, steady rhythm while he played. I told him to listen to the recording several times–every day. I moved the bow for him while he did the fingers. I asked him to imagine his bow arm going back and forth as evenly as the windshield wipers on a car. I pleaded with him. And then, at the next lesson, I did it all over again.

He would play and get the idea for the first four notes, and then everything would once again become discombobulated. His violin would sink and his bow hand would start to look like leftover Jello that someone forgot to put back in the refrigerator. Through all of my efforts, he would look at me with a blank stare. When he looked at me at all.

Henry eventually got it, though I don't know when or how. I'm not convinced that I was even remotely helpful. With Lindsey, however, I am very aware of the factors that allowed her to get it sooner and–more significantly–happily.

One important factor was me. Over the twenty years I have been teaching, I have changed my approach to various things, but especially my approach to teaching rhythm. Henry was a student I taught in the mid-80's, when I was in my early years as a teacher. I gave him the best I had to offer, but I have often wished I could have him back to do it all over again. Like the mother who once quipped that she thought the first child of every family should be disposable, I have yet to meet a teacher who doesn't feel something similar about those first students.

Lindsey is a student I have taught more recently. As Dr. Suzuki told me when I left Japan, "teaching is learning." About halfway into those first twenty years, teaching and paying attention to the results–or lack of results–taught me a great deal about rhythm. I stopped telling students to slow down (did I say telling? I mean *begging*...) and replaced those mere words with more effective strategies. Parents followed my lead and made the same changes in their home practices. During the same period of time, I also studied what other teachers had to say about rhythm, and I studied psychology.

This research has taught me that I always need to keep two things in mind when helping students develop rhythmic playing. First of all, rhythm is a complex subject. There's a lot for students and parents to know about what it is and isn't. Breaking that information into smaller and smaller pieces allows me to craft lessons and assignments that will help them develop rhythm skills in small, manageable steps.

The second important thing? Realizing that if I force myself to wait for student mastery to occur with those small steps–not force a timetable–students build genuine self-confidence as well. I'm not talking about false self-confidence, as in telling a seven year old that he can swim 150 meters underwater if he really puts his mind to it. Maybe an adult can solve that challenge. Thomas Edison, for example, kept doing the impossible over and over again. But I wouldn't hold my breath waiting for the kid. More than anything else in a child's musical education, rhythm skills have the potential to develop the genuine self-confidence that comes with control.

55

The I Can **is More Important than the** I.Q.

Alicia Lepkowski is not a cowhand by any stretch. She's a respiratory therapist who lives in a suburban ranch house. But it didn't surprise me when she said that the theme from the TV western *Rawhide*–"Rollin', rollin', rollin'"–would cross her mind as she and her husband rounded up their three boys, grabbed everything they needed, and moved on out of their driveway to go places. Over the years that all of Alicia's sons studied with me, I learned three useful things from her. The first one was a nifty recipe, "No Peek Chicken." You dump several raw ingredients into a casserole, put a lid on it, and leave it in a 350-degree oven for 50 minutes. About the only thing you can really do to mess it up is to let your curiosity and impatience get the best of you, take the lid off, and have a peek. You just have to trust that it's working. And it does, every time.

The second thing I learned from her was on a Saturday morning at the violin shop, when we were selecting a violin for one of her sons. As we were waiting for a sales clerk, Alicia picked up a parenting book and glanced at the front and back covers. "Oh," she sighed, laying it back down on the display table, "more reasons to feel guilty." It was early on in my teaching career and she was the first parent to open my eyes to the idea that increased information doesn't always relieve parental worry. Like the images in those magic eye pictures, once you are able to see this parental angst, it eventually pops out at you every time it's there.

But of all the things I've learned from parents over the years, the third thing I learned from Alicia–a slogan that she passed on to me–was one of the most valuable. We agreed that it was as corny as it was profound: "The 'I Can' is more important than the I.Q."

It's profound because helping children construct their sense of confidence, their sense that they can overcome the challenges facing them, is a crucial part of helping children develop the amazing talent they're already born with. Sure, kids may come into the world with various traits, but my experience as a teacher has convinced me that Shin'ichi Suzuki was right on the mark: all children have talent. He based this observation on the fact that they all learn their native language. If all children across the globe can accomplish this feat, then they pretty much have the basic ingredients they need in order to grow their instrumental skills to a very high level.

At the core of those instrumental skills is a well-developed sense of rhythm, so it stands to reason that developing rhythm skills makes a hefty contribution to a child's belief that he or she is capable of mastering musical challenges. It's not that understanding rhythm instantly eliminates all technical concerns and the need for practice even though I sure wish it did. It's that an ability to handle rhythmic issues sets the stage for the eventual resolution of technical issues. In other words, the ability to control the rhythmic elements of playing fuels a child's sense of hope. [For a fuller explanation, see section 67, "The Story of Dounis."]

So, the good news is that rhythm skills can help eliminate most difficulties. The bad news is that rhythm skills are more complex than playing the hard parts slower. And there's more bad news. Telling your child things such as "don't rush," and pleading with your child to "slow down" are likely to be as effective as toilet training with the words "It's down the hall and to the left."

I'll admit that the toilet training analogy can sound a little weird. But it's also useful. Parents whose children have successfully completed toilet training–a stage most parents might prefer to forget–know that there are many steps in the process. But somehow they get through them all, as a friend of mine described in an e-mail to our college gang:

> I am delighted to report that Elijah's been pooping in the Big People Toilet for two to three months. Amazing how much nicer it is to have a diaper pail with just WET diapers...Also nice to get rid of those wretched little training potties. I look forward to the time when I can go for weeks without even thinking about my children's bowel and bladder habits (though I suppose by that time I'll be focusing on whether they're abusing crystal meth or something. Hmmmm. Maybe I'll just be happy where I am!?)

Children aren't born knowing how to apply their sense of rhythm to their playing any more than they're born knowing how to flush. They're both learned behaviors. They're not like the ability to breathe, which just happens. But someone who can breath has a heartbeat, and if the heart is beating, the rhythm sense is there–it's merely a question of three basic steps: finding it, refining it, and using it. All three steps are important–a child can't use something he hasn't found in the first place. Anyway, back to the toilet training analogy. I like the way Anna Freud, a famous psychoanalyst who was the daughter of her even more famous psychoanalyst father, Sigmund Freud, described toilet training. She referred to it as a "developmental line."

In other words, toilet training isn't an event, but a sequence of events that starts with adult responsibility for the diapers, moves on to a series of attempts and accidents, and ends with control and autonomy. Anna Freud described other developmental lines as well, for example the "work" line, which begins with teddy bears, has playing with blocks and going to school in the middle, and ends with showing up at the office at 9 a.m. I like to think of playing in the violin section of an orchestra as another example of a developmental line, with many steps happening in the years before the conductor gives the down beat.

You help develop a child's sense of "I Can" by remembering that rhythm skills grow in a developmental line. As with other developmental lines, begin by working on the smaller steps first. Let your child master these micro-challenges one at a time. The sense of competency that he develops through clearing these hurdles gives him the necessary courage to return to the track, and allows him to grow into taking on the taller hurdles later.

If you're not quite sure which specific micro-challenges your child is ready for–few parents really are when it comes to rhythm–be sure to ask your teacher. You'll also get ideas from reading the rest of this chapter. At this point, however, just know that the steps need to be small enough so that the child can transform each individual difficulty into something easy–or at least manageable–within a short span of time. By "short span of time," I mean 10 minutes, which can seem short to an adult, but feel like an eternity to a child.

It's o.k. if every aspect of rhythmic control doesn't happen all at once. It's also fine if you don't know any more than the next step your teacher has given you. It's like what E. L. Doctorow said about writing: the process is "like driving a car at night. You can see only as far as your headlights, but you can make the whole trip that way." Or maybe you want to think of it like that "No Peek Chicken" recipe. You follow the recipe you're given, and then you trust.

Because I believe so strongly in the importance of developing a child's sense of competency, I have a personal teaching policy, my "Fairness Doctrine," which prevents me from pointing out a smudge in a student's playing unless I have substantial evidence that he can clear it up instantly. The exception to this policy is when I see that I can get the student in the neighborhood of the solution. If I can do that, then he can see the success that awaits him at the end of the block. He just has to do the work to get there. It's not usually effective to tell a student what lies waiting for him on the other side of the continent–and that if he will just trust me and continue trudging along, he'll eventually get there. The student's trust in me grows when I give him something manageable, something that he can sense will move him one step closer. In lessons, then, I'm the one who has the burden of dividing the big difficulties into small difficulties. And they have to be small enough for children to overcome them.

There's another way to think of my "Fairness Doctrine:" I like to respect children's blissful ignorance. My plan is to let them have their bliss as we gradually convert the ignorance into skill and knowledge. The end result, I hope, is blissful *competence*. I try to avoid that detour to sad hopelessness, which can make everything grind to a halt, and, in turn make it difficult to start up again and get back on track.

Let's take a look at Kathy, a student developing blissful competence. As we watch her lesson, we see that she's having difficulty getting her left and right hands to work together. But she's content to stop in the middle of her playing–to insert what violin teacher Ronda Cole calls a "thinking space"–to figure out how to coordinate her hands when she continues. She's also willing to repeat this practice over and over. These are good signs. Kathy is not a lazy child, but a child who is working to develop her playing. Until the two sides are working together, it's completely unreasonable for me to expect her to be able to play the entire piece slowly enough so that the rhythm is even from the beginning of the piece to the end. In fact, if I were to mention that the rhythm isn't even, I would run the risk of distracting her from the important coordination challenge she's currently happy to be overcoming.

Pointing out the uneven rhythm at this point would also run the risk of overwhelming her, and an overwhelmed child is neither happy nor confident. The violin and viola teacher Carolyn McCall, talking about this one-step-at-a-time approach, tells parents that even for her, an accomplished musician, "It doesn't help me to be distracted by yet another thing." It would be like a nurse telling the obstetrician "The feet are coming out first, the mother's blood pressure is dropping…oh, and your malpractice premium is due." It's not that the doctor is incapable of writing a check, but at the moment he's otherwise occupied.

My silence about Kathy's uneven rhythm doesn't mean that I'm not aware of it. Kathy may recognize the uneven rhythm as well, but, as is often the case with students, we usually have an unspoken agreement to ignore it for now. In some situations like this one, the child is aware of the uneven rhythm, but has an illusion that I'm not; and this illusion gives her the courage she needs to keep working away.

I certainly wouldn't build Kathy's rhythmic confidence by videotaping her and pointing out to her how uneven her rhythm was. I do like to videotape my students from time to time–usually at a recital–but not to *prove* to them that something isn't working. I think that children usually know anyway, and trying to "prove" their faults to them only damages their confidence, making the whole undertaking of studying an instrument more difficult than it needs to be. When I videotape students I ask them what they liked, which is exactly what I would do if I were to videotape Kathy. I'd let her bring up what she didn't like and wanted to change. If she herself mentioned the uneven rhythm, I'd have strong evidence that she's really ready to tackle that challenge. If not, I'm comfortable waiting until many of the smaller skills are automatic. (A slightly different kind of assignment is to have a student prepare an audio or videotape for her next lesson. That way, she has the possibility of re-making the tape several times. At the next lesson I can ask her what changes she noticed from one take to the next.)

Whether the issue is rhythm or something else, we help build a child's skills and confidence by giving her one–and only one–manageable challenge at a time. Children can sometimes handle more than one thing simultaneously, but they usually do so with a great deal of anxiety. Not good. Playing becomes an experience of "trying hard" all of the time, which erodes a child's ability to be musically expressive. Practice to make it easier instead. We don't want to encourage children to be worried about monitoring all the things that can go wrong. We help them develop their confidence, their "I Can," by letting them work on one small difficulty at a time. Although this approach is helpful with all aspects of technique, it's especially crucial when it comes to rhythm skills, because rhythm is something that must be felt in the body, not merely understood in the brain. As rhythm issues become easier, we score points for the "I Can."

While teachers need to remember that they help children by presenting them with only one manageable challenge at a time, it's even more important for parents, who can have an even bigger impact working the exact same way. Keep in mind that children aren't learning and developing skills in a sterile laboratory. The soil that they are growing in is their relationship with their parents. An important element in that relationship is the fact that children want to–need to, in fact–look good in the eyes of their parents. Overcoming obstacles in the eyes of their parents, the most important people in their worlds, creates a strong root system that can support their future success in the world. I strongly recommend that parents adopt my Personal Fairness Doctrine as their own.

But this isn't really new news for most parents. In fact, hearing the report yet again is enough to make the worry voice in a parent's head–the voice that refuses to go on vacation but was finally convinced to take a little nap–bolt upright like a night watchman who dozed off.

In an attempt to prevent your overwhelmed sense of guilt from laying this book down, I'm going deal with one of the most common set of concerns parents have: *"Why does my child say 'I can't' when I know that he can do what I just told him to do? What do I do? Is it too late? Have I already destroyed his sense of self-confidence beyond repair?"*

When given a new challenge–no matter how small it may be–there are many children whose "I Can" seems to suddenly vanish. They whine "I *can't*" either with words or with actions, and even though the parent, the teacher, *and* the child have had reasonably solid evidence that the child is ready for this next step.

In these cases, I recommend that you silently re-evaluate what you're asking the child to do. As part of this process, instead of jumping into cheerleading mode–saying things like "You can do it!" and "Go for it!"–use a strategy that allows you to get more information about what the child is thinking and feeling. Reflect her feelings back to her in a statement: *"Sounds like you're afraid you won't be able to do it."* Or ask her one of these questions: *"What makes it difficult?"* or *"What's preventing you from being able to do it?"* or *"If you really can't do it, what will happen?"* Then, in order for either of these two strategies to work, be prepared to listen to her feelings and to reflect them back to her. Don't tell her what you think she *should* feel. Just continue to listen and to reflect her feelings back to her.

Many parents worry that this approach merely encourages children to wallow in their fears; that it only helps them rehearse feeling badly. They're right about the rehearsing part. But it's not rehearsing a fear so as to be able to perform it over and over, show after show.

It's more like a fire drill. It's a child's way of sounding an alarm in order to find out what would happen *in the event of an actual emergency*. Children want to know that they're prepared to handle the bad feelings that they *imagine* would come with failing, without actually having failed in reality. We adults can get in the way of a child's preparations when we rush in to offer encouragement and/or insistence too soon. These moves of ours can backfire because they communicate that the feelings that would come with failure are so awful and overwhelming that even we big, strong adults can't tolerate even *talking* about them. In essence, blocking children's abilities to express their feelings can heighten their fears, when what they're really trying to do is reassure themselves that they are competent to deal with the results of failing at something that seems difficult.

We assist children with carrying out their emotional fire drills by helping them find the words that describe what they're feeling. It's not that they don't know the words already, it's that their little kid selves are too involved with the emotional process to hunt for them. They're so swamped just *feeling* the feeling that they forget to ask themselves: "How does that feel?" So we ask the question for them. Then we just listen. And wait. And wait. And listen some more. Skipping the listening and waiting and telling the child to "get over it" is a much easier way to go. But it's not usually effective, so we just end up being ineffective and wasting our words to boot.

Sometimes children appreciate it when we silently wait for them to talk. At other times they get nervous (especially if we've expected them to have instant answers in the past). Instead of working on the question, they get trapped in their fear that their parents will say something such as "Why is it taking you so long to figure this out?"–which may sound like a question but doesn't feel like a question to them. You'll have to be the judge, from moment to moment, of whether your silence or your talking helps relieve your child's worry.

If there's no response, or if you wait so long for the child to respond that the child gets antsy, one option is to make up a story about "another child." For instance, you could say:

> I was talking to a mom the other day who was puzzled during practice because her son didn't want to do anything new–he was afraid that he just couldn't do it. And she was really puzzled until he told her that he thought she wouldn't love him anymore if he couldn't do it. And his mom felt kind of bad because at first she thought she must not be a very good mom if her son thought she would stop loving him. But then she realized that if he felt that way, he felt that way. His mom knew that *she* would keep loving him no matter what, and that lots of kids worry about the exact same thing.

Instead of doing all of the talking, you could also ask your child questions about "another kid." For example, *"A mom asked me why I thought her son didn't think he could do anything new and I told her I didn't know. Do* you *have any idea?"*

Talking about "another kid" may not make your child gung-ho to start on the new thing or to tell you more about what he's feeling today.

But there's always tomorrow. What you've done today is tell your child that you're not afraid of the feelings themselves or the idea that he may be having them. Once your child sleeps on this reassurance, you may find that things go much better the next day. Or the next.

When we've helped children put their thoughts and feelings into words and we haven't gotten any information that lets us know we really are asking for the impossible, *only then* are we ready to go on to the next important step: loaning our insistence that they do it anyway. We know that we have chopped the food into small enough bites, but that they must still do the chewing and swallowing, even if they think it tastes horrible. We use our adult knowledge to know that while it may *feel* overwhelming to a child, it's not. We know that the child will eventually learn this fact through an experience of surviving what seemed impossible to survive.

If you *still* aren't really sure whether or not you're pushing too big of a challenge onto your child, you can always wait until the next lesson and get advice and reassurance from your teacher. You should have plenty of other things to fill your practices in the meantime. You can't go wrong with having your child play extra repetitions of review pieces that he already plays well, for example [as covered in section 16, "Review Repertoire to Help the Playing Get Easier"].

Once you understand this "emotional fire drill" phenomenon (Sigmund Freud called it "signal anxiety"), you can begin to notice that many children say "I can't get this," but then *immediately* get busy working away at it, even if the adult remains silent. Kathy said these exact words at the same time she was realizing that she could stop and put in a thinking space, after which she kept repeating her success. In the presence of a silent adult, other children will alternate saying "I'm *never* gonna get this" with one failed attempt after another until they eventually arrive at the success they were pursuing. These kids just need your silence as they run through their little fire drills, then go back to class. The important thing to notice is that they keep pulling themselves back to the work of learning. Providing them with our silent presence can be excruciatingly difficult for us to do at times, but it's the most powerfully effective work we can do at the time.

When a child is eventually successful, our work is then to say, *"Look what you can do!"* before adding an enthusiastic *"Do it again!"* Or it's also helpful to go with *"Wow! How did you do that? How did you figure that out?"* which helps the child retain the success because he's talking about it. In some cases, you may decide only to acknowledge the success and then come back to it for more repetitions tomorrow. As with any of the suggestions I'm giving you in this book, you be the judge. It's your child, and you're the one who's there. Do what makes sense to you.

I also recommend that you have your own emotional fire drills. In a sense, that's what we've done in the last few paragraphs. In your mind, I've helped you rehearse what to do when the child says "I can't" and your immediate reaction is *"Now what do I do? What if I can't help him develop his rhythm skills?"* Just as there are tumbles when a child learns to walk, there will be times when a parent feels stuck in practice, and it helps to know that you can survive them. Practices will not always go smoothly. I recently heard someone say that if a musician never sounds horrible when he's practicing, he's not really practicing.

A child who is genuinely ready to tackle the specific rhythm challenge you're working on can understand what caused the spill, learn from it, and overcome it. In other words, he can use the mistake to increase his confidence. But a child who does not have the physical skills and information necessary to change his playing the next time around will not be able to do anything except feel bad–distressing if it's in the eyes of the teacher, but even more debilitating if it's in the eyes of the parent, the person who matters the most.

When a child is able to master a challenge a few times, but then something gets out of kilter–as *often* happens–I recommend that you avoid saying things such as "that was wrong." Instead, be prepared to ask questions such as *"What did you notice?"* and *"What do you need to be sure to do the next time?"* When the child then does it the next time, you've got a good example of overcoming an obstacle. You've got another dose of "I Can" vitamins. Yet another option is to let the child just go on to the next repetition without saying a word. If the next repetition comes out just fine, then you can say *"Good job getting back on track."* You might even want to tag on that fortifying question: *"How did you do it?"*

Sometimes children's reluctance to do something new isn't about a fear of being unsuccessful. It's about a disappointment that the new thing isn't instantly easy. This disappointment is frequently served up with a large scoop of anger. There's a very common childish sense of entitlement that generates a huge upset over having to move in small steps. Children don't *want* to. They just want to be able to do it *now*. This childish reaction of theirs is normal–after all, they *are* children. We help them tolerate this disappointment by reflecting those feelings back to them and by telling stories about "other" children who had similar feelings *and moved beyond them*. And then, if necessary, we insist that they practice anyway. These strategies give upset children experiences in which they overcome their disappointment and develop their "I Can!" along with their maturity.

If all of this seems like a lot of work, you're right. It is. But if you're like most parents I know, you don't mind working, you just want to know that your work is going to matter. Let me reassure you that all of the work I'm describing here has enormous payoffs. When you build a child's ability to control the many rhythmic elements of playing, you are building that child's ability to develop and to control most musical skills. This sense of control fuels a sense of confidence.

56

Rhythm is Much More than a Steady Beat

There are many times in our day-to-day lives when we speed up. Here are some examples:

- Running across the grocery store to give Grandma a hug the instant you spot her.
- Swimming underwater as fast as you can so you go the distance before running out of air.
- Dashing down a hill so fast that you can't keep up with yourself and eventually fall over.
- Propelling yourself higher and higher on a swing.
- Challenging yourself to see how much you can elevate your heart beat during an aerobic workout.
- Pulling the cord on a lawnmower.
- Devouring the first few bites of a meal when you're starved.

There are also times when we slow down:

- A sprained ankle.
- Driving by a house that's for sale and checking for the realtor's phone number.
- Savoring a square of chocolate.
- Getting stuck behind a confused person in a turnstile.
- Hustling to get to a 3:00 appointment, but taking just a moment to look at the new merchandise in a store window.

As the above examples illustrate, things don't always go at an even speed. Sometimes we choose to change the speed; at other times circumstances force us. But the rhythms of daily life generally have a fair amount of consistency to them. You may set the car's cruise control to 65 miles per hour, but you do slow down and speed up as necessary. Perhaps you run into construction, or the scenery just gets way too beautiful to zip right by it.

Just as there's more to life than routine, there's more to rhythmic playing than merely keeping a steady beat. Generally speaking, a piece performed with a rigid beat is as artificial and stiff as a park with trees that don't wave in the wind. So it's fine, normal, and natural for a performer to make the artistic *choice* to do things like bend the beat or take a breath between phrases.

Our adult job is to keep track of *why* a child slows down or speeds up. We need to ensure that the child's technique is powerful enough to give him the *choice* to alter the rhythm. The decision to slow down, speed up, or pause needs to come from a bank account well-funded with fluent instrumental skills, not from technical poverty.

So if a student plays without an even tempo, we have to figure out why. For example, when children play through their new pieces from beginning to end, they usually have to slow down for one or more sections. These slower sections are construction areas, so they're wise to slow down. Until these projects are completed, however, it's more effective and efficient to devote plenty of time to repeating these sections exclusively. Postpone playing through the entire piece until the construction is finished. If you do allow your child to play through the piece during this phase–and I don't recommend that you allow it more than once a day–remember that we're all for accident prevention. If your child senses a need to slow down when he enters the construction zone, let him.

For many parents this slowing down makes sense. But parents are commonly perplexed when children do the opposite. And they often do. They speed up through these construction zones. To an adult's mind, you should slow down to avoid hitting the orange cones. For a child, though, the speeding up can sometimes represent a wish. It's a wish to make the difficulties of the spot magically disappear as quickly as you can say "Bach!" The adult equivalent is putting dirty dishes in the washing machine when the dishwasher is full and unexpected company is arriving in ten minutes. But just as adults have to deal with the dirty dishes sooner or later, children eventually have to deal with the challenging spots. The difference between the adult and the child is that adults are usually quicker to realize that the wish was only a wish. Children may need our help to see this reality.

There's another reason children sometimes rush through the tough sections. Their bodies sense a need to gather momentum for the challenge. It's like running to jump on a train. Of course, jumping onto a moving train is something they shouldn't be doing in the first place, but if you're going to do it, that's the way it's done.

However, if your child can prove beyond a shadow of a doubt that he has developed enough facility to play the piece with a steady rhythm, you've done your job. The choice to bend the rhythm is now his.

Rhythm is Flow

Rhythm comes from the Greek word *rhythmos*, which means "flow" or "river." Remembering this origin can do an enormous amount for us as we help children develop their sense of rhythm.

Another useful definition of rhythm comes to us from the Dalcroze Eurhythmics teachers: "rhythm is *motion*." Helping students develop the ease and fluency of their motions, then, is much more important work than merely paying attention to the strict timing of those motions.

We need to see timing accuracy for what it is–only *one* component of rhythm. We focus on helping students develop ease of motion–flow–because it's the skill that then allows them to play accurately with a steady beat. Even if they do sense a steady pulse on their insides they can't really play with it unless they have the physical skills to do so. The same thing holds true when it comes to following a conductor's baton or the click of a metronome. In the long run, placing a priority on nurturing flowing, easy motions enables children to perform with an even pulse; and it gives them the facility to alter that pulse as the musical mood dictates.

It's especially important to value fluent playing motions over timing accuracy when working with beginners. For example, Charlie, a typical beginning student of mine arrives for his lesson after having studied for several months already. Charlie has developed enough coordination to get his violin and bow to say "Mississippi Hot Dog" on the open E and open A strings with a fair amount of sparkle and evenness in his tone. He has also developed the ability to play each of the notes in Suzuki's "Twinkle Variation A." However, at his lesson I don't have him play the entire song. Instead, I work with him on a smaller section of the piece, helping him to prepare his physical balance with each new pitch in the section.

This sequence has become predictable for him, as it is also part of his home practice. He prepares the pitch with his left hand, I check to see that the bow is balanced on the string, and through it all I'm keeping a close eye on the overall balance of his entire body. Most importantly, I constantly feel a steady pulse inside myself so that when everything is ready, I say a very rhythmic "Wait! Wait! Ready! Go!" He then bows "Mississippi Hot Dog" on that pitch. At home, of course, his "home teacher"–in this case, his father–performs my role.

It's important to point out that when Charlie actually does play, the bowing is rhythmic and even. Each new pitch is like a different shot in a movie. So we examine the set before each bowing of "Mississippi Hot Dog." The idea is to get each one prepared so that we end up with what the violin teacher Irene Bozarth Mitchell calls "units of excellence." Another way of thinking about it is that we develop the pearls first, and then string them together later. Stringing them together isn't nearly as tricky as cultivating the pearls in the first place.

Getting to the point of being able to practice this small amount represents an *enormous* accomplishment for everyone involved. Let me assure you that this kind of practice is difficult for both the parent and the child. But it's even more difficult–downright impossible and unproductive, in fact–if you have to spend time fixing the bow hand, the violin hand, and the body balance before each pitch. When this is the case, the time it takes to get to the rhythmic "Ready Go" overtaxes the child's patience. The solution is to forget about "fixing" things and shift your practice focus to repeating the separate skills–creating and maintaining a bow hand, bouncing the left hand fingers, etc.

As you practice these skills you have to keep in mind the number one rule of practice: you practice to make it easier. These skills need to be so easy, in fact, that they're automatic. [For ideas about how to tolerate this amount of repetition, see section 28, "Look for Opportunities to

Play Games and Have Fun," and the games in the appendix.] Even when the separate skills are automatic, we are flirting with disaster if we ask a beginning student to play straight through one of Shin'ichi Suzuki's Twinkle variations right on the beat, right away. If we encourage students to "keep up" with a steady tempo too soon, they actually may get the timing, but their bodies are learning to expect a sequence that goes something like this: note-panic-note-panic-note.

Panic kills the flow that is essential for music making. Worse yet, when panic is rehearsed, it becomes an integral part of the playing. And this panic will eventually become the weed that takes over a garden that should be producing rhythmic flow instead.

Our goal needs to be preparing students for excellence right from the start. It may seem like I'm contradicting that idea when I recommend that you *postpone* insisting on a steady beat. I tell my students and parents that the silent spaces that come with this "stop and prepare" practice are like the tails on a tadpole. They contain nutrition. And they gradually disappear. Just as chopping off a tadpole's tail doesn't help it grow into a frog faster, we need to keep the spaces around until they're so unnecessary that they gradually disappear. If we chop them off too soon, we create problems. We won't end up further faster if we train a student to play one way–with panic built in from getting rid of the spaces too soon–and then hope that it transforms into another way later on. So at the initial stages, I would much rather see a student take time to prepare each pitch elegantly, smoothly, and gracefully than to keep accurate timing throughout the piece. That important skill comes later.

The fact is, an accomplished player will prepare for the upcoming note during the note she is currently playing. It's like the way we walk. One foot is on the ground preparing to leave it; and the other foot is in the air preparing to land. But in order for a musician to prepare for the next note as she is in the process of playing the current one, she will first need to go through a phase in which she learns how to prepare while she's *not* playing.

It can take months for a student to develop this skill. But the payoff comes when practice has made the separate parts easier, and the playing just starts to flow. With transfer students who might not have had this coordination training, it's often the cause of significant blocks in the development of their playing. Unfortunately, it's a cause that can easily escape our radar. It may be an elementary skill, but it's still one they need. I work with them in a way that's very similar to what I do with the beginning students. I may use a scale instead of one of Suzuki's Twinkle variations, but I still talk about the tadpoles.

I'm always willing to wait for a student to develop a sense of flow before working on timing accuracy. I am known to be a fussy teacher, but I like to think that I'm fussy about the things that really matter. When it comes to beginning students, I'm a real hold out for ease, flow, fluency in the body, and a good tone because I know that the payoff is astronomical for the student. Investing in the timing of the notes, however, is wasted motion. If the other skills are developed first, the timing comes later and fairly easily.

I know that I'm going against the grain of what many people have been taught when I say that rhythm is more than a steady beat. When I ran into a parent who had heard me lecture about these ideas six months earlier, she told me that she was initially angry and vigorously disagreed with me. Later, however, as she continued to reflect on the lecture and work with her child, she realized how her insistence on timing accuracy was blocking her child's sense of flow and getting in the way of the musical goals she was trying to accomplish.

I hope it doesn't take you six months to appreciate the importance of developing flow in a student's playing. But if you need to disagree with me for a while, go ahead. And notice as you practice how what I've written about in this section can apply to what is happening with your child's playing.

A Few Comments About "The Next Piece"

It's important for a student to be able to play with a steady beat from one end of a piece to the other. I pay close attention to how this ability is coming along, and every student eventually develops it. Before the rhythm in a student's current working piece is completely even, however, I might begin to add parts of a new piece to the student's assignment. Still, before a student is ready to begin working on the next piece, there are a great number of details that must be in place in the current working piece.

The first thing I look for in the current piece is smooth motions. This flow won't happen unless the child has developed the basic skills of managing his body and the instrument. Because I'm such a hold out for these things, I have a reputation as being a *very* fussy teacher. I don't think of myself as a fussy teacher as much as a teacher who believes that every child I work with is capable of playing really well. I'm willing to wait until genuine skill and ability bloom in these areas. If a student comes to me and can't make a functioning bow hand, or effectively balance the violin–or even stand in one place calmly–we need to work on these issues until they're easy. Until we do, it's unfair to expect a child to move on to the work of bringing these skills together to produce a pure tone on the instrument.

This work can sometimes take an incredible amount of time, and the most difficult part of it for me is helping parents manage the jitters that come with it. I have no qualms that the student will eventually be able to develop real skill and ability with the instrument. But I often worry that the parent's lack of trust of either me or the process–or sheer *exhaustion* with it all–will make lessons come to a halt before the student gets a glimpse of the amazing things that he is capable of. The middle of the process typically sees a downturn in the child's enthusiasm, which compounds the parent's worry. But once the child sees what he can do, the enthusiasm level pops back up. Until it does, however, that parental uneasiness and uncertainty is one of the major reasons I judiciously overlook some technical issues–even though my perfectionist streak would like to see everything perfect before moving on. I make myself fudge wherever I can. The evenness of the rhythm is one of those places.

While the rhythm might not yet be completely even, the student must be able to get a clear tone on pretty much every note. By clear tone, I *don't* necessarily mean playing in tune, although the piece must be relatively in tune, and my standards for what constitutes "relatively in tune" increase as the student continues to progress. What I *do* mean by "clear tone" is that the sound is free from blemishes and scratches. It rings. This is a very difficult concept to describe in words, but your teacher can help you with it.

Finally, the child isn't ready to move on to the next piece until he knows all of the notes and bowings *without prompting from me or a parent*. If the student hasn't practiced the notes and bowings enough to develop fluency with them, then his playing won't have those smooth, flowing motions I keep talking about in this chapter. And if the student practices and practices but doesn't listen to the reference recording daily, he's lacking the one thing that could help him the very most [For more information about the importance of listening, see section 14, "Listen to Recordings."]

If a student is very clear about what notes come next, but simply has to stop and prepare for certain sections, or slow down a bit, I'd *consider* moving on to the next piece. If some areas of the piece need more repetition than would come from daily review, however, then we can't go on. I treat those spots as construction areas. They need extra time and attention, and at lessons I work with them separately, assigning the student to do the same thing at home.

Oh, one other thing. It also almost goes without saying, but I wouldn't move a student on to the next piece unless review is a normal, routine part of daily practice. Anything less robs the child of the opportunity to discover his musical powers.

But if all of these things are in place–except rhythmic evenness–I feel that the student is ready to begin previewing the next piece.

These fledglings actually do end up playing with a great amount of timing accuracy, not just a vague rhythmic flow. However, I wait to say much about keeping a steady beat until they are pretty secure in their technical skills and I have added stepping and playing review pieces to their assignments [as outlined in section 62, "Stepping and Playing with the Pulse"]. Until that time, however, I sometimes tell students to think about the evenness of windshield wipers going back and forth, or the steady drip of a leaking faucet. Or the "drip drip drip of the raindrops"–to quote the opening of Cole Porter's "Night and Day." If these sorts of images do the trick, that's wonderful. If they don't, then I know that playing with a steady beat is going to be more of a project. It's not just a question of installing a new fan belt, but of building of an entire transmission. So I postpone work on the timing issue until the flow is really developed. You can't buy that timing; you have to build it. And it won't cost you in dollars; it will cost you in time.

Activities for Developing Rhythm Skills

When a student has acquired a fair amount of repertoire and developed reliability with technical skills, I introduce the ideas of slowing down and playing with the beat. I mean *really* playing with the beat. Before this time, however, there are lots of preparatory activities you can weave into lessons. I almost never do these kinds of exercises during individual lessons, but they figure into nearly every group lesson I teach. Please keep in mind that it will probably take you a while to learn how to do these exercises, but once you learn them, just like learning a swimming stroke, you can work them into the flow of your practices.

And, by the way, when leading these activities becomes automatic for you, you can use them to buy yourself time to think about what you can do next [see section 31, "Have Strategies for Buying Yourself Time"]. These exercises and games also have the advantage of giving students a break during practice. Those who normally sit–cellists, guitarists, and pianists–get a chance to move around; and those who normally stand–violinists, violists, and flutists–get to sit down.

Rhythm is motion, so all of these exercises involve physical motion. The first one is really simple. You play a recording and keep the beat with the music. Choose everything from pop music to music that is hundreds of years old. Ideas include recordings by artists such as Rosemary Clooney, Gil Shaham, Ricky Martin, Elvis Presley, Yo Yo Ma, and Leonard Bernstein. Use what's handy–pull stuff out of the bins at the library. And when keeping the beat, look for motions that don't make sounds, such as shaking your hands in the air, touching your knees or your shoulders, raising your eyebrows, and waving your elbows like a very rhythmic chicken.

When I do this exercise in group class, the students copy my motions. Occasionally, I've had students do the leading, but they are often either too shy or too silly for it to be useful. But check and see. If you're not doing it in a group, your child might be able to focus on inventing motions that keep the beat instead of getting lured into coming up with the silliest possible gesture. I also suspect that some children might relish doing this in a group, but be bashful to do it by themselves with their parents. If this is the case with you and your child, it's probably not because you're too intimidating or because your child is holding back. Think about how people yell and cheer at a ball game when part of a crowd, but are hesitant to do it all alone. It's the same idea. Don't force it. Move on to something else.

Another activity is having a student play an *easy* review piece with the reference recording and the simple instruction "Stop and start whenever you feel like it." It's helpful to start out with an instruction like this one, so that the child has as much control as possible. However, you may find that it works better if you tell your child to stop playing with the recording when you touch her head and then start again when she senses that she is able. Joining the recording can be a bit like jumping on a moving merry-go-round–the student has to get her inner pulse moving with the music first, then jump in when she feels she can. Teachers often do many variations of this "On/Off" game in group classes.

There are other exercises that can be done with simple, rhythmic instructions from the adult. For example,

(NOTE: I've only written out the rhythm so that **you** *know how to give the instruction rhythmically–don't show it to your child.)*

Change the speed at which you deliver the instruction, and notice how the child "catches" the beat. By the way, if your child is having difficulty catching the rhythm, the first place to investigate is the rhythmic quality of your delivery. Make sure it's perky, energetic, and clear. A next step with this is to say

and the child then claps:

Again, the child will likely have absorbed the beat in your instructions. After that is working well for the child, you can move to "Ready, set, clap to eight." I generally don't go past eight, though. Too complicated.

Doing these "Ready, set..." games is an excellent time to introduce a concept that conductor Karla Philips refers to as "Magic Lips." In other words, have the child mouth the words. It helps if you encourage children to exaggerate the lip motions. "Magic Lips" help kids keep track of where they are. And since it's pretty easy to lip-read exaggerated numbers, "Magic Lips" also help you see where a child gets confused–some children start counting at the wrong place, for example. However, as a general rule, don't offer a child a lot of explanation if you see that she is engaged in figuring it out. Give it several goes and see if she's getting closer and closer in her approximations. If she is, an explanation will likely turn her off. You'll move yourselves towards a much happier practice session if you can offer her a remark like "I'm glad to see that you're working to figure this out." Another option is to offer her the choice of your assistance, as in "Would you like an idea about how to do this?"

My violin students generally seem to enjoy doing these exercises. I think the fact that they get to sit down is one of the biggest reasons. They feel like they're getting a break. I feel like we're really getting some useful skills developed. For these reasons alone, they are useful exercises to work into a practice.

60

Early Uses of the Metronome

A metronome is as indispensable for a musician as a ruler is for an architect. However, both tools have limited use. While it's crucial that students eventually learn the skill of playing with a metronome, the piano teacher Hans Boepple notes that "metronomes don't teach rhythm any more than using a ruler teaches you to draw a straight line." What metronomes can do is help you organize the learning process.

I don't encourage students to play with a metronome until they can really sense the pulse in their bodies. I know that they have this sensitivity when they can step and play their pieces [as outlined in section 62, "Stepping and Playing with the Pulse"]. Until this ability is fully developed, however, there are some helpful places to use the metronome during lessons and practices.

Before a student is formally playing with a metronome, I sometimes use it as a tool to help home practices go smoother. In other words, I think of it as an argument stopper. For example, at William's lesson I asked him to play the beginning of his piece slower than he had been playing it. Suddenly, everything worked. As commonly happens in situations like this one, his mother said "I *told* him to play it that slowly this week, but he wouldn't listen to me." So out came Mr. Metronome.

But rather than have William play with the metronome, I had him *sing* with the metronome. Next, I *turned off* the metronome and gave William the instruction: "sing it inside at that speed while you play it." William couldn't sustain the slower speed for the entire piece, but did quite well for the first part. So I just had him play the first phrase of the piece. After this worked well a few times, I noted the setting on the metronome, and his mother wrote it down in her notes. William's assignment for the week was to sing with the metronome at that setting, turn it off, and then play the first phrase while singing inside what he had just sung out loud. It's one step removed from the parent telling the child to slow down–it's "Mr. Metronome" that's dictating the speed. Often, it can be enough of a difference to keep the parent-child practice relationship positive.

Another early use of the metronome–which doesn't involve having the child play along with it–is doing games similar to the ones I outlined in the previous section. I usually start by turning on the metronome to a reasonable speed–112, for example–and then saying, right with the metronome

Read- y! Set! Clap to four!

This is a good way to introduce the metronome, but the students' clapping generally makes too much noise for them to hear the metronome. So, I very quickly move into "Clap for four; shake for four" in which students clap four times–perhaps too loudly to hear the metronome–and then shake their hand in the air four times, like this:

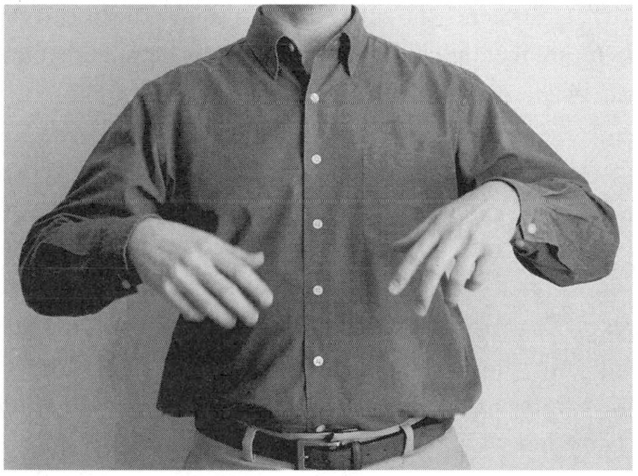

When they are shaking their hands, they can hear the metronome's beat and join it. They "Clap for four; shake for four" about six to eight times in a row before I stop them. From one round to the next, you can change the metronome setting. I often let students pick a setting between 60 and 200. Since students usually want to do it outrageously fast, we often take turns: "You pick one speed, then I'll pick the speed of the next round."

Of course, since rhythm is motion, the shaking is just as valuable as the clapping. After all, the sound of the clap isn't the rhythm. The rhythm is the *motion* you use to make the clap. The sound is merely a byproduct. Instead of having the students shake their hands, you could give them another way to move silently–for example, they could flap their arms, moving their elbows like a chicken. "Magic Lips" can really help with this exercise, by the way [see page 214].

A slightly more advanced version of these games involves using the bow. Violinists and violists can hold their bows in front of their bodies, perpendicular to the floor, and can use instructions such as "Bow for four; wait for four." Further variations could actually involve playing open strings, with instructions such as "Play for four; wait for four."

As you can see, there are many early uses of the metronome–fun ones–that don't actually involve playing *with* the metronome. However, they do put the child in nourishing situations. Even though you don't necessarily see the benefits right away, consistent exposure to rhythmic nutrients means that the child's rhythm skills are getting what they need in order to blossom later on.

Slowing Down is as Difficult as it is Important

Linda was playing through her piece way too fast for her confused fingers to keep up. "Your fingers are eager little puppies that *want* to learn the tricks you're trying to teach them," I told her, "but they need a little more time to figure out what to do." Then I told her to *sing* the piece slower– "and give those cute little puppy-fingers time to do what they know how to do." She did sing it slower. She got lost. She's typical.

As students often will do when given the opportunity, one boy summed the matter up concisely and honestly when I asked him why playing slowly was so difficult: "I lose my spot," he said.

Try it. Ask a student to sing something as slowly as you think he would benefit from practicing it. More likely than not, he will get lost. The reason is simple. Just as you have to be able to *imagine* an orange if you want to draw one, a student has to be able to *imagine* a piece slowly in order to play it slowly. In other words, the student has to be able to *sing* a piece slowly in order to be able to *play* it slowly. Sometimes the singing can be out loud–which helps the parent or teacher know what the child is singing on the inside. And sometimes the singing is "inside." In other words, as I tell children, "You sing it, but you turn off the speakers."

So until a student can step the pulse and play pieces in his repertoire [as outlined in section 62], I usually only work on the fraction of the piece he can sing slowly. I work this way because helping him grow fluency and ease takes priority over getting through the entire piece. Of course students do eventually learn the entire piece. But I only look for excellence in one small, manageable chunk at a time. Actually, I think in micro-chunks.

In addition to difficulties conceiving the piece slowly, there's another issue that makes slowing down difficult. It's the challenge of controlling slow movements. It's a bit like trying to ride a bike really, *really* slowly. Or to dribble a basketball much slower than usual. Some things just have a minimum speed that they need to go. For a string player, I'm talking about the bow. In fact, sustaining a bow stroke for the longest time possible–30 seconds or more–is one of the most ultra advanced exercises that an artist-level player can do. It's excruciatingly difficult. It's like breath control for a singer. Slowly sing all of "Twinkle, Twinkle, Little Star" in one breath and you'll get a sense of the difficulty a string player faces in slowing down. If you do the same thing using only 25% of your lung capacity you'll start to understand what a young string player with a short bow and short arms is up against in the slowing down department.

This difficulty with physical control is an important one to understand. Once in a while, I hear young string players struggle in performance because a well-meaning piano accompanist slowed down to make it "easier" for the student. But it just made it more difficult because these students either ran out of bow or struggled to control it.

But even though it's difficult for a child to slow down his bow arm, it's sometimes exactly what the fingers in his other hand need in order to keep up. Sometimes it's even what the bow hand needs.

Many parents understand why slow practice is important; and they may even understand why it's difficult. But when they ask their children to play a piece–or just a section of a piece–slower, they find themselves confused and irritated with what often comes next: the child repeats it at the exact same speed. When you sense the curtain rising on this familiar drama, the first thing you can to do to re-write the play is to remind yourself that slowing down a section of a piece is a process. Your awareness will do wonders for creating a calmer scene. Then you can use one of several options for helping your child slow down.

One is to say "Now play it *even slower* than that." (Watch your tone of voice here–it should convey "Yes, that was slower, you're right, you got it, now do it *even more...*" and *not* "THAT WASN'T SLOWER, WHO ARE YOU KIDDING, REALLY MAKE IT SLOW THIS TIME!") Keep repeating "Now play it *even slower* than *that*" until the child really slows down enough. This strategy gives the child the benefit of the doubt–maybe he really did think it was slower–at the same time that it insists "that wasn't enough...*more*!"

Another option is to ask a question such as "How do you know that was slower?" This kind of question can sometimes mine amazing bits of information you were unaware of.

If you're not down to your last good nerve, another route you can take is ignoring the fact that it wasn't slower and simply repeating your original instructions. Sometimes a child may *want* to slow down but not be able to right away. He may need several repetitions to figure out a way to get slower. Issuing a verbal penalty for not immediately solving the challenge won't help him with the task. But the repetitions may.

You may begin to notice that in the process of slowing down, your child gets confused and starts to forget notes. Don't scold her for that. Congratulate her for slowing down. Empathize with her frustration, *and forge onward!* If you're really concerned about the forgotten notes, you can have her alternate between playing the section at the speed she's used to, and playing it slowly. This back and forth usually helps to transfer the notes into the slow version.

Once your child can play the section slowly, the next step is to repeat it at the slow speed. If it takes a long time to get your child to slower, you may have to wait until the next day's practice for this step. And even then, you may have to repeat the steps for getting the section slower.

But once your child can repeat a section slowly, ask him if it's getting easier. It might not at first. There's a good reason for this. When students slow down, they often discover scratches and dents in their playing that they didn't notice–couldn't, in fact, notice–when zipping right through. Noticing all of these things can send focus in lots of erratic directions before students are able to zero in on one thing again.

While this approach, founded on kind steadfast insistence, works with many children, with others it just becomes a battle of wills. The parent keeps telling the child to slow down, and the child keeps playing at the same speed. Irritating, yes, but still not a hopeless situation. One way to think about it is that while the child may not be learning to slow down, she may be developing other skills because she's at least repeating the piece. But my concern in this situation is that she may be developing bad habits that will be difficult for her to unlearn, which is why there are still other possible approaches.

You can lay out dominos on the floor, having a child touch a domino every time she sings a note in the phrase. Then have her repeat these steps several times, gradually moving the dominos further and further apart. Eventually it will take so long to get from one domino to the other that the child will be forced to slow down.

Another option is to explain to children why slow practice is so important. I do a fair amount of talking during lessons–I'm certainly a talkative kind of guy, and I *enjoy* talking–but when it comes right down to it, I'm generally quite skeptical about the benefit of verbal explanations. Sure, I explain things to students all the time, but I'm convinced that the explanation is often more useful for the parent and me than it is for the child. It ends up being a way that I clarify for us adults what is important about the next activity in the lesson. When it comes to kids, though, *action* is where it's at. It's not that I'm opposed to explanations, it's just that I don't count on them working effectively.

Having said my piece about explaining things to kids, I now offer some of the ways that I explain to kids why slow practice is so helpful.

I sometimes compare slow practice to a basketball game or a soccer game, pointing out that it would be much easier to score points if all of the other players would just go in slow motion so that you could aim carefully and send the ball exactly where it needed to go.

It's even more effective if an adult asks a child questions about these kinds of things, such as "What would make basketball easier?" "What would happen if everyone on the soccer field moved in really slow motion?" And "What if you had a second chance at all the shots you missed AND it was in slow motion?" This last question is a good one for suggesting the power of repetition.

The basketball image is also useful in terms of letting kids know that you understand that slowing down can sometimes make things more difficult. Dribbling and throwing a ball are two examples of actions that just don't work when you try to slow them down past a certain point.

I also like to point out another encouraging difference between sports and music. In an activity like baseball, you're not allowed to play the same game over and over. But with music, you can play the same piece over and over. It's called practicing. And you don't have to do the entire piece. You can work on the separate plays in it. What drives me nuts about basketball is that you can't really take time to think when you've got the ball, you can only react, and you only get one chance. You may try to think fast, but it would be much easier if people weren't waving their hands in your face in a deliberate attempt to distract and confuse you. They would *never* be allowed to do that during an SAT test. It's also considered very bad behavior from a concert audience. So, unlike, say, a soccer game, with music you can practice and prepare knowing pretty much exactly what's going to happen at "the game" when you get to the performance arena.

This is the good news: you don't have to play music with people waving their hands in front of your face. You get to rehearse the difficult plays over and over until they are easy. When you play music, you are free to enjoy the playing without hoping that others don't get in your way. You also don't have to worry about "trying your hardest." In this respect, it's quite instructive to remember the quote from the Alexander Technique teacher Patrick Macdonald: "When at first you don't succeed, never try again, at least not in the same way." Practice isn't about working your hardest and hoping you can score even more when you try your hardest during the game. Practice is to make the playing easy enough so that it's nearly effortless, not so that if you try really hard you can get it all.

In addition to everything I've mentioned so far, there's one other strategy I can suggest at this point. It's called "fast slow practice," and it's a pretty advanced strategy. It's not advanced for the student–in fact, it's one of the first strategies we use with the very young beginners. It's advanced for the *parent*, because it can sometimes be as difficult to figure out as it is effective. So your teacher will probably need to help you with this one. In essence, the strategy involves having the child play at a speed that's comfortable for him, but stopping in specific spots in order to think and prepare for what comes next. To use the basketball analogy, it's like dribbling a few feet down the court, freezing the game while you figure out where you're going to go next, dribbling over there, freezing the action again while you aim the ball at the hoop, then shooting. With a young cellist, for example, you might let her sail through her piece until just before she gets to the phrase that has the G-naturals that she's been forgetting for the past two days. During the stop, you remind her of the G-naturals or–better yet–you ask her what she needs to notice when she plays the next phrase. Then she plays the phrase.

One of the reasons this strategy is so effective is because, when it's all said and done, often the issue isn't really slowing down as much as it is getting the left and right hands coordinated. With bowed instruments, in fact, this strategy (also known as "Stop and Prepare") is often helpful so that the child can prepare the left hand, then the right hand before proceeding. But figuring out the optimal places to stop can be a real challenge. Some places are not effective–they'd be like interrupting a basketball player the instant the ball is leaving his hands. Other places really irritate the child. So turn to your teacher for assistance!

I've given you several strategies in this section but I haven't given you a magic bullet. That's because there isn't one. But a combination of the strategies from this section and the different rhythmic exercises from the previous section usually works over time. Like multivitamins, a little bit of this work every day helps children gradually grow rhythmic control.

I hope that this section has given you a way to make sense out of a child's reaction to an instruction to play slowly. If the child can't do it right away, it's *normal* for a child to be frustrated and we shouldn't penalize him for having this very normal reaction. At the same time, it's not an excuse for either of you to give up. Slow practice is often just the thing to help a child's musical powers grow.

Also keep reminding yourself that developing the ability to slow down is one of those areas in which children learn an important lesson which is much bigger than the musical skills they are developing: it is possible for something to be difficult and frustrating at the same time that it is extremely helpful. And practicing helps to make it easier.

Stepping and Playing with the Pulse

If I were forced to say what I thought was the most important musical skill for a child to develop, this one would be it. The ramifications of a child's being able to step the pulse as he plays are enormous. Fortunately, there are only four basic steps to developing this skill:

1
Get ready to play, but wait

2
Start stepping

3
Have the playing join your feet

Do these steps with each review piece, starting with the very easiest pieces first.

While these instructions are quite simple, actually carrying them out can be rather complicated, so I wait until a child has had about two years of lessons before introducing them. When I do finally introduce stepping and playing with the pulse, some students are able to do it immediately; others require several days or even weeks just to be able to get through their very easiest piece. But it's like riding a bike. Once a student develops the coordination, being able to step with a piece is usually a fairly straightforward undertaking.

The following four sections of this chapter address the complications that frequently arise in using these four simple steps to develop a student's sense of pulse.

The Importance of Getting Ready

In the course of doing countless master classes, I have all too often encountered students who haven't truly learned how to get ready with certainty. If I ask these students "What does 'get ready' mean?" the usual response is a blank stare or something like "You know, you're just...you know...you're just *ready*." When I ask a few more questions that don't yield any more specific information, I realize that they really have no idea. They know that getting ready exists, but the ingredients are as unknown to them as the secret spices in Kentucky Fried Chicken.

Just to be sure, I do ask them to *show* me "ready." Once a student has demonstrated ready, I ask him to tell me what he's doing that tells him he is ready. Sometimes students are able to describe what they're doing. That's great, because I can then just add to what they're already doing. I'm sorry to say, however, that many students can't even *demonstrate* getting ready. Such students need instruction. In order for them to really get themselves ready, they need to know the criteria for getting ready with certainty. It can't be "I look at my dad and he tells me to start." [For more about the importance of giving children concrete, pertinent information, see section 29.]

A student who is clear about what getting ready means is a student who has a sense of power, control, and ownership. Teaching him the criteria, puts him behind the wheel, making him the driver of his playing, not a passenger.

I like to explain the importance of getting ready by pulling a rubber band out of my case, wrapping it around my finger, and aiming it at something in the room.

"Will I hit the light switch?" I'll ask the student.

"Probably" is his typical reply.

Then, the rubber band still around my finger, I aim for something far away from the light switch.

"How about now? Will I hit the light switch *now*?"

"No!" says the student, usually puzzled as to why I'm messing with a rubber band, and a bit nervous that I might hit *him*. But the rubber band remains around my finger.

Then I sort of aim for the light switch but wave my arm all over. "What about now?"

"Maybe."

I then let the student know that the point of all of this is to help him hit his target every time. I often add a demonstration on the instrument–perhaps starting the piece by throwing the bow on the string, or by not preparing the finger on the fingerboard, but sliding it all over in an attempt to find the starting pitch.

"Getting ready" means doing everything you can in order to hit the target. Everything, that is, *except* letting the arrow out of the bow. A champion archer will balance his entire body, load the arrow in the bow, aim, breathe.

For string players, getting ready means balancing the entire body, preparing the left finger to play the pitch, and making sure the bow is balanced on the string. I could easily add other ideas, such as hearing the pitch inside your head, placing the bow exactly where it needs to be on the string, etc., *but I'm going for the bare minimum here*. Your teacher can help your child know exactly what specific actions of his constitute being ready. Non-string players have their own criteria for what constitutes "getting ready," and you can get these from your teacher as well. As with any other skill, students who find it difficult to get ready to play need practice until it's easy. Keep in mind that you may need to divide the task into smaller pieces. For example, before working on balancing the bow on the string, your child may first need separate practice just with *creating* a bow hand, then with *maintaining* a bow hand.

Giving the child genuine information and knowledge that he can control and retrieve is an important step towards helping him play with rhythmic control. If he can't really get himself ready, the rhythm train is off the track before it even leaves the station.

64

Let the Student Choose how often to Step the Pulse

I'm happy to report that there are few complications when it comes to having a student step a pulse. Most students are able to do this and most students can find the pulse if they have had experience marching and stepping with a variety of musical styles. In twenty years of teaching I've only had one student not be able to do it–a university student who had about three years of lessons in elementary school as a child, and who ultimately stopped lessons when law school became too demanding of her time.

Sometime towards the end of *Volume One* of the *Suzuki Violin School*, I recommend that students begin stepping with their most familiar pieces. For most students, this piece is Suzuki's "Twinkle Variation A." I'm not attached to any particular words for this variation, but for the sake of this explanation, I'll use the words "Mississippi Hot Dog."

Some students will step one time for the entire "Mississippi Hot Dog," others will step two times for it (Once at the beginning of "Mississippi" and once at the beginning of "Hot Dog"). Still others will step four times for it (At the beginning of "Missis-," "sippi," "Hot," and "Dog.")

Any of these alternatives will be effective. What's really important is that the body–in this case, the motion of the feet–is connected to the pulse. Once students can coordinate playing and stepping, they soon develop versatility with stepping the pulse in any of these different ways.

65

Provide Reassurance when Things Get Messy

If you remodel your kitchen, you're going to live with a mess for a while. And you might find yourself eating sandwiches out of a picnic cooler. Things will get worse before they get better. That's also what will happen when students attempt to have their playing join their already stepping feet.

But if students can get themselves this far, this skill will ripen on its own. At this point, you don't need to provide much, other than a little sunshine in the form of reassuring words. One of the pieces of encouragement you can offer is empathy: "I've heard that many students have trouble with this at first." As violin teacher Joanne Bath says, "always remember that children want to look good in the eyes of their parents." She's right, of course, they do [though at times they can behave in ways that may make you think just the opposite is true–for more about this phenomena, see section 4, "Listen to the Actions First"]. So let your child know what "looking good" is to you. Say things like "I don't expect it to go neatly." Being explicit about your expectations can greatly reduce your child's anxiety, allowing the learning to happen faster.

Most students only get through a few pitches the first several times they attempt stepping and playing Suzuki's "Twinkle Variation A." They get the general idea, but they're not able to sustain it. It's a little bit like being able to stand on roller skates but only being able to go a short distance before falling over. Your only parent job at this point is to remember that getting started is a significant accomplishment in and of itself. You can offer encouragement by having your child get away from the instrument and *sing* the piece while stepping the pulse, then going back to the instrument. It may take several back and forths until your child can get through more than just a few pitches. You may just need to come back to it the following day. Developing the skill of stepping and playing is such a big deal that it doesn't have to happen in one practice session. Share this thought with your child also.

Children who are uncomfortable with having things less than perfect will struggle with this approach, and it's important to respect their struggle. Tell them things such as "I know that it's really uncomfortable for you not to get this right away." You might even want to add, "I'm glad to see you care so much about getting this!" Whatever you do, do *not* criticize your child for being "too much of a perfectionist." Perfectionism is usually fuelled by anxiety, so your criticism would only add to her worry. Your child will gradually be able to tolerate waiting for a skill to develop fluency if she senses that *you* are both willing to wait *and* willing to listen to her frustration and fears about not getting it instantly. Tacking on a disparaging label like "perfectionist"–which she's too young to do anything about anyway–will only prolong her uneasiness.

Besides, the "perfectionist" label might not be accurate. Some children don't really care about something being perfect, they just get frustrated when they can't do it the first time. They become profoundly upset with the fact that it isn't easy instantly. [If you're the parent of a perfectionist, you will likely find it helpful to pay special attention to section 4, "Listen to the Actions First," and section 20, "Develop the Skill of Acknowledging Feelings."]

So give this skill of stepping and playing plenty of time to ripen naturally. Eventually, students will be able to get a bit of the way into the piece, but then the stepping and the playing will come apart. The same advice applies: fortify your child by being very clear about why you're doing all this stepping:

"Play this again from the beginning. The goal isn't to get through the piece. The goal is for you to follow the stepping of your feet. If you notice that you're not with your feet and you stop, great! That's fantastic. It's not a problem if you can't stay with your feet. It *is* a problem if you're not with your feet and you keep going. What matters is that you notice, and that you stop when it's not all working together."

Kids need to know how they can mess up and what the qualifications are for doing a good job, especially when they're working with their parents. You may have to describe it several times–not because your child isn't paying attention, but because your child needs reassurance from you. Children feel much more secure–and are much more willing to do the work–when they know where the wiggle room is.

If you think that your child is still going too fast to get the stepping and playing coordinated, saying "slow down" is still likely to be met with growls. The solution is usually found by telling the child "Lift your knees really high." The farther his feet have to travel, the longer it takes, and the slower the piece is. Yet another option is to ask the child to pound the floor, imagining that he's wearing big boots. Take a moment to have your child step the beat away from the instrument, pretending to be wearing boots as big as the giant's in "Jack and the Beanstalk." Belting "Fee! Fi! Fo! Fum!" along with the plodding adds a nice touch. Then have him come back to the instrument, and continue working away.

Inhibition

It's always a good idea to teach new skills using familiar notes, fingerings, rhythms, etc. With a skill as complicated as stepping the pulse while playing, I first assign my late Suzuki *Volume One* students the task of stepping and playing the first piece they learned: Suzuki's "Twinkle Variation A." When they get the hang of it, we move on to Suzuki's other Twinkle variations. The order is Variation A, C, D, Theme, and then on into Suzuki's *Volume One*, going in the order that the students originally learned these pieces. It's time to come back and start thinking about "Variation B" when they've played a few pieces past "Twinkle, Twinkle, Little Star" and things are going well. When they first start stepping with "Variation B," I usually tell them this story:

"Back when I was in junior high, I was invited to a roller skating party, but I didn't know how to roller skate. At first, I would skate a little bit; then fall over. Then I'd do it again. Eventually, I was able to get around the rink without falling over, but then I had to learn how to stop. The only way I knew how to stop was by falling over. This variation is the one in which you learn how to stop because you decide to, not because you fall over."

I tell them this story because I want them to know that this task is a particularly challenging one. "Twinkle Variation B" is difficult because it contains rests; and rests present unique complications. They're complicated because the only thing that rests is the sound–the pulse needs to be very much awake. Musicians need to feel the rest clearly but not play anything. The specific skill involved here is called "inhibition"–in other words, sensing a feeling but not acting on it.

Inhibition is certainly an important skill to learn, whether it involves inhibiting an urge to play on the rest or a desire to tell your mother about the surprise birthday party your grandfather is planning for her. As with many other skills, learning inhibition can be difficult. So difficult, in fact, that according to neuroscientists, inhibition doesn't fully mature in men until their late twenties. For women who find that amusing, get this: inhibition doesn't mature in women until their early twenties. In my experience, most children are certainly capable of developing all the necessary inhibition for music-making well before their early twenties, but we need to help them do it, and we can't expect it to happen on the spot.

Feeling a beat and not playing–doing nothing–is often an enormous challenge for a child. That's why I wait to introduce stepping with "Variation B" until stepping is going well with many other pieces. There are three things that usually do the trick: just waiting is one, and the other two are following the advice outlined in section 64 ("Let the Student Choose how often to Step the Pulse"), and section 65 ("Provide Reassurance when Things Get Messy").

Once students are able to step and play "Variation B," they're well on their way to being able to go through the entire book. Please keep in mind that the challenge dotted rhythms present students is similar to the challenge rests present. If you're not sure what a dotted rhythm is, ask your teacher.

67

The Story of Dounis

When students can step and play their pieces, I tell them the story of Demetrius Constantine Dounis.

Dounis was born to a wealthy family in Greece in the late 1800's. He loved to play the violin and wanted nothing more than to be a violinist. But his father was determined that his son would *not* be a violinist, and told him he could choose between a career in law, medicine, or the church. Young Dounis was not interested in any of these options. He wanted to be a violinist. In fact, when he was ten, he sold his bike and his roller skates so that he could go to Italy and study violin. His father made him return to Greece.

Several years later, Dounis left home to play concerts in the United States. Once again, his furious father forced him return to Greece. Dounis finally gave up and went to medical school, although he continued his violin studies as well. He eventually became a doctor, specializing in neurology and psychiatry. However, during the last year of his medical training, his father died. Dounis quit being a doctor. He became a violin teacher, eventually settling in the U.S.

He was the first violin teacher who knew a great deal of factual information about the human body and how it worked. His training in psychiatry also taught him about the mind and people's feelings. With all of this in his background, he became a very famous violin teacher, and some of the world's great concert artists would study with him–even after they were already famous.

Knowing all he knew, Dounis had this to say about rhythm: "Rhythm is technique." In other words, once you understand the rhythm–the movement, the flow of a passage–other problems in the technique tend to take care of themselves. They disappear on their own. (By the way, Dounis also used to say this about the goal of technique: "If it is not easy, it is no good. It has to be easy.")

I wait to tell students this story until they have developed the skill of stepping with their pieces, because it then allows me to put words to something that they are already sensing: "Now that you can step the pulse and play your pieces, you'll still have to practice–to make things easier. But knowing where the pulse is lets you control *the one thing*–the rhythm–that does the most to help make playing *anything* easier."

Some people might want to use this story about Dounis as a way to *convince* the child that he needs to learn how to step and play. I don't. *I'm* convinced. It's my conviction talking when I insist that the child does the work necessary for developing the skill of stepping and playing.

If I were to attempt to convince the child, however, I would be squandering my energy. I'd end up putting my efforts into choosing just the right words and just the right inflection, while the child may or may not be putting forth effort to listen to what I'm saying. And even if he were to listen, there's no guarantee that he would believe me. So I'm better off putting my resources into insisting that he works on stepping and playing. *After* he has developed this skill, he's got a basis for understanding and using the Dounis story. He has either already sensed that feeling the pulse helps him organize his technique, or he's very close to it.

The student's ability to sense the pulse comes from moving, not from listening to me talk. Remember: rhythm is motion. It's not the sound your hands make when they clap with the click of a metronome. It's the motion–the quality of the motion–your hands make to come together to produce that clapping sound. Technique is the physical skills you use to produce a sound on an instrument. In other words, technique is motion. Put these ideas together and it's easy to see how Dounis came up with the idea that "Rhythm is technique."

One of the easiest places to see this concept is in skills such as shifting for string players and hand crossing for pianists. They're both techniques that depend on the moving hand having the appropriate amount of energy. It's like playing shuffleboard. Just the right amount of energy and the disc lands on the target. Too much and it goes way past. When speaking of shifting–particularly using too much energy for a shift–the violin teacher Dorothy DeLay used to tell students "It's like parking your car when you are going forty miles an hour. [You] overshoot your space...There was a cartoon in the *New Yorker* some years ago...one of those helpless women looking at her husband and saying, 'You know dear, the thing I hate about parking is that awful crash.'"

Exactly how much energy does the shift of position need? Like the basketball player practicing free throws, the solution lies in repetition, and noticing how much energy it takes to get where you're going.

When students can understand rhythm physically–not rationally–they are well on their way to being able to surmount most technical difficulties.

The Ability to Step and Play Helps Everyone

Even though I have yet to find a student who actually *enjoys* stepping and playing, once it becomes just another thing to do–like tying shoes or buttoning a shirt–students may complain but do it anyway.

This is a terrific position for teachers and parents to be in because it allows us to tell a rushing student everything that was positive about what he just played, and then add "Oh, by the way, play it again and step with it." Since it's difficult *not* to step on the pulse at this point, students quickly get themselves into a much steadier rhythm.

It's a great position for the student as well, because he doesn't have to hear a variation on "You're doing the rhythm wrong," he just dives right into a solution. Even better, it's a solution that he's immediately a part of. It's also freeing for the non-musician parents who often sense when something is a little bit lopsided in the rhythm, but aren't exactly sure what it is–let alone what to do about it. Saying, "Play that again, stepping with it," usually does the trick.

The student may sense that you're having him step with his playing because something in the rhythm wasn't quite what it needed to be, but being able to step and play gives him real power to do something about it. He'll sense that too. It's a very nourishing situation for him to be in.

I think that's why I usually don't get much more than a groan from a student before he gets busy and steps and plays. But I almost always hear the groan first. You can expect it, too. Say nothing, or merely something that agrees with the child, such as "Yes, it's icky"...and then sit there and watch him get busy.

69

Why Cutting Up an Apple Doesn't Work

A mother who practiced with her two young children–and was an intermediate-level cello student herself–attended a lecture I gave entitled "Rhythm." Afterwards, she approached me and said, "I'm finally getting the answer to my questions about rhythm. I've been trying to make understanding it with my mind the end of it. But it's not. It's really a *physical* thing and I have to understand it in my body."

Cha-*ching*! She got it. You can't think about rhythm any more than you can *think* about what it means to be in a warm bath. The thought of the feeling is much different than the actual experience of it.

But it's pathetic how easily we adults can get lured into thinking that if we can just give children the right explanation, they'll have the feeling of rhythm. We get so far into our explanations, that some of us have even been known to pull out an apple and knife in an attempt to explain how an apple is a whole note, half an apple is a half note, etc. This is good intellectual information for children to have, *but not until they have already developed a strong physical ability to sense pulse, motion, and flow* the essential ingredients of rhythm.

And it takes time to be able to sense these things. During a class I was teaching to the parents of students who were to start lessons in a few weeks, a mother seemed to be doing just fine patterning a rhythm on her arm. Then I played through an entire piece. As I did, I watched as she stayed right on the rhythm...then get off of the rhythm...then get back on. When I finished, she said "I thought I had it, and mostly I did–but no matter how hard I concentrated, I kept getting off track."

I stopped the class then and there to point out to all of the parents that Wendy had just told us something extremely significant. We had just gotten a report from an adult who said that it *looked* like she could do something, she herself *thought* she could do it, and she *understood* how to do it. Yet the physical skill wasn't solid and needed more practice until it was easy enough to be reliable.

When practicing with a child–especially when working on rhythm skills–something similar will happen. There is often a temptation to think that if the child seems to understand something but isn't doing it perfectly, then the child is either not paying attention or trying to irritate us–or both. We need to be aware that even with the best of intentions, it takes time for skills to become consistent and reliable for us mortal humans.

The neurologist Frank R. Wilson, who wrote the books *The Hand* and *Tone Deaf and All Thumbs*, made an extremely important observation:

> Twenty years ago we discovered that computers can do things that seem very much like thinking, and we argued about whether they would ever become machines that would be as smart as we are. We now seem to be convinced that we, and possibly our children, could never be as smart as computers are. We have compensated for this anxiety by turning our schools into institutions whose job is to download data into young, empty brains. It is a fatal mistake, because children are not computers.

Just because the mind comprehends something–perhaps even instantly–does not mean that the body can do it right away. Since kids aren't computers, you can't feed information into them and assume that if it doesn't work right away, something is wrong with the chips. With a kid, the chips are still in the process of growing and developing.

As I mention throughout this book, the reason people practice should be to make it easier, not so that they learn to "think really hard." [For a fuller explanation, see section 6, "Making it Easier".] Especially when it comes to rhythm, it is much more important that a skill is mastered physically than mentally or intellectually.

Admonishments and explanations from parents and teachers usually accomplish nothing more than making a child feel bad and worry, because intellectual understanding alone doesn't offer children physical control over what they're doing. Even if children understand traditional explanations about the quarters of an apple being quarter notes, or that cutting a piece of pie in half makes a sixteenth note, there is no guarantee that the information will reach its useful destination: the body. Information about rhythm is not useful if it stays above the neck.

Playing Along With "Mr. Metronome"

When a student can step a pulse while playing nearly everything in her repertoire, it's time to formally introduce her to the concept of playing with "Mr. Metronome." But not until then. If you introduce a metronome too soon, you end up with a student playing away and a metronome clicking; but they're not connected. They may as well be in two different cities.

Connecting with the metronome comes about easily, however, after students have learned to step the pulse, because a wonderful thing happens when they're doing all that stepping: they get exhausted. Playing with the metronome ends up being a welcome relief, *since the metronome does the stepping for them!* It just feels like a handy tool that makes the job easier.

This way of introducing playing with the metronome stands in sharp contrast to the many students I've encountered whose parents and teachers have used metronome assignments like a punishment, or a dose of cod liver oil. These students sense the appearance of a metronome as an adult's way of saying, "See, you're wrong, your beat isn't steady." I want to avoid having students "proved wrong" in the eyes of the people they most want to please, their parents. So I find it most productive to wait to introduce a metronome until students are able to use it as a nifty tool–not a punishment–that helps them develop the ability to keep a steady beat.

There's a strong probability that students who aren't able to access their own sense of pulse and then play along with it, haven't developed the coordination they need to truly join the click of a metronome (or even a conductor's baton, for that matter). As a violin teacher, stepping is the most effective means I have found to help my students develop this sense of pulse. Those who sit down, such as pianists and cellists, will have to get advice from their teachers about how they can learn to feel the pulse in their bodies. The piano teacher Nehama Patkin suggests having students step and sing their pieces away from the piano.

Some students can *almost* play with the metronome before they've genuinely developed this coordination. Seeing them doing this can falsely lead you to believe that they really know what they're doing. But the most that many of these students can do is *pretend* that they are playing with a metronome. This is not a good way to teach integrity–and by "integrity" I don't just mean honesty, I also mean the ability to integrate various aspects into a whole. And when it comes to developing rhythmic skills, having a student pretend to play with the metronome is about as effective as eating a Caesar salad with a steak knife. It's do-able, but can have unpleasant consequences. At best, you just end up being too careful to enjoy the experience.

So I'm thrilled when students have developed their rhythmic skills to the point of really being able to use a metronome. It is a cause for celebration. And when they really can do it–*whoopee!*–bring on the metronome assignments!

And for a delightful variation, instead of just a metronome, use the rhythm features on an electric keyboard. It's much more interesting to play a scale with a "Bossa Nova" or a "Pop Rock" rhythm set at 92 than it is to play with the mundane tick of a metronome set at the same speed.

71

Reading is Reading, not Rhythm

Please don't confuse reading with rhythm. They are two separate skills. It takes rhythm skills to be a good reader, but it's not necessary to read in order to have highly developed rhythm skills. As a prime example, take the African drummers who can perform intricate rhythms, but can't read them.

A subtler example is the rhythms that native speakers of a language have. For example, a girl who is born into an Italian family living in Canada will learn to *speak* Italian if her family speaks it at home. She will learn the rhythms of the Italian language, but without adequate instruction and practice, she will not necessarily learn to read Italian. Me, on the other hand, an adult native English speaker, may learn to read and write Italian quite fluently, but would not likely be able to *sound* Italian, even though I might get very close. I'd get nabbed as a non-native speaker when I tripped on the rhythm of the language.

So in order to read a rhythm accurately, a child has to be able to play it on his instrument. It's like a driver who sees a stop sign. In order for the sign to be effective, the driver has to be capable of actually putting his foot on the brake. Musicians reading music are in the same situation–they have to be able to execute the instructions that the notes on the page give them.

...Ideally speaking, that is. When reading, students' rhythm skills often start to wobble, especially when they're just starting to read rhythm and pitch at the same time. This wobbling is to be expected, although with effective teaching and practice students should ever so gradually be able to maintain an even pulse when reading pitches and rhythms.

They usually lose track of the pulse when they get mired in figuring out what the notes on the printed page are telling them. It's like a math test where you can zip along, answering lots of easy problems until you get to that one that stumps you. When reading music, every so often students come across a measure that's more like a differential equation than a simple problem such as eight times three.

To help parents and students understand this concept, I like to put math problems on index cards. For example, the first card I'll put on the stand might be "5 + 1" as illustrated below:

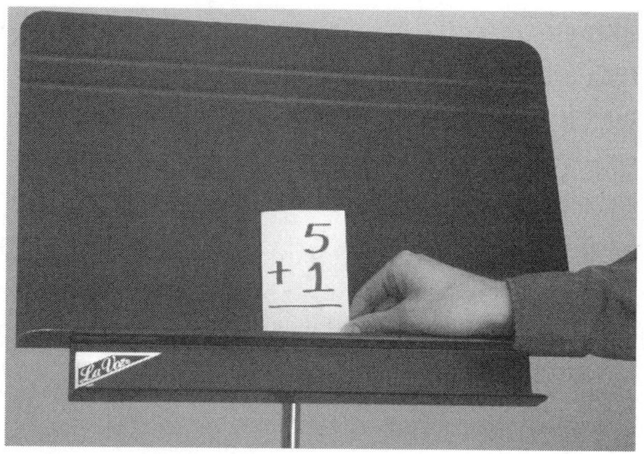

We'll then go through a series of cards, with problems such as these:

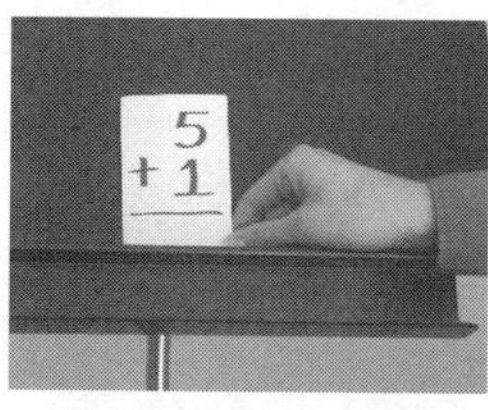

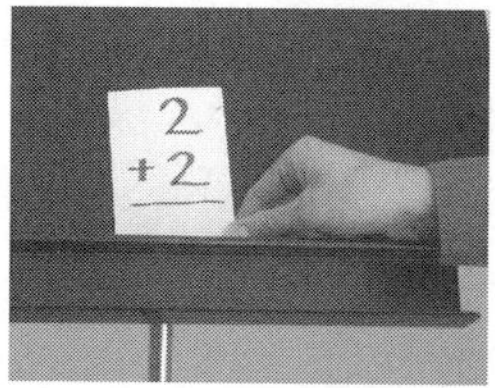

"Simple?" I'll ask the student. If the student agrees, we are finished with that step.

In the next step, I turn on the metronome and have the student answer the problems in rhythm–one answer for every four beats of the metronome. If you were to eavesdrop on a student who was doing the above series of problems at his lesson, you'd hear:

"Six" (beat-beat-beat)
"Zero" (beat-beat-beat)
"Four" (beat-beat-beat).

The student can usually do all of this fairly easily until I start tossing in some more complicated problems, such as this one:

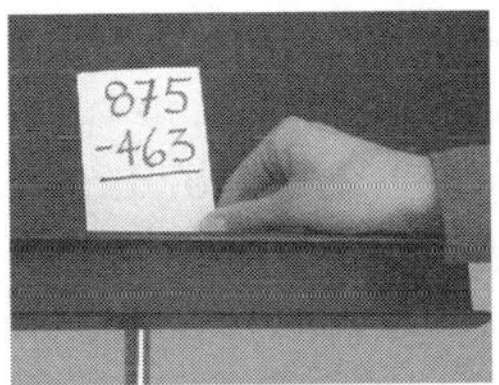

These more complex problems usually take the student a while to figure out.

"Why can't you do this one as easily as the other ones?" I'll ask.

"It's not fair! It's too hard!" is the likely reply.

But if I just put in one problem like that and give the student time to solve it–several times–the student can eventually do the following sequence in rhythm:

This demonstration works well for showing students the benefit of going back and working something out, and it also demonstrates to the parents how reading skills are similar to math skills. Much of reading happens automatically–like basic arithmetic facts–but every so often you get to some notes you have to figure out.

Which is part of what practice is about. Music students have the luxury of being able to practice fine details until they're easy and automatic. You can't practice a math exam in the same way, because you don't really know *exactly* what's going to be tricky about it until it's in front of you.

But when a math test is in front of you, you get to use an eraser. In a musical performance, however, you don't. You can't go back and change your answers. It's during *practice* that musicians get to have what violin teacher and author Susan Kempter calls "musical erasers." You can pretty much know ahead of time what you'll need to do in a musical performance, so a first step of practice is going back and erasing the answers you don't want. The next step, of course, is repeating the answers you *do* want–repeating them so many times, in fact that they become easy enough that an eraser isn't necessary. In other words, when you get to tricky stuff like the music version of 700-89, you make your best guess the first time through, then you get to go back and decipher the rhythm, erase what you had before, if necessary, and then repeat it until it's easy and automatic. Then you're ready to perform it.

(At least you're as ready as you can be. You won't actually know how your playing will hold up in front of an audience until you have an audience, which is why even the world's most experienced concert artists preview their major concerts with other audiences first.)

I can't leave this topic without adding that part of *sight*-reading, a specific kind of music reading, is learning how to do what is affectionately known as "faking." But it's not actually faking. It's really just learning how to make keeping the pulse a bigger priority than getting every note accurate. In sight-reading, it's better to bungle some of the rhythms and miss pitches than to lose track of the steady pulse–especially when playing in ensembles. Since this is the goal of sight-reading, learning to keep the eye moving is one part of learning to read music. There is a virtue in learning how to keep going, and it's a crucial skill for a mature musician to have.

Sight-reading requires quick decisions. It's like aiming the basketball towards the hoop and keeping the game going even if the ball doesn't go in. It's in individual practice that you get to re-do the game until you can reliably get it into the hoop, every time.

Counting Aloud: Not Much Fun; Enormously Helpful

Ask your eyes to draw a picture of what you look like and they will come up with something like this:

Ask your brain to draw a picture of what you look like and it will come up with something like this:

A huge percentage of our brain space is devoted to our face–especially the mouth–and to our hands. When students sing things, they're covering a lot of brain space. They must be, because when they return to playing something on their instrument after singing it, many problems seem to disappear magically.

Counting out loud while playing is another practice activity that helps enormously, and for similar reasons. I've observed that my students hate to do it as much as I do. So I often tell kids that "I have always hated to count aloud." I'm quick to add "At the same time, I do it on occasion because nothing helps with rhythmic reading quite like it." Then it's time for the empathy and insistence: "It feels awful and I don't expect you to like it," I'll tell them, "but do it and we'll see what happens."

This is a slick approach in concept, but actually getting them to count aloud takes a lot of effort and resolve on my part. I'm willing to take a stand that they cross the rapids of this stream, however, because I know that counting aloud helps. I know that they will be able to see the benefit of it once they have the vantage point of having actually counted out loud. My insistence helps them cross the stream.

"Magic Lips"–mouthing the words [see page 214]–can sometimes be a substitute for counting aloud, but there's no guarantee that a student will like it any more than actually counting aloud. It's difficult as well. I know I keep telling you that the goal of practice is to make things easier. It is. It's just that sometimes you practice in ways that make it harder. Then the regular way feels easy. This is one of those times.

I don't have students play and count aloud for everything, only when there's something not working in a rhythm they're reading. When students play and count aloud, they usually realize what needs to change, and then they change it. I don't generally have to say anything except "Congratulations!" at the end. Working with students in this way is a big deal to me. I like to create nourishing and fortifying situations in which the students face challenges that they can surmount if they take a moment to engage their brains and figure out the problem. But I don't do the figuring-out for them–that would be like me trying to give you the benefits of exercise by running on the treadmill for you.

Although they detest doing it, I insist that they count out loud for the same reason we have to do lots of things in life–eat vegetables, for example. Or stand in a 75-minute line for the most popular ride at the amusement park, as the conductor Winifred Crock tells her high school orchestra when they complain about the time it takes to practice. These unpleasant things enrich us, just not right away.

When you're trying to decide if the count aloud battle is one worth choosing, remember that the skill of counting out loud is really useful and allows the child to move into self-reliance and a sense of accomplishment. Then go for it!

My Almost Secret Motto Applied to Rhythm

As a teacher, I have a motto for myself. It's something I almost never say to students, and rarely to their parents, because in addition to having minor concerns that they'll miss the point and think I'm lazy, I have major concerns that they'll use the idea in inappropriate ways as they work with their children. Trusting that you will read (and re-read!) this section carefully and use this information wisely, here's the motto: "If I'm working harder than the student, something's wrong."

Another conviction of mine is that telling kids things–giving them explanations, commands, and warnings–is one of the least effective tools we have for either creating changes in their behaviors or for developing their skills. If it worked to merely tell kids things, we could just record ourselves saying things like "Always remember to say thank you," "Pay attention in class," "Look both ways before you cross the street"–and then have them wear headphones attached to Walkmans all day long.

Much more effective, however, is to create experiences in which children can discover things for themselves. In other words, children benefit more from actually living through things than they do from having them explained to them.

Which brings us to the primary reason I have students learn to step the pulse to what they're playing. We parents and teachers can wear ourselves out telling students "Keep a steady beat," "Slow down," and "Don't rush!" One alternative to these words, pounding out the beat, is also a lot of work. So is tensing up your entire body as if doing so could somehow make the child play more evenly.

And some of us adults–I used to be one of them–do *all* of these things. When we do, we are working harder at keeping a steady beat than the student. Furthermore, these strategies don't really work. So we get as frustrated as the child does, because neither one of us really knows what to do. But when students step with their playing, *they* have to keep the steady beat, otherwise it just doesn't work. Students get the heebie-jeebies when their stepping and playing don't fit together. It's not our words that teach them about the rhythm, it's this experience along with the resources to put things right that does the heavy lifting.

Students often display a great deal of resistance and irritation when I have them stepping and playing their pieces. As far as I can tell, this reaction comes from at least two sources: 1) it's really hard work–especially working out the initial coordination; and 2) it can also be exhausting.

As with working on anything else that's difficult and irritating, I don't try to talk my students out of being irritated and upset about doing the work. At the same time, I don't let them ditch the work either, because rhythm is at the heart of technique in general. I'll say "I know it's frustrating, but it's nutritious," or "This stepping practice is your musical spinach. It's not appetizing, but it *will* fortify your playing." Also, reminding them that the goal of practice is to make things easier, I predict that stepping will become second nature, as did other things that were once difficult for them. Statements like these contain empathy because they acknowledge–instead of deny–how the situation feels to the child. These statements also contain an insistence that the child does it. And I'll admit that they also contain trace elements of explanation, but I don't think of the explanation as being nearly as substantial as the empathy and insistence.

The thing that holds me steadfast during the students' upset is my knowledge that when something isn't working in the playing, the malfunction can often be traced to losing the pulse. I know that in spite of the medicine's bad taste, it's ultimately a soothing tonic.

When students step and play pieces, they are working harder at keeping a steady beat than either the teacher or the parent. Not that we adults don't work hard. *Our* work often involves being able to tolerate the student's frustration and upset over the fact that nailing the rhythm isn't instantly easy and it takes work to get it that way. In general, our work often involves creating situations in which the students can learn, rather than having us tell them things. [Section 19, "Don't Just Do Something, Stand There," offers similar advice.]

The Ability to Step with the Pulse Gives the Student Traction

One winter Sunday when I was eight, we were returning home from church when my father accidentally hit a patch of ice and the car slid into a ditch full of snow. We were lucky that it happened in front of a farmhouse, it was broad daylight, and the farmer's tractor got us out quickly. We were also lucky that my father wasn't driving all that fast. Still, it was pretty scary at the time. And my eyes got really big when I saw my father slip the farmer a $10 bill–which seemed like a fortune to me (and probably was, given that it was the late 1960's).

As much as I hated that experience, I have always enjoyed roller coasters. For some reason, I've just known from early on that roller coasters are built to be both safe and thrilling. I remember a trip to Cedar Point when I rode the "Blue Streak," which, at the time, was about as scary as roller coasters got. But I wasn't scared as much as thrilled.

"So," I'll say to my students, after telling them about roller coasters and the car sliding into the ditch, "it has to do with the way things are prepared. If you accidentally hit a patch of ice when you're driving, that's scary. But if you're on a roller coaster that's designed to be safe, the speed and the curves are thrilling.

I go on…"There's no speed limit in music," I then tell them. "You're allowed to play your pieces as fast as you want, as long as there are no accidents. In fact, one of my goals is that you learn how to play really, really, *really* fast. A slow roller coaster wouldn't be much fun or very exciting.

But it's safe excitement. A car sliding on a patch of ice isn't exciting. It's scary, because you're out of control. So you need to drive through your pieces at a speed that will allow you to keep the notes safe. You have to choose a speed that prevents a wipe-out."

And even though I don't usually count on explanations helping that much, I still go on…"If you're zipping through a piece, the audience will usually enjoy it more if they know you're safe. It's like the magician who saws someone in half. We don't really want the person to get sawed in half, and we know it doesn't really happen. We don't want the show to turn bloody. But we get to believe that it might happen, though all the while we know it won't. The audience needs to know that you won't wipe out, even though it might look like you will. Practicing this section of your piece slower will help you build the safe structure it needs for exciting/fun speed, not scary/dangerous speed."

"But I *like* to play it fast!" a student like Ella will insist.

She's right. Ella *does* like to play things fast. When students say things like this, I need to remember that slowing down a piece can zap all the fun out of it. It's like having to learn to spell "supercalifragilisticexpialidocious," when all you really want is the buzz you get from saying it over and over.

I also need to remember that my job as an adult is to make sure that Ella gets the nourishing experiences that she can't give herself. So I tell her that there's no speed limit, only that she has to stay safe. I empathize with her thrill instead of telling her that it's wrong to play the piece at a certain speed.

I let her have her feelings *and* I insist that she learn to step and play. I know that running down a hill is fun, but if you don't have control over what you're doing, you can end up running faster and faster until all you can do is wipe out. Roller-skating down a hill would be even worse. When students can step and play with pieces, the strong sense of pulse that it develops gives them the traction they need to in order to go lickety-split *and* keep things safe.

So that's the student's experience. What about the parent's? Ella's father usually finds it really irritating when his daughter turns Suzuki's

"Perpetual Motion" into "Perpetual Grating." It's pretty awful to listen to because it's so, well, *grating*. But Ella's father also recognizes that his daughter *feels* like she's playing something thrilling–she's not yet aware that she doesn't sound like the violinist Midori flying through a Paganini caprice at a dizzyingly fast speed. Ella is blissfully ignorant.

And Ella's father, like many parents, worries that pointing out what Ella doesn't know–her ignorance–will rob her of her bliss. He's concerned that if he insists that Ella slow down, he'll drain all the joy out of her feelings about playing the piece. Ella's father doesn't yet know that although the process of stepping and playing with a piece may temporarily drain the joy out of it, like changing the oil in a car, it also has the possibility of replacing it with something fresh that will make things run smoother and, likely, more *joyfully*.

The process goes something like this: Children usually have to slow down in order to be able to step and play with it. Once they can do this step, they can go a bit faster, and then faster yet. If that sequence still doesn't get them up to speed, one way to help them to go even faster is to have them think of the pulse in larger units. In other words, have them step less often–Instead of stepping once every beat, for example, have them step once every two beats. Then, speed that up gradually. The beats are like sticks of gum–they're easier to move around if you can group them in packs than if you have to deal with each one individually.

If this explanation makes sense, wonderful; if not, your teacher can help you. In fact, you should probably ask your teacher if your child is ready for this is a kind of practice. If the answer is "yes," then your teacher can also answer your questions about how to do it.

By getting students connected with the pulse of the music and really sensing it in their bodies, we are giving them a kind of traction, which makes a huge contribution to their ability to control their playing. The more a student has this kind of control, the more the student has the capacity to own his playing, to be musical, and to be secure in performance. Learning to sense the pulse, along with other aspects of rhythm, ultimately helps a student to discover and to develop his own musical soul. It's a huge task, and well worth the effort it takes.

Can you recommend some games to make practice more fun?

appendix: games

A6

appendix: games

The Penny Game

When you have had good, solid evidence that a child can do something if he sets his mind to it, the penny game can be a fun way to get the child to focus himself without your having to bark out something like "Come on! Snap to it!"

For example, say a child keeps zipping sloppily through a chunk of music, dropping several notes in the process. You know that he needs to practice this chunk slowly enough so that all the notes that belong in it have time to show up.

Here's how you play:

Get out a small stuffed animal. Lay out a row of five pennies for the animal, and a row of five pennies for the child. Using specific language that the child can understand, tell the child exactly what has to happen.

If he plays through the phrase slowly enough for all the notes to show up, he gets one of the stuffed animal's pennies. If all of the notes don't show up, the animal gets one of his. Both you and your child have to agree that the child either did or did not get all the notes. If the child says he did and the parent says he didn't, nobody gets a penny. If the parent says he did and the child thinks he didn't, nobody gets a penny.

You can often reinforce the point by asking the child "O.K., who gets the penny?"

When the child says, "I do!" you ask "Why?"

The child will then give you an explanation of what he did to win the penny. Verbal reinforcement–especially the kind in which the child is the one doing the talking–can't hurt.

Remembering that you're not going to even start this game unless you truly know that the child can win if he chooses, don't give in, saying things like "Well, that was a pretty good try, so I guess you get the penny."

No. He may lose a round or two until he senses that you are serious.

He will likely win some rounds. At some point, you can start begging him to please mess up so you don't lose the game. What happens? He digs his feet in even more, determined to play slowly enough so that he gets all of the notes.

Play until someone wins all the pennies.

Don't cheat. If the rule is that he has to play slowly enough to get all the notes, don't withhold a penny if he rushes a bit in one small part of it but still manages to get all of the notes. If his bow slides around a bit, you can't hold that against him either. Stick with the original rules–*think like an attorney, but talk like Mr. Rogers.*

You can sometimes fudge a bit by saying "The rule is, you have to focus on the thing I give you before each round," which will allow you to go from talking about preparing the bow hand, keeping the bow hairs in one spot, remembering the D-sharp, etc. But this version of the game is better left for older students. The principle is still the same: you have to choose points that the child can either choose to do or not, instead of points that the child can do if he tries really hard or struggles. It should be a point that is as easy as standing up or sitting down. You wouldn't say to a child "*Try* to sit down." You'd just say "Sit down," and the child either does it or doesn't do it. Focus the technical points of the game on something your child can either do or not do.

Sometimes students lose because I choose the wrong point. I had thought they could do it if they really wanted to, but it turns out, I was wrong. Even though I messed up, they still lose the game. The consistency and predictability of the rules, in this case, are much more important than whether the child wins or loses. However, it is equally important to *play another round of the entire game, this time choosing something that you know the child can win.* Then stop. Let the child be a winner.

I tend to use pennies because they're easier to find than checkers, poker chips, or other game pieces. Sometimes, when I don't have enough pennies, I'll use whatever I have in my pocket, including dimes and nickels. Maybe there will be six pennies, three pennies, and a dime.

I was once teaching under a tree at an institute in the woods, and I didn't have any pennies, so we used acorn tops. I've even done the game with scraps of paper. Kids engage the same way.

What I have found interesting is that children often forget to take their pennies at the end of the lesson. Others who do take them don't spend them; they just keep them in their violin cases. Oliver once had about 50 pennies fall out of his violin case. They had been there for years–he had transferred them from one case to another as he outgrew his violins.

I'm not a big one for giving students "rewards" for their work at lessons. It's not that I never give students things–I enjoy giving them treats now and then, but the treats are not connected to "how they did" at the lesson. I think the work and the accomplishment of the lesson need to be their own reward. I suspect that what students enjoy about the way I play this game is that it's fun and that it is very specific and they get a feeling of accomplishment that is much more valuable than the pennies.

If giving students these pennies bothers you, you can simply say at the start of the game "These pennies aren't for you to keep, they're just for playing the game, since I don't have checkers." I have approached the game this way as well, and have gotten the exact same results.

One time, when I was teaching in a studio across from a football field, instead of competing with a stuffed animal for the pennies, I had the child compete with the football team that was practicing during her lesson. It turned out that I didn't have to take any pennies across the street to the football players–she ended up winning all of them.

Cards

Many years ago, a first grade boy walked into a lesson, looked at a deck of cards that someone had left behind and said "Oh, are we going to play cards today?" My immediate reaction was to say "NO! We're not going to play cards! Now start paying attention to what you need to pay attention to and stop looking around the room!"

I'm happy to report that I didn't actually say that. Instead, just before I was about to say it, I thought "Hmmm, let's see what we can do with cards..."

What I actually ended up saying was "Yep, we're gonna play cards at your lesson." Then I had to figure out how we would do that. The game that emerged at that lesson is one turned out to be a keeper–I have continued to use it for nearly two decades. It's a handy strategy for getting a lot accomplished in a way that lets children feel like they're in control, but that actually gives me a great deal of ability to make sure that the important things that need to get repeated get repeated.

The rules of the game are quite simple. "Here's how this game works," I'll tell a student. "You pick a card. Whatever number is on the card is how many times you get to do the next thing. If you get a face card, then I get to do the next thing. An ace counts as a one."

That's pretty much the game. Make sure you don't announce what "the next thing" is until the student has picked the card and you see what the number is. You'll need to decide quickly after you see the number. If the student draws a 10, you probably won't want to say, "O.K., play your song ten times through." But you might want to say "Repeat the 'Moon Exercise' your teacher gave you 10 times." Since the "Moon Exercise" only takes 3 seconds to do, it's a good candidate for a ten. When the child picks a four, you can say "Play 'Twinkle, Twinkle, Little Star' four times."

Do not let your child know that you are making up the assignments as you go along. Just act as though you have the entire deck memorized. I've never had a student catch on. Students like the game because they feel like they're in control. I like the game because they are much more likely to willingly repeat an exercise seven times if they pull a seven than if I say, "Do this seven times."

Face cards are particularly fun because students think they're getting a break, but I know that they're an opportunity for me to do some real teaching. Five-year-old Ricky, for example, was having trouble keeping his bow hand together, so when he pulled a face card, I decided that I would make a bow hand. Except I made a mess instead. He was delighted! "No, not like that!" he insisted. So, I tried again, asking him "Please, please tell me what you like about what I'm doing." Even though things looked a mess, I did have a bent thumb. I did this messy bow hand a few times. Each time, I would ask Ricky what he wanted me to change, but I kept pretending not to get it. Finally, I asked him if he would please show me what he meant. He took his time and made a gorgeous bow hand. I took some time to "ooh" and "ahh."

If kids have been working quite intensely, when they get a face card, sometimes I'll just let them sit down while I play. All they have to do is be quiet. If you are a parent who doesn't play an instrument, you could let the child sit down while you play a song...on the stereo. Just one song. The child will most likely appreciate the break.

In recent years, I have been playing this card game by having the child pick four to seven cards at a time. Then we line them up side by side and the child gets to choose which one to do next. The kids really seem to enjoy getting to choose which one they're going to do next.

If there is a face card or two in the line-up, students will often want to go straight to it. I'll often say "You know you can do the face card next, but think about if you'd rather have a break in the middle of all of this." Whatever they choose, I think it's useful to introduce the idea of delayed gratification. Through experience, they learn that it may be better to have a break in the middle. However, I have to say that students generally don't complain if they do a face card first and then have five more cards where they have to do it.

The advantage of having your child pull several cards at a time is that it gives you time to think. For example, the child pulls the cards in the photo on the right-hand page, then chooses the two of spades as his first choice. You respond with:

"Yes…the two is 'Twinkle, Twinkle, Little Star.'"

You chose "Twinkle, Twinkle, Little Star" because it was the first thing that popped in your head when you were coming up with a song that your daughter plays easily. You're buying yourself time. While she's playing it, you think about what you can do for the other numbers. "Hmmm…," you think, "Her teacher pointed out that the pinkie in her bow hand still needs attention, and assigned us 16 pinkie taps a day, so I'll have her do pinkie taps for the nine and we'll pick up seven more later on today…I'll do pinkie taps for the Queen…for the seven she can play the first part of her new piece, since she seemed to have a difficult time with it at her lesson…and for the Jack…the Jack….um…I'll just play her new song on the CD while she sits down."

Your daughter finishes playing "Twinkle, Twinkle, Little Star" and you ask "What did you notice when you played that time?" She tells you that she had a clear sound on all of the notes, and then you tell her that you liked the way her bow floated off the string at the end of the last note. You're off and running as she chooses her way through the rest of the cards. When they are all done, you have her pick six more, and continue.

If you wish, before you do six more cards, you can take a break for something silly. For example, I've got some flip-back books and I sometimes give students the option of "watching a movie" before we go on to the next six seconds. I only flip through the book once–they really have to pay attention, and it takes all of about five seconds. But you can buy a lot of goodwill with five seconds.

Stickers

Playing "Stickers" is a great deal like playing cards. Instead of drawing the number from a deck, the child gets the number by peeling a removable sticker off of a circle, which has a number in the middle of it. Whatever number is under the sticker; that's how many times the child gets to do the next thing. The removable stickers are available at most office supply stores. Just in case the student might be able to see through the white stickers, I scribble on them.

The advantage of the sticker game is that you can decide what numbers to put under the stickers, allowing you to know in advance what is going to be coming up in practice. In essence, you can plan the practice. Since the stickers are re-useable, you just put them back on for practice the following day.

Another option with the sticker game is that you can write "free" instead of a number and the child gets to choose the next activity.

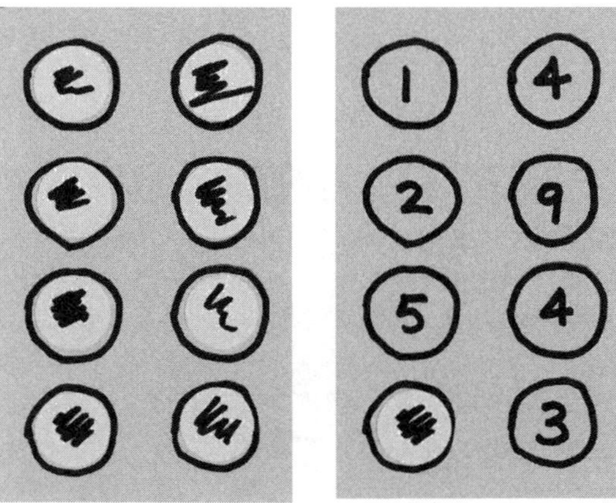

A4

Drawing

You can often get a lot of practicing done pleasantly by taking many breaks for drawing and coloring. For example, you yourself could draw a simple vase with three or four stems coming out of it. Every time your child completes a portion of practice, you draw another petal on a flower. You could do something similar with a face. You draw a circle on a piece of paper, and after every activity, you draw a new part on the face. You could also take turns–you draw after one activity; your daughter draws after the next.

Tic-Tac-Toe is another possibility. Every time your child completes the first part of his practice, it's time for him to take a turn; when he completes the second part of his practice, it's time for you to take a turn, etc..

Some young children love having their names spelled out. Do one activity for each letter in the child's name.

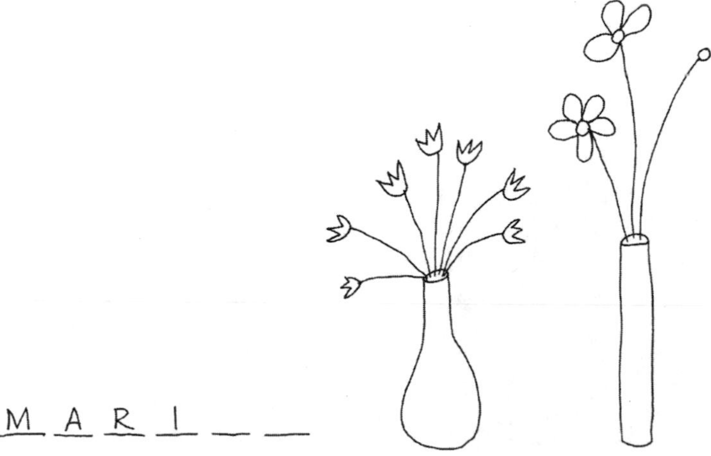

Dominos

Dominos can be great fun during practices. Have a student do something for each domino that you set up. When all of the repetitions are done, the student gets to knock the first domino over and watch the chain reaction as they all go. Sometimes you can even manage to line the dominos up in the shape of the first letter of the child's name.

You can also use dominos to help a child slow down her playing, something most children find very difficult to do. When you ask a child to sing something as slowly as you think she should practice it, she'll often get lost. One way to get around this is to lay a bunch of dominos down flat on the floor, one next to the other, and have her *sing* just one small section of the piece, touching a domino for every note in the piece. Then spread the dominos out a bit and have her touch and sing again. Keep repeating this, spreading the dominos out farther and farther. It becomes a silly game–you might even end up with the dominos so far apart that she has to walk from one to the other. The secret, however, is that in all of this silliness, she's learning how to control the speed at which the notes come out. For the final step in this game, she plays this small section of the piece at the speed she just sang it. Rather than you telling her to slow down, it is her own slow singing that is the boss of her playing.

A6

Paper Chains

Get a sheet of letter paper and cut strips of paper that are about 1 inch wide and 8 inches long. Each time the child completes a practice task, staple the ends together to make another link on the chain. For instance, the child might get a link after making six bow hands or after playing a scale three times.

I sometimes like to clip the first link to the music stand, so that a child can see that the practice will be done when the chain reaches to the ground. The next day of practice, you can just remove one link every time the child completes a task. The practice is over when all of the links are gone.

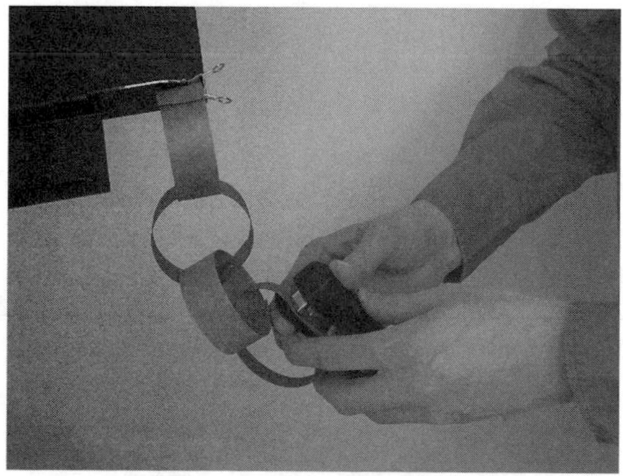

notes and sources

notes and sources

I want to take this opportunity to gratefully acknowledge the authors, editors, publishers, and agents who gave me permission to reprint passages.

decoding

page 1 "Every kid 'talks' in code…" Peter Ruderman, MSW, in a lecture at the St. Louis Psychoanalytic Institute, 16 December 2004.

5 "writing a novel is like driving a car at night…" Anne Lamott, *Bird by Bird* (New York: Anchor Books/Doubleday, 1994), p. 18. © 1994 by Anne Lamott. Used by permission of Pantheon Books, a division of Random House, Inc.

5 "[Practice] is intensely personal..." Lon Sherer, AMusD, *Practicing: A Liturgy of Self-Learning* (Goshen, IN: Pinchpenny Press/Goshen College, 1988), p. 3 & p. 5.

8 "Each second we live…" from *Joys and Sorrows: Reflections by Pablo Casals* (as told to Albert E. Kahn) (New York: Simon & Schuster, 1970), p. 295. Copyright © 1970 by Albert E. Kahn; copyright renewed © 1998 by Harriet E. Kahn. Reprinted with the permission of Simon & Schuster Adult Publishing Group.

24 "It costs a lot..." Dolly Parton, in a speech to the National Press Club, March 23, 2000.

page 37 the "first task for the student is to develop the ability to focus...*assisted by a proper environment and willing adults.*" [emphasis added] Kay Collier-Slone (McLaughlin), PhD, *They're Rarely Too Young and Never Too Old to Twinkle* (Ann Arbor: Shar Products Company, 1985), p. 58.

57 Edward Kreitman, *Teaching from the Balance Point* (Western Springs, IL: Western Springs School of Talent Education, 1998), p. 68.

59 "Ultimately love is everything..." M. Scott Peck, MD, *The Road Less Traveled* (New York: Touchstone/Simon & Schuster, 1978), p. 13. Copyright © 1978 by M. Scott Peck, MD. Reprinted with the permission of Simon & Schuster Adult Publishing Group.

61 "pushing a movement to the limit is reinforcing the limitation," Margaret McIntyre, "Lesson 4: Easy Weight Shift & Improved Angulation," *Integrated Skiing* (Paia, HI: Integrated Movement Systems, Inc.), http://integratedmovementmaui.com/)

61 In addition to her work as a ski instructor, Margaret McIntyre is primarily a Feldenkrais® practitioner. According to http://integratedmovementmaui.com/, Feldenkrais Method® "is not exercise for the body, it is sensory-motor education for the brain...[stemming] from a simple reality: once you feel how your body moves, you use the information to improve your actions and create new ones! ...Typical benefits to expect from this work are improvement in posture, balance, movement efficiency, coordination and flexibility, reduction in pain and accelerated recovery from injury."

65 "If I had eight hours to chop down a tree…" Abraham Lincoln, http://www.websters-online-dictionary.org/definition/english/az/az.html

69 "People have said, 'Don' t cry' to other people for years and years, and all it has ever meant is, 'I'm too uncomfortable when you show your feelings. Don't cry'…" Fred Rogers, *The World According to Mister Rogers: Important Things to Remember* (New York: Hyperion, 2003), p. 58. Copyright © 2003 by Family Communications, Inc. Reprinted by Permission of Hyperion. All Rights Reserved.

69 "Should we allow name-calling…" Selma Fraiberg, MSW, *The Magic Years*, (New York: Fireside, Simon and Schuster [orig. Scribner' s], 1959), p. 279. Copyright © 1959 by Selma H. Fraiberg; copyright renewed © 1987 by Louis Fraiberg and Lisa Fraiberg. Reprinted with the permission of Scribner, an imprint of Simon & Schuster Adult Publishing Group.

76 "Every parent can understand…" conversation with parent educator Carol Kaplan-Lyss, 9 September 2004.

78 "the ' right' to have a feeling is not the same as a license to inflict it on others…" Selma Fraiberg, MSW, *The Magic Years*, (New York: Fireside, Simon and Schuster [orig. Scribner' s], 1959), p. 278. Copyright © 1959 by Selma H. Fraiberg; copyright renewed © 1987 by Louis Fraiberg and Lisa Fraiberg. Reprinted with the permission of Scribner, an imprint of Simon & Schuster Adult Publishing Group.

78 "The principle needs to be this…" Selma Fraiberg, MSW, *The Magic Years*, (New York: Fireside, Simon and Schuster [orig. Scribner' s], 1959), p. 281. Copyright © 1959 by Selma H. Fraiberg; copyright renewed © 1987 by Louis

Fraiberg and Lisa Fraiberg. Reprinted with the permission of Scribner, an imprint of Simon & Schuster Adult Publishing Group.

81 Adele Faber and Elaine Mazlish, *How to Talk So Kids Will Listen and Listen So Kids Will Talk* (New York: Avon Books, 1980).

81 "The true opposite of depression is not gaiety or absence of pain…" Alice Miller [translated from the German by Ruth Ward], *The Drama of the Gifted Child* (originally published as *Prisoners of Childhood*) (New York: Basic Books/Harper Collins, 1990), p. 57. Copyright © 1979 by Suhrkamp Verlag am Main. Reprinted with the permission of Suhrkamp Verlag am Main. All Rights Reserved.

88 "…to be a teacher in the right sense is to be a learner…" Søren Kierkegaard , *The Point of View From My Work as an Author* (1848), as found in *A Kierkegaard Anthology* [edited by Robert Bretall], (Princeton, NJ: Princeton University Press, 1946), p. 335.

92 "When parents are direct and honest in their expectations for a child…" T. Berry Brazelton, MD, *Touchpoints: Your Child' s Emotional and Behavioral Development* (Reading, MA, Perseus Books, 1992), p.275. Copyright © 1994 by T. Berry Brazelton. Reprinted by permission of Perseus Books PLC, a member of Perseus Books, L.L.C.

101 "it is so much easier to embrace absolutes than to suffer reality..." Anne Lamott, *Bird by Bird* (New York: Anchor Books/Doubleday, 1994), p. 104.

126 "[A] great deal of the elegance and dignity…" Marc P. Keane, *Japanese Garden Design* (Boston: Charles E. Tuttle

Publishing Co., Inc./Periplus Publishing Group, 1996), p. 128. Copyright © 1997 by Marc P. Keane. Used by permission of Charles E. Tuttle Publishing Co., Inc.

musicianship

page 131 "The first obligation of a teacher…" conversation with Seymour Fink while having ice cream at the Capital Suzuki Institute, Columbus, OH, in the mid-90's; clarified over a personal e-mail exchange in March 2005.

134 "We believe that we should hold to our theories lightly rather than tightly..." the psychoanalyst Robert Stolorow, PHD, in a lecture at the Michigan Psychoanalytic Institute, May 18, 1996.

149 "Rules carry handcuffs; principles are free…" Elizabeth A. H. Green, with Judith Galamian, Josef Gingold, and Meadowmount Musicians, *Miraculous Teacher: Ivan Galamian and The Meadowmount Experience* (Fairfax, VA: American String Teachers Association, 1993), p. 129. Reprinted with permission from ASTA with NSOA, 4153 Chain Bridge Road, Fairfax, VA 22030.

157 the Bourrée from Händel's Flute Sonata in G Major, as found in *Elf Sonaten für Flöte und bezifferten Bass* [herausgegeben von Hans-Peter Schmitz] (Kassel, Bärenreiter, 1955).

166 "What I once thought was a single step…" Mills, Elizabeth, "Advice to a New Mother," in *The Suzuki Concept* (Berkeley, CA: Diablo Press, September 1973), p. 18.

rhythm

page 195 Anna Freud, a famous psychoanalyst…referred to it as a "developmental line." Anna Freud, "The Concept of Developmental Lines," *Normality and Pathology in Childhood* (New York: International Universities Press, 1965), pp. 62-92.

196 "writing a novel is like driving a car at night…" Anne Lamott, *Bird by Bird* (New York: Anchor Books/Doubleday, 1994), p. 18.

221 "When at first you don' t succeed, never try again…" Patrick Macdonald, *The Alexander Technique as I See it* (Brighton: Rahula Books, 1989), p. I, as quoted in Pedro de Alcantara, *Indirect procedures: A Musician' s Guide to the Alexander Technique* (New York: Oxford University Press, 1997), p. 191.

231 Dounis was born to a wealthy family in Greece …became a violin teacher, eventually settling in the U.S. Chris A. Constantakos, PhD, *Demetrios Constantine Dounis: His Method in Teaching the Violin*, (New York: Peter Lang, 1988), pp. 19-28.

231 "Rhythm is technique." Chris A. Constantakos, PhD, *Demetrios Constantine Dounis: His Method in Teaching the Violin*, (New York: Peter Lang, 1988), p. 87.

231 "If it is not easy, it is no good. It has to be easy." Chris A. Constantakos, PhD, *Demetrios Constantine Dounis: His Method in Teaching the Violin*, (New York: Peter Lang, 1988), p. 51.

231-232 "It' s like parking your car when you are going forty miles an hour..." Dorothy DeLay quoted in Sylvia Gholson, DME, *Proximal Positioning: A Strategy of Practice in Expert Violin Pedagogy*, (Ann Arbor: UMI Dissertation Services, 1994), p. 197.

235 "Twenty years ago we discovered that computers can do things that seem very much like thinking..." personal e-mail from Frank R. Wilson, MD, 9 March 2005.

The Suzuki Violin School ®
by Shin'ichi Suzuki,
is published by
Summy-Birchard, Inc.,
sole publisher for the world
except Japan.

The Suzuki Association of the Americas, Inc. (SAA) is the official organization authorized to support and develop Suzuki education in North, Central and South America. For locating a Suzuki teacher, learning more about Suzuki education or obtaining Suzuki method teacher training, please contact the Association for information.

SAA
P.O. Box 17310
Boulder, Colorado 80308

1-888-378-9854

www.suzukiassociation.org
www.suzukimethod.org